Deborah Kennedy

Deborah Kennedy

SHOPPING AT HOME
For Camping and Outdoor Equipment

SHOPPING AT HOME
For Camping and Outdoor Equipment

By
BEN BACHMAN

ADDITIONAL MATERIAL

David Kendall
Rich Larocco

Richard Gottlieb
GENERAL EDITOR

FACTS ON FILE PUBLICATIONS
460 Park Avenue South
New York, N.Y. 10016

Published by Facts On File, Inc., 460 Park Avenue South,
New York, N.Y. 10016

Library of Congress Cataloging in Publication Data

Bachman, Ben
  Shopping at Home for Camping & Outdoor Equipment.

  Includes index.
  1. Camping—Equipment and supplies—Catalogs. I. Title.
GV191.76.G67   688.7′654   81-12556
ISBN 0-87196-541-0
ISBN 0-87196-535-6 ppk   AACR2

Printed and bound in the United States of America

9 8 7 6 5 4 3 2 1

Author's Introduction

Good equipment is critical to most outdoor pursuits, but few activities owe as much of their popularity to equipment as backpacking. Take, for example, the goose-down sleeping bag. A premium-quality down bag is warm in sub-freezing temperatures, weighs as little as three pounds, and stuffs into a bundle that is not much larger than a loaf of bread. Used in conjunction with a lightweight nylon tent, an aluminum pack frame, freeze-dried food and a small gasoline stove, the sleeping bag becomes the nucleus of a portable life-support system that is adaptable to a wide variety of wilderness environments and weather conditions. No special skills are needed to use this equipment. With a modicum of experience and common sense, the modern backpacker can be instantly at home virtually anywhere he chooses. Technology, in other words, has taken most of the drudgery and frustration out of camping. The backpacker is free to enjoy himself.

It wasn't always this easy. As recently as the late 1950s and early 1960s, a five-day camping trip in the mountains could involve a substantial amount of physical discomfort. In the first place, one's gear was likely to weigh upwards of 75 pounds. The standard sleeping bag was a cotton or dacron model that itself weighed 10 or 12 pounds. Above timberline, you went to bed bundled in every stitch of clothing you owned and still ended up shivering most of the night. Your tent, if you had one, was a primitive affair that lacked such refinements as mosquito netting, a rain fly, or a built-in floor. It was made out of leaky canvas and would probably blow down in a moderate wind. All cooking was done over an open fire in Army mess kits or recycled tin cans. Cast-iron skillets were not uncommon either, and you probably carried an axe and perhaps even an entrenching tool. The pack used to transport this equipment was either a canvas rucksack or a wooden packboard. In the case of the latter, tying down the load required a substantial amount of rope and no small measure of ingenuity. Most of the weight rode on your shoulders, and at the end of the day you were sore, stiff, and exhausted.

The remarkable thing is how much fun a trip like this really was, but roughing it has always had a peculiar kind of charm. In addition, a backpacker who ventured into the wilderness in the early 1960s was likely to have whatever mountain range he chose entirely to himself. In fact, "backpacking" did not really exist as a sport in its own right. The primary outdoor recreational activities were hunting and fishing, and the dominant method of travel for extended backcountry trips, especially in the West, was horsepacking.

But mountain climbing was gaining in popularity, and knowledgeable climbers had access to a better class of equipment. A serviceable line of relatively lightweight camping equipment had been developed during World War II for the famous 10th Mountain Division (David Brower's old unit), and was available here and there as Army surplus. European equipment was also available if you knew where to look for it. On the domestic front, high-quality down bags, aluminum pack frames, and nylon tents were available from such venerable suppliers as REI, Kelty, Camp Trails, Gerry, Trail Wise, and Holubar. Indeed, the fundamental technology of modern backpacking gear had already been established, but, again, the major problem was access. Unless you happened to live near Boulder, Colorado; Seattle; or San Francisco, good gear was very hard to find.

The answer, of course, was mail-order shopping. Information about the new equipment spread by word of mouth and through advertisements in mountaineering club journals, and before long, the ritual of sending away for catalogs and poring over their contents became an important part of the backpacking/climbing experience. Many an enjoyable winter night has been spent leafing through well-thumbed catalogs in anticipation of the summer to come. And many a backpacker outfitted himself completely without ever so much as setting foot inside an outdoor specialty shop.

By the mid-60s, however, the situation had begun to change. Climbing and backpacking both experienced a tremendous growth in popularity. A number of different factors were responsible, the most obvious of which was a simple increase in population. As the post-war baby boom generation graduated from high school and went on to college, they encountered the mountaineering clubs that tended to flourish in an academic environment. Since the typical college student of the 60s had grown up in a city or a suburb, he was ready for a little wilderness adventure. Prosperity and automotive mobility put such things within almost everyone's reach.

The successful 1963 American Mount Everest Expedition shoved climbers into the public eye and gave the sport a new glamour. At the same time, the strong bonds that already existed between mountaineering and environmentalism were reinforced by organizations such as the Sierra Club. An additional element was provided by the emergence of the counterculture. Proto-environmentalists such as Thoreau and John Muir had preached an anti-establishment, anti-business message from the beginning, and this had great appeal to the flower children. They were also attracted to the backpacker's self-sufficiency, to his ability to set up casual housekeeping at a moment's notice, and before long, hiking boots and goose-down parkas became common sights not only in the mountains but on the streets of Berkeley and Cambridge. This, incidentally, was probably the beginning of backpacking chic, a phenomenon that is still with us today.

The 1960s were the Golden Age of American rock climbing. No longer content to imitate Europeans, American climbers developed a technique of their own and perfected it on the colossal rock walls of Yosemite Valley. A few climbers, such as Yvon Chouinard and Royal Robbins, became virtually legends in their own time. To understand why, all you had to do was gaze up at those forbidding cliffs. The things these climbers did were incredible. And they did them with style. It would have been easy to make a week-long ascent of El Capitan or Half Dome into a media circus, but the Yosemite climbers went about their business with self-effacing modesty and adhered to a strict set of rules that made their climbs, which were difficult enough to begin with, even harder. In published accounts, they dwelled not so much on the dangers involved as on the glories of nature and the spiritual rewards of sustained effort. Their approach was almost mystical. Some of this rubbed off on backpackers, perhaps because it dovetailed so nicely with the high moral purpose professed by environmentalists. There was pleasure to be had in the wilderness—nobody denied that—but it was as much as intellectual pleasure as a physical pleasure. A backpacking trip was an "enriching" experience, something akin to listening to a great symphony. The magnificent Sierra Club "Exhibit Format" books published at the time capture the spirit of the thing. They are big, beautifully printed volumes with voluptuous photographs and filled with quotations from Shakespeare, Muir, and the Bible.

By the same token, backpacking equipment suppliers were expected to be above the sordidness of commercialism. The hard sell belonged on the used-car lot, not in an outdoor catalog. Equipment makers were presumed to be dedicated outdoorsmen who put excellence and craftsmanship above profit. To a surprising degree, this was actually true. And if the realities of the business world inevitably intruded on such lofty ideals, a lot of quality gear still managed to find its way onto the market. And the market was ready for it. The backpacking boom had begun.

It was almost a chicken-and-egg sort of thing. If the right equipment had not been available, backpacking would never have grown, but if there hadn't been a lot of backpackers, there would have been no reason to produce much quality gear. Fortunately, the gear *was* produced and people bought it. By the late 1960s, new suppliers were springing up all over the country, although Boulder, Seattle, and California were still the most popular locations. Firms such as North Face and Sierra Designs typified the new wave. Equipment became more sophisticated, as did consumers and marketing techniques. Quality, however, was still the primary selling point. Backpackers and climbers had never had it so good. The problem was no longer one of finding gear, but of selecting what was right for you among the many available options.

In the process of all this excitement, backpacking itself began to mature. Politically sophisticated to begin with, backpackers were instrumental in promoting wilderness-oriented legislation. The other side of the coin, however, was that it had suddenly become a lot harder to find solitude in the woods. Even in remote areas such as the Wind River Range of Wyoming it was not at all unusual to find 50 or more cars parked at every trailhead. In national parks, the problems of backcountry overcrowding were particularly severe. The "wilderness permit," which amounted to adventure by reservation, was becoming a fact of life.

The type of person attracted to backpacking seemed to be changing also. Just as environmentalism had broadened its scope beyond the immediate issues of wilderness preservation, backpacking and climbing now had a much wider appeal. As the influence of the counterculture waned, backpacking became a family activity. The down bag and the aluminum pack frame were gradually becoming badges of middle-class affluence.

The decade of the 1970s was a period of phenomenal growth for the equipment industry. The older companies expanded their operations (Eastern Mountain Sports, for example, opened branch stores all over New England and the Northeast), and new manufacturers and specialty stores appeared at a bewildering rate. New products, such as Gore-Tex clothing, synthetic-fill sleeping bags, and internal-frame packs, were introduced and won wide acceptance. Canoeing, kayaking, and whitewater rafting also experienced a tremendous surge in popularity during the 70s.

Not everyone was happy with the boom. Cynics would see the same thing happening to backpacking that had already happened to downhill skiing, a once simple and inexpensive sport that had been "spoiled" by fashion and flashy merchandising. Indeed, there was some justification for these fears. A few of the larger suppliers had grown to the point where they resembled department stores. They were a far cry from the friendly little backpacking shops of the old days. These were firms that did millions of dollars worth of business every year. They had standard corporate hierarchies, marketing departments, and big advertising budgets. It was only a matter of time before some larger, non-backpacking-related company would buy them out.

Somewhat remarkably, this happened in only a very few cases. While it is true that the big equipment manufacturers have gotten even bigger, they are still owned, for the most part, by individuals with a direct stake in the business. The conglomerates and multinationals have been held at bay. It is also true that there are more small suppliers than ever before. The industry has not become impersonal. In fact, it is probably easier to obtain custom-made gear now than at any other time.

As far as the average consumer is concerned, the major effect of industry growth in the 1970s is twofold: variety and availability. Virtually every medium-size city in the United States now has an outdoor specialty shop. So do many resort and college towns. In addition, most general sporting goods stores now carry backpacking equipment, although it is not always of the best quality. The same is true of discount stores and Army/Navy stores.

So why is there a need for a book like *Shopping At Home for Camping and Outdoor Equipment?* Why send away for catalogs when you can simply go downtown and see the gear for yourself? Indeed, a number of equipment manufacturers have deemphasized their mail-order business or gotten out of it entirely. A few firms no longer sell to retail customers at all, preferring to distribute their products exclusively through dealers.

Nevertheless, mail-order shopping remains popular, and for several good reasons. In the first place, there are so many different brands on the market that a single retail store cannot possibly carry all of them. When you walk into a store, even a large store like REI or Eastern Mountain Sports (both of which have large mail-order departments), you are only seeing a small fraction of what is available. Moreover, retail stores naturally tend to emphasize the products of the larger manufacturers. There is no way that the smaller companies can match the distribution networks of their big cousins. Quite a few small companies don't even try. A backpacker in New York or Boston is just not going to learn about the products of a small manufacturer in Montana or Idaho unless he sends away for their catalogs.

This is not to say that the products of large companies are necessarily less desirable than those of small companies. Far from it. But it is to the consumer's advantage to examine all the options. Another, no less important benefit of mail-order shopping is that it allows you to compare products at your leisure. Most of the companies in this book offer detailed product information in their catalogs—the kind of information that is not always easy to come by in a crowded store. With several catalogs in hand, you can better see how various brands stack up against one another. Even if you do end up buying the item in a retail store, this process of catalog comparison shopping will be an invaluable aid toward making an intelligent purchase.

Please note, however, that this book is not a consumer guide in the strict sense of the word. In the pages that follow we do not rate companies or individual products. We have attempted to maintain a tone of informed neutrality, our main purpose being to let you know who and where the suppliers are and what they sell. On the other hand, if a specific item (such as the L. L. Bean Maine Hunting Shoe or the Sierra Designs 60/40 Parka) has a generally recognized reputation, we have mentioned it. One further note: No paid advertising has been accepted. We are in no way beholden to any manufacturer.

Product rating systems or charts have a certain kind of usefulness in some fields, but the backpacking equipment industry is not really one of them. There are, for example, a great many pack frames on the market. Most employ the same basic design, are made out of the same or similar materials, and fall into the same price range. Any attempt to rate these packs is going to have to rely, to a large extent, on personal preferences, and personal preferences, thank heavens, are hardly ever identical. Thus, each pack has its own band of partisans, each convinced that they are right. Moreover, a good deal of hairsplitting is involved. You can argue from now until the cows come home about how one fabric is superior to another, or why one design is more efficient than anything else, and lose sight of the fact that all of them get the job done.

The marketplace itself is actually the best rating system. With so many companies competing against one another, bad products simply don't survive. We have mentioned it before, but it's worth repeating: Product quality in the backpacking industry is exceptionally high. Parkas and pack frames, after all, are a different class of merchandise from soap or underwear. Nobody *has* to buy backpacking equipment. Consumers can afford to be choosy. There isn't much demand for seriously deficient items. This doesn't mean that second-rate products don't exist; you can find them in any discount store, but not, as a rule, in the mail-order specialty market.

There are a number of excellent books in print today about the techniques of backpacking, mountaineering, canoeing, kayaking, and rafting. If you are new to the sport, we recommend that you read some of them. It is not our purpose here to provide a how-to manual of wilderness travel. But before moving on to company-by-company descriptions of the equipment suppliers, a general survey of the various types of products that are currently available would seem to be in order.

Sleeping Bags

As has been true for the last 25 years, goose-down-filled sleeping bags are still probably the first choice among outdoorsmen. Down bags are certainly the most expensive. In fact, a goose-down bag is likely to be the single most costly item of equipment that the average backpacker ever buys. Expedition down bags intended for ultra-low temperatures are now up in the $300 price range. Nevertheless, down offers a lot for the money. With proper care, a down bag will last for many years, and nothing else is as lightweight or as warm or packs into a smaller stuff sack.

On the other hand, synthetic-fill bags have become immensely popular in the last decade. The most obvious advantage of a synthetic-fill bag is a substantially more economical price. But there are other reasons to choose synthetic, most of which have to do with the fact that the synthetic insulating materials absorb very little water. This is a factor that can become critical in a rainy climate. Once a goose-down bag becomes damp, it loses much of its efficiency, and if a down bag gets soaked, it is virtually useless. Moreover, a wet down bag takes days to dry out. Synthetic bags retain warmth when wet and dry out very quickly. Synthetic bags also tend to be less fragile than down models, and improving technology is gradually narrowing the warmth/weight advantage of goose down.

A number of bags combine synthetic and goose-down fill, with down on the top part of the bag and synthetic on the bottom. This arrangement makes sense because the down on the bottom half of an all-goose-down bag is crushed flat by a sleeper's body weight and loses most of its insulating value.

Another development, which has been advocated by Jack Stephenson for years and is now gaining wider acceptance, is the "vapor-barrier" bag. Vapor-barrier bags feature a thin layer of waterproof material in addition to or in place of the normal inner lining of the bag, which results in a substantial increase in thermal efficiency. Vapor-barrier bags are usually available as "modular sleeping systems" that can be adapted to a wide range of temperatures. The vapor-barrier principle has been applied to clothing as well.

Packs

The big news in packs during the 1970s has undoubtedly been the internal-frame rucksack. First developed for rock climbers and ski-mountaineers, internal-frame packs have won acceptance among trail hikers too. Some of these packs have an "X"-type internal frame, others, a pair of parallel staves, and still others use the contents of the pack as a frame, but all of them ride close to the hiker's natural center of gravity and are much less likely to throw him off balance than a standard external-frame pack. Nor is there any sacrifice of load-carrying capacity or comfort. Most internal-frame packs feature sophisticated wraparound waist belts and harness systems. Internal-frame packs are also better suited to air, bus, or train travel, since they are more compact than pack frames and do not have any protruding metal parts to snag on luggage racks or airport baggage conveyors.

The aluminum pack frame, however, has not been rendered obsolete. It was a great idea when first developed back in the 1940s, and remains popular today. Improving technology has made frames stronger than ever before, and new types of frames that feature either high-impact plastic material or flexible-frame joints have added a certain amount of elasticity that makes it easier to carry big loads.

Tents

As with the internal-frame pack, the freestanding dome tent came into its own during the 1970s. The advantages of the dome tent (increased shoulder and head room, lack of external guy lines, remarkable stability) are perhaps most applicable to the larger three-, four-, and six-person models and to expeditionary tents, but successful one- and two-person versions are also on the market. Elsewhere on the tent scene, variations and refinements of the standard single and double A-frame designs are setting new standards for light weight and fast set-up time. Tent prices cover an extremely wide range ($100-$500), and an alert consumer can save a good deal of money simply by selecting a tent that is not overdesigned for his own particular needs.

Clothing

Advances in clothing have occurred on two fronts: Gore-Tex fabrics and synthetic insulating materials. As with sleeping bags, synthetic-insulated garments have an advantage over goose down in both price and wet-weather utility. Goose-down parkas simply are not very practical on a trip where you expect a lot of rain. If a synthetic-fill garment gets wet, you can wring it out, put it back on, and it will be warm. Hollofil II, Thinsulate, and PolarGuard are the most popular insulators. Pile clothing, another synthetic, is also quite popular. Pile looks something like woolly sheepskin, absorbs very little water, is extremely lightweight, and is very versatile since it can be worn by itself or in combination with windshells or other garments.

Gore-Tex is a remarkable material that is permeable to water vapor but not to liquid water. In other words, Gore-Tex is both breathable and waterproof and thus ideal for rainwear and mountain parkas. It is also used in tents, sleeping bags, and hiking boots.

Speaking of boots, we ought to mention that the once universally accepted rubber lug sole (Vibram or otherwise) has been getting some bad press of late. Too many hikers wearing heavy lug-soled boots, it seems, are destroying popular trails. For summer trail hiking the trend is definitely toward lighter boots with much shallower tread patterns. Actually, this doesn't involve any sacrifice on the hiker's part, since the lighter boots are more comfortable. According to backpacking folklore, a pound on the feet is equivalent to five pounds in the pack and this is probably true. Some hikers have taken to wearing running shoes on the trail. For cross-country travel and mountaineering, however, lug soles and sturdy boots are advisable.

Climbing Gear

Just as the passage of too many lug-soled boots can rip up a trail, too many pitons pounded into and pried out of cracks can damage a popular rock-climbing route. This is what led to the "clean climbing" revolution in the 1970s. Climbing nuts and chocks have now largely replaced the offending pitons (which remain useful, however, when employed with moderation in the proper circumstances). But clean climbing is more than hardware; it's a whole attitude toward climbing and the mountains. Ample literature is available on the subject. When you come right down to it, though, the essentials of climbing technique and the proper use of equipment are best learned in a hands-on situation under the guidance of experienced mountaineers. We cannot emphasize this point enough.

Canoes, Kayaks, and Rafts

Canoes made out of five materials—aluminum, fiberglass, Kevlar, Royalex and wood—are available today. Aluminum was once extremely popular, but has declined somewhat of late. Aluminum canoes tend to stick to rocks, to be noisy, to be cold or hot according to the temperature, and to be difficult to repair in the field. It is easy, however, to make too much out of this. Aluminum canoes have been paddled millions of miles by an uncountable number of perfectly satisfied owners. To their credit, aluminum canoes are sturdy, economical, relatively lightweight, and virtually maintenance-free.

Fiberglass is the most popular canoe material in use today, but there are almost as many different kinds of fiberglass as there are boat builders. Quality varies, but a properly laid-up fiberglass canoe is light, strong, quiet, responsive, sturdy, aesthetically pleasing, and economical. The lightest canoes are made of Kevlar, while the strongest canoes are made of Royalex, a "memory" plastic that springs back into shape after being dented. Kevlar and Royalex boats are more expensive than fiberglass or aluminum. Wood is the most expensive canoe material, but a well-made wooden canoe is an object of astonishing beauty. It is also fairly light and can be surprisingly durable.

Most kayaks are made of fiberglass or Kevlar. There is great variety in the design of kayaks. Some models are general purpose, while others are extremely specialized. Perhaps more than in any other type of boat, the weight and height of the paddler is of critical importance in choosing a kayak. You do not sit in a kayak; you put it on. Kayakers, of course, are aware of this already. We suspect that most of them have a definite idea of what they want in a boat and we will attempt no further advice. As with rock climbing, kayaking is something that you can't really learn from a book. It would be a serious mistake to go out and buy a kayak of any kind before you have mastered the fundamentals of the sport.

The same thing is true of whitewater rafting, although the choice among rafts is much more limited than with canoes and kayaks. Because some rafts are much more expensive than others (although none of them will seem cheap to the novice rafter), it is important to pick a boat that will meet your needs but is not overdesigned. The requirements of a weekend tripper are obviously not the same as those of a professional guide on the Middle Fork of the Salmon or the Grand Canyon of the Colorado. Raft dealers can offer valuable advice, and you can also learn a lot by taking a guided raft trip, even if the trip is only a day or two long.

Odds and Ends

Some sort of small cooking stove has become a necessity for most backpacking. Basically, there are two types of stoves: those that burn liquid fuel (gasoline, or the like) and those that burn a gaseous fuel that comes in a sealed canister. The canister-type stoves are easier to light and to operate, but liquid-fuel stoves burn hotter and are more efficient at high altitudes or in very cold weather. All in all, liquid fuel stoves are more popular, and new designs have eliminated or reduced many of the problems associated with gasoline stoves in the past. Some of them are surprisingly expensive, but winter campers and mountaineers won't mind paying for quality and convenience. The average backpacker can make do with something less elaborate.

Knives—pocket, folding, and otherwise—are available in astonishing variety. Virtually all of them will handle the jobs normally associated with backpacking, so choosing a knife usually comes down to picking out one that appeals to you on an aesthetic or emotional level. Some campers want a lot of accessory blades, others don't. Anglers, of course, have more specialized needs, but again, there are many fishing knives to choose from, too. A knife that has a corkscrew can be worth its weight in gold, both in the wilderness and elsewhere.

Knives and stoves only begin to cover the range of accessory items that are offered to backpackers. In fact, one of the great pleasures of mail-order shopping consists of looking at the incredible array of odds and ends and gimmicks and gizmos. Some are useful and some are not so useful, but they are all appealing. These catalogs contain everything you ever dreamed of and a good deal that you never imagined.

But whether you are looking for a sleeping bag, a tent, a

canoe, or a pair of shoelaces, it is advisable to keep in mind the danger of becoming bogged down in technological details. Every manufacturer naturally likes to claim revolutionary breakthroughs for his own product, and such claims usually have at least some basis in fact, but that does not mean that everything else on the market is obsolete. We would point out that if all the technological improvements of the last 10 years were suddenly erased, you could still completely outfit yourself with excellent gear. On the other hand, there is no reason not to take advantage of new developments if they are something you can really use. Nor is there necessarily anything wrong with being an equipment freak. To a certain type of person, cleverly designed equipment is a pleasure in and of itself. The important thing is to get the gear you want. It is with that end in mind that we put together *Shopping At Home for Camping and Outdoor Equipment.*

Guide to
Shopping at Home

Catalogs

Shopping at home begins with the catalog. This can range from a simple price list to a comprehensive source of information with photographs and descriptions. Many catalogs are free; those that do cost vary in price. Some companies will refund the price of their catalog as credit toward your first purchase.

When ordering a catalog, be sure to indicate which catalog you want, since a company may put out several, and include your return address in the letter. If the cost is over one dollar, it is best to pay by money order, since a personal check will take two weeks to clear. For catalogs priced at under one dollar, send coins taped between two pieces of cardboard. Alternatively, the company may request a self-addressed, stamped envelope, which should be sent with your letter.

A general principle which holds true in any transaction with a mail-order company is that you should keep records of all communication, whether it is by phone or by letter. In the event of later complications, you will have clear evidence to support your case.

Ordering

In making purchases from a catalog, you should give the specific information required by each firm. This can include model numbers, style numbers, colors, sizes, quantities, and so on. These specifications should be recorded on the order blank accompanying the catalog, or printed clearly on a blank sheet of paper. At this point, it is a good idea to check the combined prices and any delivery charges against the cost of the item in a normal outlet. Although a discount is likely, it is not assured. You should also make sure that the stated prices are up to date; a phone call to the company will usually get you verification.

Payment

Each company will indicate its preferred method of payment. Some request that you pay only by certified check, but most firms will accept a personal check or a money order. Most companies take Interbank charge cards, such as Visa and Mastercard, or regular credit cards, such as American Express and Diner's Club. Although a personal check is the cheapest form of payment for you, you will have to wait an extra two weeks while the check clears before the order can be sent out. A bank or postal money order requires no clearance, and has only a minimal cost. Like a personal check, it can be stopped if you have to cancel the order, provided the firm has not yet shipped the goods. If you use a charge card, you have the convenience of ordering by phone, and a simplified bill at the end of the month, but you must of course avoid the finance charges on unpaid bills.

Shipping

Companies in the United States have three options for shipping your merchandise: the Postal Service, the United Parcel Service, and truckers. The cost for delivery by UPS is established according to distance and to the dimensions and weight of your package. UPS provides the Common Carrier Rate Chart, which gives shipping costs as determined by these three variables, in case a company asks that you determine shipping costs to be included in a bill. Parcel Post shipping is more expensive than UPS, but allows delivery to a post office box, unlike UPS, which needs a street address. If you require shipment by Parcel Post, this should be stated both on the order form and on your check, for in cashing the check, the company is agreeing to your terms. Truckers are used when an order exceeds the standard 50-pound mailing limit. The charges are based on weight and distance, and must be paid upon delivery, either in cash or with a certified check. This charge can be quite high, and in some cases, REA Express may be a faster and cheaper alternative. It is worthwhile to contact both REA Express and your local carrier to compare their shipping costs for your particular case.

Finally, you should know that U. S. companies must respond to your order within 30 days, either by shipping your purchase, explaining the delay, or refunding your money. If a firm fails to do so, call or write, give them your order number and a description of the items, and ask for an explanation.

Problems
In case you are not satisfied with the merchandise, you may have a 30-day option to return it to the company. Some firms require that you give the reason for your dissatisfaction before they will authorize the return, others have a no-return policy, so it is advised that you know the terms before making your order. If the merchandise has been damaged during delivery, then the carrier is responsible, and you should file your complaint with them. However, if your complaint is with the mail-order company, either for non-delivery, fraud, or misrepresentation, and the company refuses to give satisfaction, then there are several recourses available. The U. S. Postal Service will investigate every complaint, and has the power to refuse mail delivery to a company if it doesn't cooperate. The Federal Trade Commission is unlikely to offer immediate aid, but will investigate if a company has a record of fraud and poor service. The Direct Mail/Marketing Association is a trade organization that will refer your complaints to the appropriate agencies and will itself put pressure on the firm in question. You may write to these organizations at the following addresses:

Chief Postal Inspector
U. S. Postal Service
Washington, DC 20260

Bureau of Consumer Protection
Federal Trade Commission
Washington, DC 20580

Mail Order ActionLine
Direct Mail/Marketing Association
Six East 43rd Street
New York, NY 10017

ADVENTURE 16 WILDERNESS CAMPING OUTFITTERS

4620 Alvarado Canyon Rd.
San Diego, CA 92120
714-283-2374
Accepts MC,VISA. Annual. Est. 1962. Mic Mead, Pres.

East Coast and Midwest backpackers may not be familiar with A16, but it's worth investigating. The first thing you notice is the catalog. It looks like a tabloid-size newspaper and is written in an enthusiastic, down-home style. The interiors of A16's southern California stores are set up to resemble old-time backwoods trading posts. The manufacturing facilities, however, are up to date, and expanding to meet demand. A16 products are backed by a lifetime guarantee.

During its 20 years in the business, A16 has pioneered such concepts as the "hip-hugger" pack frame, the lightweight two-layer dome tent, parkas with underarm zippers, and a 2½-gallon waterbag that weighs three ounces.

A16 says that its half-dome tents have more usable room per ounce than any other two-layer dome tent on the market. The four-person half-dome weighs 6½ pounds. The 2½-person half-dome weighs 5½ pounds. The two-layer design with inner breathable wall allows moist air to escape without condensing.

The curved poles have most of their bow at the side of the tent rather than the top, to give more usable shoulder room. Sit-up room is not confined to the center of the tent. The wide door allows entry and exit even when someone is already sitting in it. There is a "bay window" in back. A16 also carries Black Ice brand tents.

A16 goose-down sleeping bags feature true differential cut, 1½-ounce ripstop nylon fabric, slant stretch net baffles placed five inches apart (instead of seven or eight inches), and two double zippers located on top of the bag. According to the catalog, the down in these bags lofts up to 750 cubic inches per ounce. A16 also carries PolarGuard sleeping bags and Black Ice brand down bags.

The waist belt on the A16 hip-hugger pack frame is attached to a forward carry point rather than the bottom of the frame rails. This arrangement provides a more comfortable carry and better weight distribution. The frame itself telescopes to adjust from 29 inches to 35 inches. Shoulder straps are self-aligning. Sliding shoulder bars permit automatic adjustment to keep weight off the top of the shoulders. The pack bag has two zippered side pockets with double compartments. A16 also offers a number of internal-frame packs including the Lowe expedition pack, as well as a variety of day packs and soft luggage.

The A16 goose-down parka and Gore-Tex parka round out the mail-order line, along with a selection of outdoor clothing, cookware, stoves, and books.

PRODUCTS: Tents, sleeping bags, outdoor clothing.

AIR LIFT COMPANY
2217 Roosevelt Ave.
Berkeley, CA 94703
415-845-1195
Brochure. Est. 1974. Johnathan Francis, Owner. Kathy Marrelius, Cust. Svc.

Of all the things that backpackers can put between their sleeping bag and the ground, an air mattress is the most comfortable. Traditional air mattresses, however, are too bulky and too heavy for most modern hikers. In addition, old-style air mattresses tend to puncture easily or to develop slow leaks that let you down during the night.

The Air Lift modular mattress system is a different kind of

air mattress. Depending on the model, it has nine or 10 separate flotation chambers that run the length of the mattress from head to toe. This allows the sleeper to vary the inflation pressure in each chamber for a customized sleeping surface. The modular system also prevents the air from shifting from one side of the mattress to the other as the sleeper changes positions.

Each chamber has a push-pull valve and fits into its own sleeve within a ripstop nylon cover. A portable repair kit allows in-the-field repairs to be made quickly and conveniently. The separate air tubes prevent a single puncture from deflating the entire mattress.

The Standard vinyl mattress comes in two models: a 20-inch by 42-inch size that weighs one pound, four ounces and packs into a 3½-inch by seven-inch storage sack, and a 22-inch by 72-inch size that weighs 12½ pounds and packs into a 4½-inch by 8½-inch storage sack.

The Air Lift Blue Wing modular mattress is made of rugged but extremely lightweight 3.5 mil. extruded polytensilon plastic film. The Blue Wing comes in the same sizes as the Standard model but weighs only 11 ounces or one pound, five g. All Air Lift mattresses come with nylon carrying sacks, one spare tube and a strip of repair tape. The patented Air Lift inflation valve has an easy closure system that prevents air from escaping between breaths. One mattress takes approximately 75 seconds to inflate.

PRODUCTS: Air mattresses.

ALASKA WILDERNESS
P.O. Box 450
Girdwood, AK 99587
Catalog on request.

Most down sleeping bags on the market today are pretty much alike. Alaska Wilderness offers something different—a multi-top sleeping system. Basically, it consists of three components: a bottom, a lightweight top and a heavy top. Both of the tops are completely removable and can be used separately or together. The lightweight top is adequate for three-season use. The heavy top is for colder nights, and both tops together will protect a sleeper in extreme conditions down to minus 70 degrees. Fine-tuning for various temperatures can be achieved by opening and closing the various zippers.

The innovative design of the Alaska Wilderness bag does not end with the multi-layer concept. The inner shell of the bag is metalized, waterproof nylon fabric that prevents the sleeper's body moisture from passing into the goose down. This layer of vapor-barrier insulation increases the effective temperature range of the bag by 15-20 degrees. It also prevents skin oil and dirt from soiling the down. The only other bags on the market using this principle are the ones made by Jack Stephenson in New Hampshire. Understandably enough, some people are skeptical about vapor-barrier insulation. It sounds as if the person inside the bag will end up soaking wet, but this is not the case. The skin is naturally moist, and once it reaches optimum humidity it stops producing sweat.

In addition to the vapor-barrier fabric and the multi-layer top, the bottom of the Alaska Wilderness bag incorporates an integral foam pad. There is no sense putting goose down underneath a sleeper, since his body weight crushes it flat. Foam is a more effective insulator than fiberfill in this situation, too.

Alaska Wilderness bags use prime-quality white Polish goose down with a fill power of 700 cubic inches per ounce. The bag itself is built with box baffles and eleven stitches per inch on all seams, with triple lock stitching in critical areas. Every piece of fabric is individually hot cut. Every bag is custom sized to the purchaser's individual measurements.

A Gore-Tex outer shell, a fire-retardant top cover, a high-visibility metallic top, a heavier bottom, and a waterproof envelope are available as options.

PRODUCTS: Sleeping bags.

ALPENLITE (Division of Wilderness Group)
39 W. Main St.
Ventura, CA 93001
805-653-0431
Accepts MC, VISA. Illustrated. Est. 1970. Don Douglas, Pres. Sean Collins, Cust. Svc.

For most people, the legs and thighs are stronger than the arms and shoulders, so a pack that takes advantage of this lower-body strength is going to be easier to carry. Any pack frame with a waist belt transfers a certain amount of weight to the hips, especially when the hiker is walking downhill, but it was not until 1970, when Alpenlite pioneered the wraparound stand-up frame pack, that the idea of weight transfer began to realize its true potential.

They call it a stand-up frame because it does just that—the frame stands up by itself. They call it a wraparound frame because the frame itself—not just the waist belt—reaches around the hiker's hips.

Alpenlite frames are made of seamless aluminum aircraft tubing (6061T6 and 6063T832) with double-walled tubing at the main bend (where the frame reaches around the hips) for extra durability. Heliarc welds insure strong joints. Shoulder straps and waist belts are padded with ensolite, and the waist belt has a differential cut. Pack bags are made of coated Cordura or Parapac nylon, and pack-bag zippers are continuous coil, self-healing models with storm flaps. Every pack bag is hand sewn with #69 heavy-duty nylon thread, and stress points are reinforced.

The Pac Eze bag, with 3,100-cubic-inch capacity in the standard size and 3,800-cubic-inch capacity in the extra-large size, is a top-loading model with six outside pockets and Delrin quick-adjust hardware. The Pac Zip, with the same capacity as the Pac Eze, is a front-loading model with internal shelf positions, six pockets, accessory straps, and an ice axe loop.

The Pac Master is slightly smaller in capacity than the Pac Zip or the Pac Eze (3,000 cubic inches standard size), and has a top-loading bag made of eight-ounce waterproof Parapac nylon and four side pockets.

The Monterey is an internal-frame pack with compression straps, Fastex buckles, waterprooof 1,000 denier Cordura pack bag and a 3,100-cubic-inch capacity. The Visa, with a 3,900-cubic-inch capacity, is an internal-frame pack that functions well in the backcountry, and with its hideaway harness and lockable zippers works as a piece of luggage, too. The Pacifica is a large-capacity (4,500-cubic-inch) internal-frame pack with independent floating suspension, differential cut waist belt, sternum strap across the chest, expandable sleeping-bag compartment, compression straps, and sturdy construction with waterproof 1,000 denier Cordura fabric.

In addition to wraparound frame packs and internal-frame packs, Alpenlite also makes rucksacks, ski-boot bags, ski bags, book bags, bike packs, racquet packs, fanny packs, soft luggage, gaiters, water bags and stuff sacks.

PRODUCTS: Packs.

ALPINE ADVENTURE
11 Kensington Ave.
Salt Lake City, UT 84115
801-466-6061
Catalog. Est. 1978. Les Ellison, Pres. Mark Bradakis, Cust. Svc.

On multi-day technical rock climbs, a device called a haul bag replaces conventional packs. Rather than carrying their food and equipment on their backs, the climbers load their gear in the haul bag and pull it up behind them. Obviously, the haul bag needs to be tough. The Alpine Adventure Mountain Dream double-bottom haul bags are made out of 16-ounce ballistics nylon. They are further reinforced with strong nylon webbing. The bag also has a set of padded shoulder straps for carrying it to the base of the climb. The straps stow away in a special pouch. A foam-padded waist belt is available as an option. The Grade V Mountain Dream haul bag has a 6,200-cubic-inch capacity. The Grade VI bag has a 9,000-cubic-inch capacity.

The Alpine Adventure Apex Hammock Fly is designed to fit over the single-point suspension hammocks used by big-wall climbers. The upper portion is Gore-Tex, the sides are coated oxford nylon for abrasion resistance. Most of us probably cannot even begin to imagine what it's like to sleep in a hammock hanging 1,500 feet up some rock face, but those who can will appreciate the thoughtful design of the Apex Fly.

The Alpine Adventure Clearwind and Lone Peak parkas are practical shell garments of interest to backpackers and skiers as well as climbers. Off-the-shoulder seams increase weather resistance. Zippered handwarmer pockets add convenience. A large kangaroo pocket in the front of the Clearwind is Velcro sealed. The Lone Peak, on the other hand, is a zipper-front jacket. Both have visored hoods and draw-cords at the waist.

The Redpine, Whitecap, and the Wildcat are good-looking waist-length jackets. The Whitecap is a pullover model with a zipper coming partway down the front. The Wildcat has a synthetic pile lining. Like all Alpine adventure jackets, these garments are made of Gore-Tex or Klimate.

Alpine Adventure Super Bibs are heavy-duty foul-weather pants in a bib overall design. The knees and seat are double layer. Full side zippers (protected by a storm flap) run down each leg, allowing the wearer to put on or take off Super Bibs while wearing crampons or skis.

Other Alpine adventure products include a sleeping bag cover, wind pants, a fanny sack, a fanny sack for camera gear, AWOL-style carrying bags, a climber's rucksack, gaiters, overmitts, stuff sacks, compression stuff sacks, and nylon brief cases.

PRODUCTS: Haul bags, hammock fly, parkas, foul-weather overalls, climbing accessories.

ANTELOPE CAMPING EQUIPMENT MANUFACTURING COMPANY
21740 Granada Ave.
Cupertino, CA 95014
408-253-1913
Accepts MC, VISA. Annual. Est. 1962. Edward Goddard, Pres.

A hiker all his life and an aircraft hydraulics design engineer by profession, Ed Goddard began building packs when his son joined a Boy Scout troop in 1954. The pack frames used in those days were poorly designed and prone to failure in the field. Mr. Goddard decided to find something better. For the frame he came up with a nonwelded mechanical joint. This allowed the replacement of damaged parts without scrapping the entire assembly. A mechanical joint is also stronger than a welded joint, and this led to the design of a frame with a lighter overall weight. Moreover, the mechanical joint permits the frame to expand with the addition of new parts.

Mr. Goddard also found a product called Vivatex which he used to impregnate marine-grade cotton duck. This resulted in "boy-proof" pack bags. It also produced a water-repellent pack bag that breathed and thus eliminated internal condensation. Waterproof nylon is unsatisfactory in this regard.

In 1964 the "boy-proof" packs became Ed Goddard's full-time business. He called the company Antelope Camping Equipment. In the early 70s, Mr. Goddard began experimenting with 500-denier urethane-coated Cordura as a pack-bag fabric. Cordura performs well, but it is expensive. Eventually Ed found something just as good at the reasonable end of the price scale. It is called Parapack, a waterproof synthetic used by the Air Force for parachute packs.

Today Mr. Goddard's company offers a full range of pack frames for adults and children. The basic Antelope frame is made of five-eighths-inch diameter 6061-T6 aluminum alloy tubing fastened together with the exclusive Antelope tubing joints. It features a three-inch back band, padded shoulder straps, wrap-around padded hip belt with quick-release buckle and permanently attached sleeping-bag straps. The frame comes in four sizes: small expandable, medium expandable, large expandable and extra long expandable. Pack bags, of Vivatex cotton canvas or Parapack nylon, come in various configurations and in medium and large sizes. The model 3275 pack frame is designed with special features to give adult hikers a true custom fit. There is also a Model 3280 Expedition frame and bag. In addition there are two frames specially designed for very young hikers.

Besides pack frames and pack bags, Antelope stocks child carriers that attach to the Antelope pack frame, a full range of stuff sacks, day packs and hip packs, hanging food bags, a collapsible grill, plastic bottles, waterbags, windscreens for small stoves, tent pegs, gaiters, and overmitts.

PRODUCTS: Packs, stoves.

AQUABUG
100 Merrick Rd.
Rockville Centre, NY 11570
516-536-8217
Accepts MC, VISA. Annual, four-color, free. Est. 1972. B. J. Kaufman, Pres.

Many times I've been trolling for trout when the outboard engine conked out. That's often more than an inconvenience, especially if it happens in January in a big, mean reservoir like Flaming Gorge, Utah, where a friend and I often fish for trophy-size brown trout. Our problem was that our outboard was not designed for the extremely slow trolling speeds we demanded of it. The fuel would not burn completely, carbon deposits would build up on the sparkplug and other engine parts, and then we were struggling to start out the main engine in time to steer our boat away from hull-crushing cliffs. We always carried half a dozen sparkplugs and frequently changed them just to keep our trolling motor running. An electric motor would not have had enough power for us, not to speak of the problems of using batteries, particularly in sub-freezing and sometimes sub-zero weather.

Evidently a lot of other fishermen have had similar problems. Most outboards, even small ones, just can't operate consistently at low RPMs. Aquabug's engineers set out to invent the little motor that could. Not only did they do that, but they designed three of them, and at surprisingly low prices. Two of Aquabug's outboards even feature a special two-speed automatic transmission that allows the motor to purr smoothly even while the propeller is turning so slowly that you can see it. If you troll slowly or have a small boat or canoe, you ought to look into Aquabug's little wonders. A three-horsepower outboard weighs only 24 pounds and costs $320. A 1.75-horse model, the Superbug 175, weighs only 19 pounds and costs about $250. Reportedly, the least expensive outboard on the market is the Aquabug 120, which produces 1.2 horsepower, costs about $190, and weighs only 13 pounds. The 120 doesn't have automatic transmission.

Another Aquabug product that has outdoor application is a 19-pound generator. Two models are available: the AQB 300, which provides 300 watts of AC power and 10 amps of DC, and the AQB 250D, which produces 20 amps of DC power. Both models are priced at $275.

Aquabug products are guaranteed for one year.

PRODUCTS: Small outboard engines, portable generators.

ASOLO SPORT
8141 W. I-70 Frontage Rd.
North Arvada, CO 80002
303-425-1200

Asolo Sport specializes in backpacking, climbing and ski-touring boots. They are specifically designed for hard wear in a variety of wilderness conditions. Leather for the boots' uppers comes from Eduard Gallusser, AG, a Swiss firm with seven generations of tanning experience. The hides of mature dairy cows are first chrome tanned, then vegetable tanned, and finally impregnated with waxes and oils for water resistance. Full-grain leathers are used in boots intended for wet conditions. Split-grain leathers are used in Asolo Sport's lighter weight boots intended for use on dry trails. All boots are built on lasts that are designed to accommodate a wide range of widths, lengths, and gender characteristics.

Three different welts are used in Asolo Sport boots. The Norwegian welt is the traditional way of making heavy-duty mountain boots. The insole and the upper are sewn together first, then the midsole and the outward-turned upper are sewn together on the outside edge of the boot.

In the Littleway construction method, the insole, midsole, and the uppers are sewn together inside the boot. This method is used in lighter boots; it also guards against damage to the stitching because of sole wear.

In cemented construction, the upper is folded under the midsole and then the upper and the midsole are cemented together, rather than stitched. Norwegian welt, Littleway, and cemented Asolo Sport boots are all repairable and resolable.

Asolo Sport makes four basic types of boots: dry-climate backpacking boots, wet-climate backpacking boots, climbing and mountaineering boots, and ski-touring boots. The dry-climate backpacking boots are intended for summer trail hiking. There are three models. The wet-climate backpacking boots are intended for more demanding conditions such as spring mud and off-trail cross-country use. They weigh a little more than the dry-climate models. Uppers are full-grain leather with Norwegian welt or Littleway construction. The top-of-the-line Yukon features 3.5-mm full-grain, one-piece, rough-out uppers, Norwegian welt, full-grain lining, double tongue, Celastic toe box and heel counter, and Vibram Montagna block outsole.

There are three models in the climbing and mountaineering boot category. The Chouinard Canyon is a technical rock-climbing shoe with canvas-reinforced suede uppers, leather insole, and Vibram 7.0-mm outsole. The Cervino is a general-purpose mountaineering boot with 3.8-mm full-grain, one-piece, rough-out uppers, Norwegian welt, full-grain leather lining, double tongue, a long steel shank for stiffness, laminated rubber and leather midsole, and a Vibram Montagna block outsole. Size eight medium weighs five pounds, 13 ounces. The Pro is a double boot for winter or high-altitude mountaineering. The inner boot is lined with synthetic fleece. Size eight medium weighs eight pounds, two ounces.

Asolo Sport makes two styles of ski-touring boots, neither of which should be confused with the low-cut shoes used by weekend cross-country skiers and racers. These are first-class boots for multi-day trips in the backcountry. The Snowfield is a single boot that weighs about three pounds, three ounces. The Summit is a double boot for severe weather. Both feature a Vibram 7.5-mm Nordic Norm Touring outsole.

PRODUCTS: Backpacking, climbing, ski-touring boots.

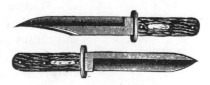

BANANA REPUBLIC
76 E. Blithedale
Mill Valley, CA 94942
415-383-4900 (415-777-5200 for orders)
Accepts AMEX, MC, VISA. $1.

The Banana Republic is not really a backpacking store, but we can't help but feel that people who like wilderness sports will be intrigued by some of the items in the Republic catalog. The seven-foot-long French aviator scarf is a good example. The genuine British Blitz Jacket made out of 100 percent British Melton wool and rescued from a warehouse where it had lain, untouched and forgotten for 30 years, is an item that seems easily adaptable to moutain wear. The same goes for the commando beret or the khaki cargo pants. Good uses for the "Artist and Writer Sweater" seem obvious. The safari shirt belongs in anyone's kit.

Style is the essence of the Banana Republic. Low prices are not. But where else do you find an authentic goatskin flight jacket exactly the same as the one worn by Douglas MacArthur? Enough said.

PRODUCTS: Outdoor clothing.

BLACK ICE
120 Woodland Ave.
Reno, NV 89523
702-747-6806
Full-color.

Black Ice offers three down sleeping bags. The White Light, a bag good to approximately minus 10 degrees, weighs three pounds, 14 ounces in the regular size. It features a down-filled collar, side-block baffles, an overfilled draft flap to protect the zipper, differential baffle depth, slat-wall baffles, triple-chamber foot section, and a waterproof stuff sack. The Aurora bag is for more moderate temperatures. The Quicksilver is a ultra-lightweight (three pounds, four ounces) down bag that is comfortable to 20 degrees.

All Black Ice PolarGuard bags feature six to nine layers of insulation, each one differentially cut. This increases the loft by creating air spaces between the layers. All five bags are of the modified mummy type with a hood that draws up over the sleeper's head. Construction details include number seven two-way YKK Ziplon coil zippers and interior overlock reinforcements at every seam. The bags range in temperature rating from 20 degrees to minus 30 degrees. The lightest bag weighs three pounds, 14 ounces; the warmest and heaviest weighs seven pounds, eight ounces.

The Black Ice UFO is a two-man tent that weighs an even four pounds. High in front and low in the rear, it features shock corded fiberglass poles, a full rain fly with Velcro closures, and guy lines with tension adjusters. It is very easy to set up.

The Black Ice St. Elias parka is a completely baffled cold-weather down jacket that is not as bulky or expensive as an expedition-style down parka, but is much warmer than the typical down sweater. Nineteen ounces of down give this garment six inches of loft.

The Dark Star parka features a tough outer shell, 10½ inches of down fill, inside pockets, cargo/handwarmer pockets outside, an optional hood, weather skirt, inset polyester cuffs and raglan sleeves. The Trinity vest has six ounces of down fill, inside pockets with Velcro, weather skirt, and a tough exterior shell.

The Earthlight parka has double-layer Thinsulate insulation for a trim fit and cold-weather utility. This jacket has the same attention to detail as Black Ice down garments, but is less bulky and more suited to damp climates. The Tenaya parka and the Windstar vest are also Thinsulate garments, cut for active uses.

The Moonrise vest has plaid wool lining backed up with two layers of Thermalite insulation. Thermalite is a polyester fiber insulator developed by Black Ice. It offers a superior weight/loft efficiency ratio and is easy to stuff. The Sunset parka also features Thermalite, a box quilted interior, a high collar, and slash handwarmer pockets. The Lightning parka is a rugged shell garment meant to be worn alone or over a jacket or a vest.

PRODUCTS: Outdoor clothing, sleeping bags, tents.

B & L DISTRIBUTORS
8645 E. State Route 36
Conover, OH 45317
513-368-2305 or 2306
Accepts VISA. Brochures, four-color, free. Est. 1977. Willis Barnhart, Pres.

B & L Distributors sells two kinds of products that are useful to many sportsmen: kerosene heaters and a hand-held searchlight said to be the world's most intense hand-held light.

There are four Toyostove heater models. The KSA-105 produces 19,500 BTUs an hour and can operate for as long as 18 hours on less than two gallons of kerosene. It weighs about 26½ pounds. The KSA-851 puts out 13,000 BTUs an hour, can burn for 20 hours on 1.99 gallons of fuel, and weighs 22 pounds. Also capable of burning 20 hours is the 30-pound RCA-36C, which yields 9,600 BTUs an hour. Even longer-burning is the RSA-10G, which can produce heat for 30 hours on less than two gallons of kerosene. It weighs 28½ pounds and produces 9,600 BTUs an hour.

The Search Light features a sealed-beam quartz/halogen lamp and a nickel-cadmium power cell. All parts but the lamp are guaranteed to function properly for three years. The battery is said to power the lamp at full intensity for four continuous hours. Shaped like an extra-long flashlight, the Search Light is made of one-eighth-inch-thick anodized aircraft aluminum. The light can be seen from more than 30 miles away and has enough power to illuminate a newspaper to reading levels at distances of more than a mile. It can be used under water to depths of more than 100 feet. If that's not enough, the battery is designed to last 20 years and is rechargeable. A plug-in recharger is included.

PRODUCTS: Hand-held searchlights, kerosene heaters.

BLUE PUMA OUTDOOR EQUIPMENT
650 10th St.
Arcata, CA 95521
707-822-5856
Accepts MC, VISA. $1. Est. 1972. Steve O'Mgara, Pres. Suzanne Shulman, Cust. Svc.

All pieces of fabric used in Blue Puma garments are individually cut with a hot knife to prevent unravelling at the edges. Seams are double sewn with 10-12 stitches per inch. Blue Puma goose down has a lofting power of 600-plus cubic inches per ounce.

The Blue Puma down parka features 11 ounces of down fill, raglan sleeves for freedom of movement, stretch knit nylon cuffs, waist drawstring, storm flap, Velcro-sealed, down-insulated double handwarmer pockets, and a #9 Talon ladder coil zipper.

The Blue Puma down jacket—somewhat shorter than the down parka—is filled with seven ounces of goose down. An optional snap-on down hood is available for both the parka and the jacket.

The newly redesigned Blue Puma down vest is filled with 5½ ounces of goose down and features a corduroy collar, inside zippered pockets, extended rear panel, brass snap-front closure, and handwarmer pocket.

Blue Puma's Thinsulate parka with Gore-Tex outer shell is an ideal garment for cold, wet climates. Thinsulate—manufactured by the 3M Company—is one of the best synthetic insulating materials because its very fine polyolefin/polyester fibers trap more dead air in a given space. Thinsulate also absorbs less than one percent of its own weight in water. The Blue Puma Thinsulate parka has Velcro cuffs, a brass snap/Talon zipper front closure, a built-in visored hood, raglan sleeves, slash pockets outside, a zippered pocket inside, double-sewn lap felled seam construction, and a clever storm skirt inside the parka itself.

The Blue Puma paddling jacket is available in Super K-Kote or taffeta/tricot Gore-Tex. Both models have six-inch neoprene cuffs with YKK zippers and neoprene necks with Velcro closures and zippers. The Blue Puma paddling sweater has a 12-ounce Antron pile body with three-quarter length sleeves for use with the neoprene-cuff paddling jacket.

The Bear Necessity personal shelter is designed to give a person in a sleeping bag complete protection from rain, snow, or bugs without the fuss or the weight of a tent. The top of the Bear Necessity is Gore-Tex laminate and—depending on the model—the bottom is either coated nylon or Gore-Tex. The Bear Necessity, in other words, is a bivouac sack, but it is an unusually well-designed bivouac sack.

Blue Puma goose down sleeping bags are available in four models for conditions ranging from summer use when the temperature does not go below freezing to severe winter conditions. Blue Puma also makes an attractive down quilt in king, queen, double, and twin sizes.

PRODUCTS: Sleeping bags, down jackets, vests, parkas.

BLUE SPRUCE JAMMERS

222 Linden St.
Ft. Collins, CO 80524
303-493-2826
Accepts MC, VISA. Illustrated brochure. Est. 1977. Kendal Scudder, Pres.

Blue Spruce Jammers makes pants, The idea originated at a jam session—hence the name "Jammers"—when several of the participants complained about the poor fit of the conventional pants they were wearing. Jammers feature a unique system of Velcro fasteners that replace all zippers, snaps, buttons and belts. A patented cord-and-loop waistband allows the wearer to custom-tailor the fit to accommodate what he is doing, how he feels or the thickness of the clothing he wants to tuck inside.

The Classic model pant features deep front pockets and a back pocket that fastens with Velcro. These pants are available in a lightweight, quick-drying 65 percent polyester/35 percent cotton blend or in 84 percent/cotton 16 percent polyester mid-wale corduroy.

The special Jammers hiking pants feature six front pockets, two back pockets with flaps, and a utility loop for knives and the like. The fabric is either 65 percent polyester/35 percent cotton or a khaki mid-wale corduroy.

The Jammers hiking shorts are similar to the pants and feature a full cut for freedom of movement.

PRODUCTS: Hikings pants, shorts.

BOB HINMAN

1217 W. Glen Av.e
Peoria, IL 61614
309-691-8132
Accepts MC, VISA. Semi-annual, four-color and B&W, free. Est. 1959.
R.K. Hinman, Pres.

Bob Hinman used to be a food broker who spent his profit hunting and fishing around the world, so it was natural for him to start selling sporting goods. His first mail-order catalog was published 21 years ago. You might recognize his name from outdoor magazines or books, for Hinman has published more

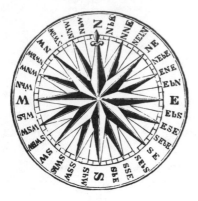

than 600 fishing and hunting articles and two books. He is co-author of four other books.

His catalog's emphasis is on high-quality hunting clothing, especially attire for waterfowl hunters and wingshooters. He also sells clothing for backpackers, anglers, and canoeists, and has a large line of down clothing.

He says his company was the first to introduce Bama Hair boot socks, Polar gloves, New Zealand Swann Dri jackets, Hinman's dove call, and a folding, stainless steel pocket axe.

The latest catalog features such other items as duffle bags, packs, gun cabinets, tents, sleeping bags, boots, and Dutch ovens. Hinman promises fast delivery because he stocks everything he sells and has a money-back-if-not-satisfied guarantee.

PRODUCTS: Outdoor clothing, camping supplies.

BOWEN KNIFE COMPANY

P.O. Drawer 590-A
Blackshear, GA 31516
912-449-4794
Color, 50¢. Est. 1971. W. Stephen Bowen, Jr., Pres. Jack R. Lippert, Cust. Svc.

The Bowen Survivor Belt combines a heavy-duty leather belt with a buckle that is also a quality knife. The point and blade of the knife-buckle are of course designed so they cannot come in contact with the wearer's body. The advantages of this setup are obvious—if you remember to put on your pants, you won't forget your knife.

The blade is 440 stainless steel and comes in single- and double-edged models. The double-edged model requires a special 1⁹/₁₆-inch belt. The belts are black or russet brown in sizes 26 to 48 inches.

Initials can be engraved on the bar portion of the buckle or imprinted on the leather belt. Deluxe buckles are available with a number of different scenes etched on the blade, including mallards in flight, a wild pig, the frigate *Old Ironsides*, a bear walking in front of some mountains, deer standing in the woods, bald eagles in flight and at rest, a jumping brook trout, the clipper ship *Flying Cloud*, full-curl bighorn rams, and running buffalo. These scenes are produced in limited editions. When the supply becomes exhausted, they are discontinued and new scenes are introduced.

Along with the Survivor Belt, Bowen offers knives of more conventional design. The 126 Model sheath knife has a 3¾-inch blade, a Stag or Pakkawood handle, and a top-grain eight-ounce leather sheath. The 124 Model is a smaller version of the 126 with the same features and quality.

Model R1306-S is a folding knife with a 3½-inch blade that locks in the open position for safety. Model R1306-BS is a bit smaller. Model R1306-B is like the R1306-BS, but features a handle made of Delrin rather than stag horn.

A second line of folding knives is made in Solingen, Germany, to Bowen specifications. They have bone handles, 440 C steel blades and come in seven models: 4½-inch (closed length) Drop Point Lockback, four-inch, three-blade stockman knife, 3¼-inch, three-blade pocketknife, 3⅜-inch, three-blade deluxe whittler, 4⅛-inch, two-blade trapper's knife, 3⁹/₁₆-inch, two-blade canoe pattern, and a 2¾-inch, two-blade penknife.

The Bowen Knife Company began as a custom knife maker in Atlanta. The products were popular enough to cause demand to exceed supply, thus necessitating the introduction of modern production techniques. Eventually, Mr. Bowen had to discontinue the custom knife business. In 1975, he moved the entire operation to his boyhood home in south Georgia near the Okefenokee Swamp and the headwaters of the Suwanee River.

PRODUCTS: Knives.

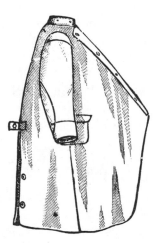

BRIGADE QUARTERMASTERS
266 Roswell St.
Marietta, GA 30060
404-428-1234
Accepts MC,VISA. Illustrated. Est. 1976. Mitchell WerBell, Pres.
Frances Chupp, Cust. Svc.

During the years after World War II, when backpacking and mountaineering were first becoming popular as recreational activities in the United States, Army suplus was a prime source of equipment. It was cheap, durable and available. If it was good enough for GIs, it was good enough for climbers. For the most part, this has long since ceased to be true. Backpackers, after all, are not soldiers. Their needs are different. Army issue equipment is expected to stand up to combat conditions. Lightweight pack frames and $200 goose-down sleeping bags are not. Nevertheless, certain kinds of military gear can still be extremely useful to civilian outdoorsmen. Army fatigue

clothing, for example, has always been popular in the backcountry. The "P-38" can opener is a very handy gadget. And if you plan to tramp around in a mangrove swamp, the U.S. Army jungle boot—the kind used in Vietnam—is indispensible.

Brigade Quartermasters offers the cream of the crop of outdoor-related military items. Perhaps they are best known for their "Wooly Pully" sweater. The Wooly Pully is the original British Commando sweater that is now used by all British forces. Various styles and colors have been approved for optional uniform wear by U.S. military units and by the U.S. Fish and Wildlife Service. Every Wooly Pully imported by Brigade Quartermasters is manufactured according to British Ministry of Defence specifications. The sweater is 100 percent pure virgin wool with reinforced shoulder and elbow patches and double stitching or cover stitching on all seams. It comes in a variety of colors and styles including crew neck, mock turtleneck and V-neck.

The "Commando Watchband" is made in Brigade Quartermaster's own shop. It features a crystal cover flap to protect a watch from shock and abrasion. Other Brigade Quartermaster products include belt pouches, nylon wallets, checkbooks, and map cases. The catalog also features knives, White Stag tents, Madden packs, camouflage clothing, cooking gear, military-type boots, and a host of unique specialty items.

And then there are some distinctly unspecial things that any ex-GI will recognize. This is the place to go for an entrenching tool or a mess kit. Or for C-rations or dog tags. As a matter of fact, you could get a pretty good start here toward outfitting your own platoon. Well, not quite. We were never issued Wooly Pullys or camouflage checkbook covers at Fort Dix.

PRODUCTS: Outdoor-related military clothing, implements.

BRISTLECONE MOUNTAINEERING
P.O. Box 5396
Akron, OH 44313

The bristlecone pine does not grow very tall, but it is extraordinarily well-adapted to survival in the high mountains. Bristlecones that are nearly 5,000 years old have been found in California and Nevada. They are among the oldest living things on the planet.

Bristlecone Mountaineering products may not last 5,000 years, but they are sturdy, cleverly designed items. The White Mountain parka—presumably named after the White Mountains of western Nevada where the ancient pines grow—is a triple-layer garment filled with goose down. The triple-layer construction rules out cold spots. The outer shell is 60/40 cloth. The parka features hand warmer and cargo pockets, zippered breast pocket, a draw cord at the waist and a knit inner collar.

The Green Mountain Zip-Out parka is several garments in one. The lining (filled with goose down) zips out to be worn as a down vest. The outer shell—made of 60/40 cloth—can be worn as a mountain parka. Together, the shell and the lining make a warm jacket.

The Hebrides Mountain parka is a shell garment that comes in a man's and a woman's version. It is fully lined and has a hood, waist draw cord, four front pockets, Velcro at the cuffs, and leather sliders at the hood and the waist. The Trossachs Tartan parka is like the Hebrides parka, but has a wool-blend Stuart plaid three-quarter lining. It comes in men's and women's models.

The Berkshire vest is filled with goose down. The Padre vest is filled with PolarGuard, an insulating material that will not absorb more than two percent of its total weight in water. This is a very good rainy-climate garment. PolarGuard booties are also available. They feature coated Cordura on the bottom.

The 500 Expedition sleeping bag is filled with Hollobond II. It is rated to 35 degrees below zero. The regular size (long is available too) weighs six pounds, 10 ounces. The Model 400 sleeping bag is filled with PolarGuard and is good to minus 10 degrees. The loft is 7½ inches. The bag weighs five pounds, 6 ounces in the regular size.

The Model 300 sleeping bag is an extremely roomy sleeping bag that will accept an inner bag for very cold conditions. By itself, the 300 is rated to 10 degrees. It is also available in a rectangular (instead of mummy) shape. The fill is Hollobond II. The Model 200 sleeping bag is a PolarGuard mummy rated to 10 degrees. The Model 50 sleeping bag is a lightweight (three pounds, 6 ounces) mummy rated to 30 degrees.

PRODUCTS: Outdoor clothing, sleeping bags.

BUCKHEAD OUTFITTERS
3130 Maple Dr.
Atlanta, GA 30305
404-261-4429
Accepts MC, VISA. B&W.

Buckhead Outfitters stocks brand-name products for backpackers. Pack frames include models by Coleman Peak 1, Alpenlite, and Himalayan. Alpenlite was instrumental in developing the wraparound frame that takes the weight of the load off the wearer's shoulders and back and puts it on the legs and hips. Pack bags come in top- and front-loading models. Himalayan packs feature an adjustable suspension system and through-the-wall heliarc welds at frame joints. Pack bags are Cordura nylon. The Peak 1 Ram-Flx frame is molded of one-piece high-impact plastic-type material that flexes with the backpacker's body as he moves. Numerous slots in the frame allow nearly 2,000 different combination of suspension-system parts. Pack sacks come in three different models including a 4,700-cubic-inch expedition version.

Buckhead also carries internal-frame packs by Alpenlite and other makers, as well as fanny packs, kid's packs, day packs, duffle bags, shoulder bags, camera cases, and soft luggage.

Sleeping bags are offered with goose down and synthetic fill. Down offers the most warmth for its weight and it can be compressed into a smaller stuff sack. On the negative side, down loses insulating capability when damp and offers almost no warmth at all if the bag gets seriously wet. Goose down bags are comparatively fragile and need careful hand washing to maintain loft. They are also expensive.

Hollofil II and PolarGuard are the most popular synthetic insulating materials used in quality bags today. Synthetic bags weigh about one-third more than a comparable goose-down bag, but they stay warm when wet. If the bag gets soaked, you can wring it out and body heat will dry out the insulation during the night. Synthetic bags are less expensive than goose-down bags. Buckhead Outfitters offers various models of sleeping bags filled with synthetics or goose down, and one bag with goose down on top and PolarGuard on the bottom. This is an eminently sensible arrangement because down compresses flat under body weight and loses insulating power. Along with sleeping bags, Buckhead Outfitters carries air mattresses, foam pads, and bivy sacks.

Tents in the Buckhead Outfitters catalog include A-frame and dome models. Compasses, stoves, knives, cooking gear, food, and clothing round out the line. A complete backpacking outfit is offered that includes pack frame, sleeping bag, ensolite

pad, trail tarp, stove, cookware, compass, first-aid kit, flashlight, and other items, all at a money-saving package price.

PRODUCTS: Packs, sleeping bags, tents, knives, food, outdoor clothing, stoves, medical supplies.

BUCK KNIVES
P.O. Box 1267
El Cajon, CA 92022
Illustrated brochure and knife instruction booklet.

Stone cutting tools and spear points were among the first objects to be made by man. These primitive implements gradually evolved into knives, and they have been indispensible to outdoorsmen ever since. Modern knives, like most things, have benefited tremendously from technological advances, especially in the field of metallurgy, but there is still no substitute for honest craftsmanship in knife-making. And unlike many other types of equipment used by present-day outdoorsmen, a good knife made in 1982 still looks pretty much like a good knife made 100 years ago. A knife, in other words, is a piece of tradition you can hold in your hand. It is a link to the past, and this is one reason that outdoorsmen tend to have strong emotional attachments to their knives. Another reason is that a good knife can easily give a lifetime of service. You really have a chance to get used to it.

So it isn't surprising that sportsmen are finicky when it comes to selecting a knife. The Buck family has been meeting the requirements of these finicky outdoorsmen for three generations, and today they offer a line of knives that look as good and perform as well as just about any on the market. All Buck knives come with a lifetime guarantee against defects in materials or workmanship.

There are 11 models in the Buck 300 series of pocket-knives. None of these knives feature corkscrews, nail clippers or other gimmicks. What they do have is the dependability you need out in the field. The Stockman, with clip, spey and sheepsfoot blades, is an excellent choice for backpackers. It is 3⅞ inches long. The Trail Blazer is a sturdy two-blade model 5¼ inches long. The Bird knife has a gutting hook and the Muskrat has a slender skinning blade and a spey blade.

The 500 Slimline series offers heavy-duty folding knives with single lock-open blades. The 700 series of extra-sturdy pocketknives feature stainless steel bolsters, non-rusting springs and stainless knife liners and laminated wood-epoxy handle inserts.

Buck makes a complete line of hunting knives in many different sizes and blade shapes, including two folding hunters with Macassar ebony handles and solid brass bolsters.

Buck sharpening equipment includes a variety of Arkansas honing stones, sharpening kits, sharpening steel and Buck honing oil.

PRODUCTS: Pocket knives, hunting knives.

BUCK-SPIN PRODUCTS
6010 Kew Park
Manitou Beach, MI 49253
517-547-6326
Annual, four-color, free. Tom Dalton, Pres.

Many hunters have asked me where they could get camouflage fabric. One company that sells it by mail is Buck-Spin Products of Manitou Beach, Michigan. It sells camp mosquito netting, two camo nylon fabrics, and six other camouflage cloths. Patterns include marsh brown, Vietnam, winter, and orange. For extra-soft garments, there is flannel camo cloth. The nylon fabrics are said to be water-repellent. Most fabrics are sold in four quantities from five to 100 yards. Prices vary from $3.33 to $6.90 a yard. Four fabrics are $4.25 a yard.

Other Buck-Spin items include four camouflage ground blinds. Prices range from about $30 to about $70. The top-of-the-line blind is a three-person model that is six feet long and three feet wide. It is self-standing.

Two kinds of camouflage hunting seats are offered. One is mounted on a square plywood platform and can be mounted on a tree stand. The other is a tripod model and is not recommended for use in elevated stands. Both are portable and compact.

Buck-Spin offers some items ready-made from camouflage cloth: four heavy-duty duffle bags, a fanny pack, a compound-bow case, a duck-decoy bag, a shoulder bag, gun sleeves, duck-call holsters, two knife sheaths, a hand bag, a tote bag, and a wallet.

PRODUCTS: Camouflage fabric, camouflage bags and hunting accessories, ground blinds, hunting seats.

BUGABOO MOUNTAINEERING
170 Central Ave.
Pacific Grove, CA 93950
408-373-6433
Accepts MC, VISA. Est. 1960. Richard & Shelly Risko, Pres.

Bugaboo Mountaineering makes high-quality goose-down jackets and sleeping bags. Every item is sewn by one person, start to finish, to eliminate assembly-line sloppiness. Designs are simple, functional and efficient, with meticulous attention to detail. The prices are competitive with mass-produced items.

The Bugaboo down jacket is typical of the line. It features a two-way heavy-duty nylon coil zipper with a double draft flap, a snow and wind skirt, an inside slash pocket with Velcro closure, down-filled cargo/handwarmer pockets, sewn-in knit cuffs, reinforced snaps, double-sewn seams, and special raglan sleeves for freedom of movement.

The Alpine jacket is a lighter weight model with a chevron quilt pattern, down-filled pockets, and an elasticized back. The California jacket is a waist-length jacket with down-filled pockets, a down-filled snap-closure front draft flap, elastic waist in back, and sewn-in knit cuffs. The Bugaboo down sweater is a pullover design with rib knit cuffs, rib knit V collar, and front pouch pockets. The Bugaboo down coat is a full-length robe-style wrap coat with chevron quilting, contrasting liner, and a belted waist. Not intended for outdoor use, the down coat makes a luxurious robe for wear around a cold house or cabin in the winter.

All Bugaboo sleeping bags feature slant box construction, two-way nylon coil zippers, double sewn seams with 12-14 stitches per inch, and top-quality goose down with a fill power of 600 cubic inches per ounce. The bags come in blue, rust or burgundy nylon taffeta or in blue Gore-Tex. All bags are available in regular or long sizes. Custom-sized bags are available on request.

The Bugaboo Superlight bag weighs 2½ pounds in the regular size. The temperature rating is 20 degrees. The Mountaineer is a lightweight four-season bag with differential cut and side block baffles. It weighs 2.9 pounds regular. The California bag is a roomier four-season bag that weighs 3½ pounds in the regular size.

The Traveler is a rectangular four-season bag with a zipper that extends around the bottom so the bag will open flat like a quilt. The Traveler weighs 3½ pounds. The Number One is an expedition bag, pure and simple. With differential cut, side block baffles, double baffled head and foot sections and a down-filled collar, the Number One is rated to minus 40 degrees. It weighs 4¾ pounds in the regular size. The Bugaboo Double Mummy is a two-person bag that weighs 5¾ pounds and is warm enough for four-season use.

PRODUCTS: Down jackets, sleeping bags.

BYRD INDUSTRIES
South Industrial Park
Ripley, TN 38063
901-635-9122
Annual, four-color, free. Est. 1960. John McLaughlin, Pres.

Byrd Industries specializes in electric fishing motors. It sells 10 models. Five are 12-volt models, while the others can be used at either 12 volts or 24 volts.

The dual-voltage models are called Double Eagles. Each has a 33-pound thrust, an 18-amp draw at full speed, six forward speeds, an automatic circuit-breaker switch, and a 36-inch standard shaft. Optional at no extra charge are 30-inch and 42-inch shafts.

The 12-volt models, called Magnum Eagles, have three forward speeds, 23-amp draws, 24-pound thrusts, automatic circut breakers, and the same shafts as Double Eagles.

In each line is a foot-control motor with a long bow bracket, a hand-control model with a short bow bracket, a hand-control with a long bow bracket, a hand-control with a short deluxe bow bracket, and a hand-control with a transom bracket.

Other Byrd products include a universal bow-mount bracket, a gadget that holds a trolling motor securely when not in use, an outboard-engine-support arm, four models of rod holders, and an electronic surface-water thermometer.

Byrd says it produces only top-of-the-line products and does not manufacture or distribute economy models.

PRODUCTS: Electric fishing motors and accessories, rod holders, electronic surface-water thermometers.

CALIFORNIA MOUNTAIN COMPANY

P.O. Box 6602
Santa Barbara, CA 93111
805-964-2462
Accepts MC. Annual. Est. 1978. James A. Frank, Pres. Jerry Smith, Cust. Rel.

California Mountain Company sells a wide range of rock-climbing and ice-climbing equipment and specializes in mountain rescue equipment. The hardware selection includes Chouinard and SMC carabiners, Russ Anderson rescue pulleys and belay plates, figure-eight descenders, Chouinard hexentrics and stoppers, Chouinard pitons, Forrest climbing nuts, etc. A variety of piton hammers are offered. There is a wide array of rope webbing and climbing harnesses, as well as ice axes, crampons, ice hammers, Sherpa snowshoes, Dolt packs, Forrest gaiters, and Chouinard packs.

California Mountain Company stocks one of the most complete selections of mountain rescue gear in the nation. A sphygmomanometer, for example, is not something you normally expect to find in an outdoor equipment catalog. California Mountain Company carries two models. (A sphygmomanometer, by the way, measures blood pressure.) Other first-aid items include stethoscopes, bandage scissors, forceps, laryngeal mirrors, disposable gloves, ammonia inhalants, emergency blankets, various splints, and Stokes litters (the classic device for lowering an injured person down a steep rock face).

Rescue operations are often complicated by darkness, so California Mountain Company carries an exceptionally wide range of headlamps and flashlights and long-life batteries, including the Streamlite, the most powerful hand-held flashlight available. With this light you can read a newspaper 500 yards from the light itself. The catalog also lists a number of strobe lights, flares, and smoke markers.

Perhaps more important than the equipment—which we have listed here only in part—is California Mountain Company's expertise in the rescue field. Most of the employees are actively involved in volunteer search-and-rescue teams. They have used virtually every item listed in the catalog and can offer invaluable advice concerning it. They are not selling anything they do not believe in.

Besides climbing and rescue equipment, California Mountain Company carries knives, stoves, cookware, freeze-dried foods, and a large selection of books, including many search-and-rescue titles.

PRODUCTS: Mountaineering equipment, rescue equipment.

CAMILLUS CUTLERY COMPANY
Camillus, NY 13031
315-672-8111
$1. Est. 1876. Nilo Miore, Pres. Thomas Williams, Cust. Svc.

After more than 100 years in the business, Camillus now employs 350 workers who produce nearly three million knives a year. The line includes fixed-blade hunting knives, folding knives, skinning knives, folding hunters, and a large selection of specialized and general-purpose pocketknives and jackknives.

The No. 31 Angler's Folder, for example, includes a stainless steel sabre clip blade, hook disgorger, scaler, and cap lifter, while the No. 99 Camp knife looks just about like the pocketknife you had—or wished you had—when you were in the Boy Scouts. This knife, with its can opener, punch, and combination screwdriver/bottle opener is an ideal backpacking knife. The closed length is 3⅝ inches.

But there are at least a dozen other knives in the Camillus catalog that backpackers may be interested in. The No. 67 Premium Stock knife with three blades—clip, sheepfoot, and spey—is one. The folded length is 3⅞ inches. The No. 18 two-blade jackknife is another. The No. 51 Barlow is a classic in its own right.

Specialized knives by Camillus include four models of wood-carvers, a pruning knife, an electrician's knife, a lineman's knife, a Coast Guard knife, the No. 695 and 697 Marlin Spikes, and the No. 17 Wildfowler knife with gut hook.

The American Wildlife Series of premium-grade knives feature 440A high-carbon steel blades and special handles. They come in folding hunter, wildfowl, and "Lok Back" models.

Sheaths, pouches, and sharpening tools are also available. Given the range of knives offered by Camillus, and the years of experience that have gone into making them, it seems unlikely that a serious outdoorsman could not find something here to fit his needs.

PRODUCTS: Knives.

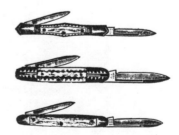

CAMO CLAN
3005 Elm St.
Dallas, TX 75226
214-742-9260
Accepts MC, VISA. Semi-annual, four-color, free. Est. 1978. Robert Hoague, Pres.

Camo Clan says it offers the world's most complete line of matching camouflage items. Indeed, where else could you order camouflaged bow covers in seven different camo patterns and colors? Besides the familiar World War II leaf-pattern camo, there are Tiger Stripe, bright orange, Viet Nam, Snow Camo, Autumn, and Tree Stand Camo patterns. Insulated clothing is made in another camo pattern, the new military Woodlands.

Each kind of camouflage is suited to a certain terrain or cover. World War II, for example, works well in a leafy area, but Tiger Stripe is better after trees have lost their leaves. Tree Stand Camo is characterized by vertical stripes and is therefore hard to see against a tree trunk.

The company's hunting clothing is designed especially for bowhunting but, of course, is effective for other kinds of hunting, too. Special features include a gathered left sleeve (to prevent sleeve from catching on bowstring), lots of pockets (seven in the trousers alone), a bow rest on the left thigh, hidden buttons, and flap pockets that stay closed without buttons or snaps. Garments are made for left-handed archers, too.

Available are pants, jackets, coveralls, caps, gloves, parkas, head covers, drawstring bags, bow covers, belt pouches, bow-stabilizer covers, insulated jackets, insulated pants, insulated head covers, and waterproof foul-weather gear. A unique offering is the Bug Buster, an insect-proof coverall with a matching button-down mosquito head net.

Camo Clan has added some hunting accessories to its line, including Weems game calls and electronic callers, two kinds of tree stands, arrowheads, two bow sights, custom arrows, deer scents, and an elk call.

PRODUCTS: Camouflage hunting clothing and accessories.

CAMPMOR
206 West Shore Ave.
Bogata, NJ 07603
201-488-1550
Accepts MC, VISA. Est. 1946.

From tent pegs and water bottles to sleeping bags and packs, Campmor offers a full selection of backpacking equipment. The products are described in a 65-page information-packed catalog.

In the last few years, Thinsulate has emerged as one of the most popular synthetic insulating materials for outdoor clothing. Unlike goose down, Thinsulate absorbs virtually no water and remains warm in wet conditions. Because Thinsulate consists of a network of millions of ultra-thin polyolefin fibers, it can trap more "dead" air in a given thickness of material than other synthetic insulators. Thus, a Thinsulate garment does not have to be bulky to provide warmth. The Woolrich Thinsulate parka offered by Campmor features 200 grams of Thinsulate and an outer shell of 82 percent polyester and 18 percent cotton poplin with four outside pockets, removable hood, Velcro cuffs, and a zipper front closure with a snap-closed storm flap. The Bremmerton Gore-Tex Thinsulate parka features Thinsulate insulation and a waterproof Gore-Tex outer shell with Velcro cuffs, hood, handwarmer cargo pockets and a waist drawcord. The Woolrich Thinsulate vest has four outside pockets, corduroy collar and a 65 percent polyester/35 percent cotton outer shell. Campmor also offers a down vest by Woolrich.

Borglite Pile is another synthetic insulating material that has gained great popularity among backpackers, climbers and canoeists because of its practicality in wet, cold conditions. Campmor carries pile garments by Because It's There in vest and jacket styles. An attractive feature of pile is its versatility. Pile garments can either be worn by themselves or underneath a windproof/waterproof shell.

Gore-Tex has emerged as the premier material of the eighties for making windproof/waterproof shells. Gore-Tex itself is not actually a fabric but a thin polytetrafluorethylene film with billions of tiny holes per square inch. Each of these holes is smaller than the smallest drop of liquid water but much larger than a water vapor molecule. Thus, water vapor can pass through, but rain cannot. In other words, Gore-Tex is both waterproof and breathable. Campmor offers garments made of Gore-Tex laminates by Wilderness Experience, Log House and Woolrich.

Other outdoor clothing in the Campmor catalog includes

ragg wool sweaters, hats, socks and gloves; Duofold underwear; SXC polypropelene underwear; gaiters; and ponchos. Campmor carries boots by Timberland and Pacific Mountain Sports.

Campmor carries a complete selection of tents by Eureka! The Campmor sleeping bag line includes bags by Wenzel, Coleman Peak 1, Bristlecone Mountaineering and Camp 7 in goose down and synthetic insulated models, plus a full range of mattresses, foam pads, stuff sacks, sleeping-bag straps, etc.

In the pack department, Campmor has external-frame packs by Kelty, Camp Trails, and Coleman Peak 1, and internal-frame packs by Wilderness Experience, Tough Traveler, Camp Trails, and Lowe Alpine Systems, plus day packs, camera packs and soft luggage.

The array of knives, compasses, cookware, stoves, water bottles, flashlights, trail food, and accessory items carried by Campmor is far too complex to be summarized here. This is one of the best mail-order selections available anywhere.

PRODUCTS: Backpacking equipment.

CAMP TRAILS (Johnson Camping)
P.O. Box 966
Binghamton, NY 13902
607-723-7546
Full-color.

Camp Trails has been making packs since 1946. In 1973, the company was acquired by Johnson Wax Associates. The frames of Camp Trails packs are fabricated of aircraft-quality aluminum alloy with heliarc welded joints. A special V-truss design adds strength under heavy loads and dampens corner-to-corner stress. YKK ziplon coil zippers are used on all pack bags. Lock-stitch construction is used throughout, with double and triple stitching at stress points. Depending on the model, pack bag fabric is eight-ounce 500 denier Cordura, 11-ounce 1,000 denier Cordura, or eight-ounce or five-ounce nylon pack cloth. All fabrics are coated for water repellency.

The Orion and the Centuri are Camp Trails' top-of-the-line external-frame packs. The Orion is a large-capacity pack with a single main compartment and an integral extension sleeve at the top of the pack bag. The Centuri functions as a divided-compartment pack or a single-compartment pack. It also has an extension sleeve for protecting extra-large loads

from the weather. Both the Orion and the Centuri feature the Camp Trails deluxe suspension system that allows the hiker to adjust the pack's weight from the hip belt to the shoulder straps while the pack is being worn.

The Astral and New Horizon packs use Camp Trails' time-tested standard suspension system. The New Horizon is a front-loading model, and the Astral is a top-loader with an extendable top compartment. Both packs have compression straps to stabilize the load.

The Camp Trails adjustable packs are for growing hikers. The Compack II frame is suitable for children and for smaller adults too. The Camp Trails Freighter Frame is specially designed for extremely rugged use. A fold-away shelf on the bottom of the frame supports heavy, bulky loads that will not fit into a pack bag.

Camp Trails also makes a complete line of internal-frame packs. Internal stays are 6061-T6 aluminum. The wide, padded waist belt, free-floating shoulder straps, stabilizing straps, and sternum strap provide maximum adjustability and custom-controlled weight distribution. The internal-frame packs come in seven models with various capacities and features.

Day packs, mountaineering packs, fanny packs, camera packs, and soft luggage complete the Camp Trails line.

PRODUCTS: Backpacks, day packs, fanny packs, camera packs, soft luggage.

CAMP WAYS
12915 S. Spring St.
Los Angeles, CA 90061
213-532-0910
Accepts MC, VISA. $2. Est. 1968. Steve Hornstein, Pres. John Mills, Cust. Svc.

Camp Ways offers one of the largest selections of whitewater rafts available in the United States. The rafts fall into two basic categories: the Red Line and the Blue Line. The Red Line rafts are heavy-duty models that come in a wide range of sizes and capacities, while the Blue Line rafts are lighter and less expensively priced.

The smallest Red Line raft, the Nantahala, is 11 feet long and features 840 denier DuPont Hypalon coated nylon tube material and a 1,200 denier DuPont Hypalon coated nylon floor.

With a weight of 88 pounds, this raft can accommodate five paddlers, or one oarsman and two passengers when set up with a rowing frame. Standard equipment includes wrap-up floor, repair kit, motor mount brackets, and mounted D-rings.

The Youghiogheny is a lightweight (65-pound) 12-foot Red Line raft designed for paddling. Maximum capacity is five people. A wrap-up floor is optional.

The Hopi is a 12-foot, two-inch Red Line raft that is ideal for overnight trips with two or three people. It can be paddled or rowed. It weighs 66 pounds and has a maximum capacity of five people. The tube and floor material is DuPont Hypalon coated nylon.

The Chattooga is a 13-foot raft that weighs 123 pounds. It can be paddled or rowed and has a maximum capacity of eight persons. A wrap-up floor is standard. The Apache Red Line rafts come in two lengths, 13 feet and 15 feet, and weigh 134 and 141 pounds, respectively. These are popular designs for longer trips or bigger rivers.

The two Miwok Red Line rafts, 13 feet, six inches and 13 feet, 10 inches long, are about as large a boat as a private party will need. They can be paddled or rowed.

The 14-foot and 14-foot, six-inch Ocoee rafts are heavy-duty boats meant to be paddled. The Havasu Red Line rafts, which come in four sizes ranging from 14 feet to 18 feet, are designed for use with a rowing frame. These are big-water rafts.

The 15-foot and 16-foot Shoshone rafts and the 16-foot, six-inch Navajo raft are heavy-duty, big-water rafts with large crew and cargo capacities. The 20-foot El Grande raft is the biggest raft Camp Ways makes.

Camp Ways Blue Line rafts come in four models, ranging from a 10-foot raft to a 15-foot raft. Tube material is 420 denier DuPont Hypalon coated nylon. The floor is 840 denier Hypalon. Standard equipment includes a wrap-up floor, repair kit, motor mount brackets, and mounted D-rings. They can be paddled or rowed. Camp Ways also offers a Blue Line inflatable kayak.

PRODUCTS: Whitewater rafts.

CANNONDALE CORPORATION

35 Pulaski St.
Stamford, CT 06902
203-359-1705
Accepts MC, VISA. Color. Est. 1970. Joseph Montgomery, Pres. Robert
Choquette, Cust. Svc.

One of the best-known and most respected manufacturers of
bicycle-touring gear, Cannondale also manufactures its own line
of backpacking equipment.

Cannondale tents feature light weight and quick set-up.
The rain fly of Cannondale tents is joined to the inner wall by a
six-inch ripstop baffle. Dead air trapped between the fly and
the inner wall acts as a layer of insulation. Other tent features
include a waterproof coated floor that extends 12 inches up the
walls, mesh insect screens, a roomy vestibule entrance, and an
aerodynamic tent shape to increase stability. The tents come in
four models.

Cannondale sleeping bags feature Hollofil II insulation,
1.9-ounce ripstop nylon shells, nylon taffeta linings, offset draft
tubes over the zippers, drawstring hoods, differential cut, and
triple-layer sandwich construction. Sleeping bag weights range
from two pounds to four pounds, seven ounces. All bags come
with waterproof stuff sacks.

The Cannondale Adirondack vest has a 80/20 polyester/
cotton outer shell and a taffeta lining. It is insulated with
Hollofil II quilted in a chevron pattern, and has a YKK zipper-
front closure with a snap-closed draft flap.

The Appalachian parka has a 80/20 cloth shell, taffeta
lining and Hollofil II insulation, plus set-in sleeves, a drawstring
at the waist, two-way YKK zipper, snap-closed draft flap, Velcro
cuffs, two-way outside pockets, and an optional hood.

The Cannondale Winan's Camel pack features an internal/
external frame, a 3,000-cubic-inch capacity, and design features
that allow you to strap additional items on the outside without
disturbing the pack's balance. The wraparound suspension
system, sternum strap, and the contour waist-belt reduce
shoulder and back strain. A full front opening panel and outside
compression straps allow precise packing.

Cannondale also makes a number of different day packs
and belt packs, along with a line of soft luggage.

PRODUCTS: Backpacking and cycle-touring gear.

CASCADE DESIGNS

568 First Ave. S.
Seattle, WA 98104
206-623-4400
Illustrated brochure.

What you sleep *on* is second only in importance to what you sleep *in*. By this we mean that the best sleeping bag in the world will lose efficiency if placed directly on the ground or snow. Some sort of pad is a necessity, not only for comfort but for insulation.

Traditionally, there have been three ways to go: air mattresses, foam pads, or ensolite pads. Foam pads are comfortable and provide fairly good insulation from the ground, but they take up a lot of space in the pack when they are rolled up. Ensolite pads are compact and lightweight, but they are not very comfortable on rocky ground. Air mattresses are quite comfortable, but they are also heavy, bulky, and subject to puncture. An air mattress is also a poor insulator, since the air inside the mattress becomes cold and draws heat away from the sleeping bag.

Therm-A-Rest by Cascade Designs, however, is a different kind of air mattress. It inflates itself simply by opening a valve. It can also be breath-inflated to adjust the level of support and comfort. To solve the insulation problem, Therm-A-Rest has an open-cell foam core bonded to the airtight/watertight mattress cover. Therm-A-Rest is more comfortable than a conventional air mattress and warmer than a conventional foam pad.

The Backpacker size Therm-A-Rest is 19 inches wide, 47 inches long and 1½ inches thick when inflated. It rolls up into a bundle 20 inches long and four inches in diameter. It weighs 1½ pounds.

The Expedition Therm-A-Rest is 20 inches wide, 72 inches long and 1½ inches thick. It rolls up into a 21-inch-by-five-inch bundle and weighs 2¼ pounds.

If a Therm-A-Rest is ever punctured, it can be repaired with contact cement.

PRODUCTS: Air mattresses.

CASCADE OUTFITTERS
Route 1
Box 524
Monroe, OR 97456
503-847-5762
Accepts MC, VISA. Annual, color. Est. 1977. Ron Mattson, Pres. Jackie Crowson, Cust. Svc.

Recreational boats for river running fall into three basic categories: canoes, kayaks and inflatable rafts. The canoe is the most versatile craft. It is the most comfortable to paddle on long stretches of flatwater and, in the hands of a skillful paddler, can negotiate fairly difficult rapids. It is easy to load and can handle large amounts of duffle. Kayaks are superb whitewater boats that are also fast on placid parts of the river. There is no way, however, to fit two people in a one-man kayak. The amount of baggage a kayak can carry is limited. Rafts are the boats for the really big whitewater. Depending on the size of the raft, it can accommodate 10 or more people. Rafts are cumbersome to paddle or row on flatwater, particularly in a headwind.

Cascade Outfitters offers one of the most comprehensive mail-order selections of whitewater rafts in the country. The basic raft fabric is nylon or polyester. It is coated with Hypalon, neoprene, or PVC. The construction of a raft is more complicated than you might think at first sight. It involves as many as 40 or 50 separate pieces that are glued together. The main tubes of most rafts are divided by baffles into separate flotation compartments. Materials and construction determine the durability (and expense) of a raft; design determines how the raft performs.

Cascade Outfitters catalogs rafts from four manufacturers. Raft packages (raft, rowing frame, oars, cooler) qualify for a 10 percent discount.

Avon is an English company with more experience than any raft maker in the world. Avon rafts are expensive, but unsurpassed in quality. Cascade stocks three models.

The Campways Blue Line is a very popular, moderately priced line of rafts. Six models are offered. The Campways Red Line is a heavier duty raft. Five models are offered. Maravia rafts, a line with excellent stiffness, come in three models. UDISCO builds a nice line of economy rafts in six models.

Rafts are maneuvered by oars or paddles. To row a raft, you need a rowing frame, and Cascade Outfitters manufactures its own high-quality design. They are built from TIG welded zinc-plated thinwall tubing for rust resistance and strength. Each frame is custom-made to fit on a specific raft.

Cascade Outfitters also stocks Perception and Seda kayaks,

Sea Eagle inflatable kayaks, Seda canoes, and Gruman canoes. In addition, Cascade outfitters carries a complete selection of oars, oarlocks, paddles, footpumps, repair kits, coolers (indispensable on a hot-weather raft trip), roof racks, life jackets, wetsuits, helmets, rescue ropes, waterproof bags, waterproof camera cases, stoves, knives, and books about river running.

PRODUCTS: Rafts, kayaks, canoes.

CHINOOK SPORT
E. Rogers Rd.
Box 1076
Longmont, CO 80501
303-772-5251
Accepts MC, VISA. $2. Est. 1975. Monique Kitinoja, Pres. Nancy Grimes, Cust. Svc.

Formerly known as Banana Equipment, Chinook Sport manufactures Gore-Tex shell clothing, pile clothing, Nordic ski wear, Early Warning reflective garments, polypropelene underwear, Thinsulate jackets, Borglite mittens, overmitt shells, and gaiters.

Pile clothing, which retains warmth when wet and dries out quickly after hand wringing, has gained popularity with mountaineers in recent years. A pile jacket is much more durable than a down jacket or vest, and, when combined with a windshell garment, is more versatile over a wide range of temperatures than a bulky synthetic-insulated jacket. Chinook Sport offers vests, jackets, pants, and pullovers made from Borglite pile, which features DuPont Hollofil 808 fiber. Chinook Sport's Highland series of pile garments are made of 100 percent polyester Trevira in pullover, pants, and mountain jacket models.

Chinook Sport was one of the first outdoor equipment manufacturers to introduce Gore-Tex shell garments. The current selection includes three basic lines of clothing. The Scirocco line features a Gore-Tex membrane sandwiched between an Antron knit layer and a soft brushed-nylon tricot. Pants, anoraks, and jackets are available. The lightweight Zephyr line features two-layer Gore-Tex ripstop with taffeta lining. Jackets, pants, pullovers and knickers are available. The Zipfront jacket is a heavy-duty Gore-Tex mountain parka with sealed seams, visored hood, two-way zipper, waist drawstring, seven pockets, and a full taffeta lining. Wind pants with a coated pack-cloth seat and knee patches are available too. The Super Generic jacket and pants are durable mountain garments made of Gore-Tex and designed for economy.

Polypropylene underwear is outstanding for its ability to wick perspiration away from the skin without absorbing any moisture itself. The skin thus remains warm and dry. Chinook Sport offers both tops and bottoms.

Nordic ski wear from Chinook includes pullovers, jackets, knickers, and bib knickers made from a combination of nylon stretch knit and a polypropelene terry fabric. There are also Gore-Tex ski jackets lined with wool or Borglite.

Chinook manufactures two Thinsulate-insulated jackets, the Ptarmigan and the Juneau, with Gore-Tex outer shells, two-way zippers, hoods, clever pockets, and factory-sealed seams in the critical areas.

PRODUCTS: Nordic ski wear, pile clothing, polypropylene underwear, Gore-Tex shell garments.

CHUCK ROAST EQUIPMENT
Odell Hill Rd.
Conway, NH 03818
603-447-5492
Accepts MC, VISA. Quarterly, color. Est. 1974. Charles A. Henderson, Pres. Donnette Charest, Cust. Svc.

Goose-down clothing provides the most warmth per pound of weight, but it loses its insulating qualities when wet. Wool does not, and it is for that reason that wool jackets or shirts are indispensible to outdoorsmen in rainy parts of the country, such as New England or the Pacific Northwest.

In the last few years, however, fiberpile clothing has gained acceptance as a suitable replacement for wool. Fiberpile is a synthetic insulating material that looks something like the fleecy side of a sheepskin. First developed by Scandinavian fishermen for use in the North Sea, fiberpile is as warm as wool but weighs only half as much and dries out faster. Like wool, it is breathable, and fiberpile retains warmth when damp. If a fiberpile garment becomes completely soaked, it can be wrung out and put back on immediately. It will continue to dry out with body heat alone.

Chuck Roast Equipment of Conway, New Hampshire, was one of the first manufacturers to introduce fiberpile to North

America. Chuck Roast fiberpile garments have earned high marks from loggers, hunters, construction workers, ski mountaineers, winter campers, members of Himalayan expeditions, commercial fishermen, and recreational sailors. The crew of the *Freedom*, the 12-meter yacht that successfully defended the America's Cup in 1980, wore Chuck Roast fiberpile.

Chuck Roast fiberpile is a blend of 65 percent polyester and 35 percent acrylic. The primary line of clothing includes a zipper-front jacket, pants, mittens, and a pile hat with big earflaps. There is also a Yankee vest with pile on the inside and windproof cotton/acrylic outside. The vest has pile-lined handwarmer pockets. The Yankee Bomber jacket looks something like those fine old Air Force sheepskin bomber jackets from World War II. The body of the jacket is lined with fiberpile and the sleeves are lined with Thinsulate. The outer shell is water-repellent Storm-Cloth, a polyester/cotton blend. The jacket has elastic knit cuffs and waistband, Action-Back panels in the shoulders for freedom of arm movement, a high pile collar, and front pockets closed with heavy-duty YKK zippers. A Yankee hat is made from the same materials as the Bomber Jacket.

Chuck Roast Equipment also offers wool sweaters, floating nylon wallets, a Cordura briefcase, a cushioned log carrier, cotton webbing belts, reflective jogging vests, slipper socks, day packs, expedition packs, and gaiters.

PRODUCTS: Outdoor clothing, packs.

CKC PRODUCTS COMPANY
1011-2 Chester
Grand Rapids, MI 49506
616-456-1926
Annual. Est. 1977. Brian VanderPloeg, Pres.

CKC kayaks, which all have Yakima footbraces, foam-padded knee braces, and suspended molded seats, come in five models. The Chelan is a 14-foot, nine-inch, 35-pound (in standard layup) high-volume touring kayak that excells on flatwater. The Rogue is an all-purpose whitewater boat with good stability and easy handling. It weighs 32 pounds in the standard layup. The Steelhead is a radical design for playing in big water. It is 11 feet long, 24 inches wide and weighs 30 pounds. The Ferret is a low-volume slalom racing kayak that weighs 19 pounds. The Surfin' kayak is a specialized design for ocean waves. It weighs 27 pounds.

CKC kayaks are available in five different layups. The standard fiberglass layup has a four-layer deck and hull, blended isophthalic resin, and gelcoat finish. It also comes in a kit version. Type 1 and Type 2 layups, which come in kit versions too, feature four-layer decks and five-layer hulls. The Type 1 layup includes one layer of Kevlar, local reinforcement, chine strips, vinylester resin, and a clear finish. The Type 2 layup is 90 percent Kevlar and includes a layer of S-glass, local reinforcement, chine strips, and XD-8084 resin, etc. Type 3 is the top of the line. The rental layup, which is the most economical, is specially designed for ruggedness and buoyancy.

CKC will also design layups to the customer's own specification. Kayak accessories available from CKC include spray skirts, flotation bags, dry-storage bags, life vests, helmets, and repair materials. Paddles are offered with fiberglass or graphite shafts and Kevlar blades.

CKC Royalex canoes come in three models. The Riverman canoe is 16 feet long and weighs 65 pounds. The Riverman 17 is 17 feet, four inches long and weighs 70 pounds. The Whitewater is 16 feet, two inches long and weighs 72 pounds. All three have white ash rails, cane seats, nice hardwood decks, and contoured ash portage yokes. Aluminum rails are available at a reduced price.

The Aramid Cruiser is a 16-foot, four-inch canoe that weighs just 57 pounds, making it suitable for solo wilderness paddling as well as two-man use. The Kevlar 49 hull is reinforced in stress areas and features vinylester resin, S-glass skin, a gelcoat finish, integral flotation chambers, and a lifetime warranty against breakage. Like the Royalex canoes, the Aramid Cruiser has ash rails, cane seats, hardwood decks, and a portage yoke. This boat is suitable for lake or river use.

The Crawdad Solo canoe is 13 feet, one inch long and weighs 37 pounds with a 400-pound capacity. It tracks well despite the short length and the lack of a keel, and it is dry and quick-turning in whitewater. The hull material is Kevlar 49 with S-glass skin, as in the Aramid Cruiser. Ash rails, hardwood decks, cane seat, integral flotation chambers, and portage yoke are standard. As with their kayaks, CKC is happy to do custom canoe work.

PRODUCTS: Kayaks, paddles, accessories, canoes.

CLARK CRAFT BOAT COMPANY
16 Aqua Lane
Tonawanda, NY 14150
716-873-2640
Annual (three catalogs), B&W, $2. Est. 1957. John Clark, Pres.

Clark Craft offers kits and plans for building a wide variety of boats, and at least 50 of the boats and five of the canoes would be suitable for fishing or hunting. A few Clark Craft kayaks also could be used by sportsmen.

Suggested boat-building materials include canvas-and-wood, fiberglass, Fibershield, wood, and steel. Styles include runabouts, center-console fishing boats, jet boats, houseboats, cabin cruisers, and sport-fishermen. Prices seem reasonable. Plans, bill of materials, and fastening schedule for a 16-foot deep-V boat, for example, cost $279. Complete plans for the same boat and full-size patterns for many of its parts are priced at $35.

Clark Craft says it is the only company in the boat-building industry offering complete hull kits for plywood designs. "We have spared no expense to come up with the ultimate in boat design and performance," says company president John Clark. All materials, plans, and patterns are guaranteed to be exactly as advertised. Several books explain how to assemble boat kits and other details.

PRODUCTS: Boat kits and building materials.

COLD RIVER (Greylock Mountain Industries)
937 Saw Mill River Rd.
Yonkers, NY 10710
914-965-7011
Color.

Cold River specializes in building synthetic-insulated sleeping bags for backpackers. The insulation in most Cold River bags is DuPont Hollofil II Dacron polyester. Hollofil compresses and regains loft well, but unlike goose down, it absorbs practically no moisture when exposed to wet conditions. A goose-down bag that becomes even slightly damp loses a great deal of warmth, and if a down bag actually gets wet, it is useless. In addition, wet down bags take a long time to dry out, perhaps as long as several days in humid, rainy weather. This could easily spoil an entire trip, as indeed it has for many an unfortunate backpacker.

Cold River's Alpha Prime bag is a rectangular bag for summer use. It uses single-layer scroll quilt construction and weighs four pounds. The Alpha is similar to the Alpha Prime, but has a layer of nylon covering the outside of the bag. The Beta is a mummy-shaped bag with a squared-off foot section. It is designed for summer use and weighs 3½ pounds.

The Gamma is a double-layer rectangular bag for use when temperatures are above freezing. It weighs 4¾ pounds. The Gamma Prime is similar, but features an Antron shell and a soft trinyl lining. Trinyl is a blend of cotton, polyester, and nylon.

The Delta is a good summer bag for the high country that is also suitable for spring and fall use in milder climates. It has a double layer of Hollofil II insulation and a tapered mummy shape like that of the Beta. Weight: four pounds.

The Kappa, Iota and the Iota Junior (a child's bag) are "2½ season" bags. The Kappa is a tapered mummy, the Iota, a rectangular bag. The Lambda is a rectangular bag with triple-layer offset quilting and a Hollobond II layer top and bottom. Hollobond II is a multi-layer bonded version of Hollofil II manufactured by the E.R. Carpenter Company. The Sigma is a sophisticated three-season mummy with triple-layer top, double-layer bottom, and differential cut; weight: four pounds.

The Omicron is similar to the Sigma but with added features, such as a thick layer of Hollobond II in the foot section and the top section. It weighs 4¼ pounds.

The Omega 1 is a true four-season mummy with specially shaped foot section, soft trinyl lining, differential cut, integral collar, zipper draft baffle, and a layer of Hollobond II. It weighs 4½ pounds. The Omega 2 weighs the same as the Omega 1, but sleeps about 10 degrees warmer. Sophisticated design, especially in the head and collar areas, makes the difference.

The Omega 3 is warmer still, the warmest bag Cold River makes, and with a total weight of four pounds it is lighter than the Omega 1 or 2. In fact the Omega 3 is equivalent or superior to a good goose-down bag in terms of warmth and weight. A special new material—composed of fine mesh netting and aluminized mylar—quilted between the lining and the Hollobond II insulation gives the Omega 3 this superb efficiency by curtailing radiant-heat loss.

PRODUCTS: Sleeping bags.

THE COLORADO TENT COMPANY
2228 Blake St.
Denver, CO 80205
303-825-3855
Accepts MC, VISA. Annual, B&W, free. Est. 1899. Robert C. Gutschall, Pres.

Many big-game-hunting outfitters in the Rockies put up their clients in spacious wall tents heated by folding woodstoves. A good number of those tents are made by the Colorado Tent Company of Denver, Colorado. Established in 1899 by Robert S. Gutschall, the business is still run by the family and reportedly still has the same dedication to quality and service that originally made it successful.

The company makes four models of wall tents: the Guide, the Woodsman, the Outfitter, and the Herder. Various sizes are available, all the way from eight by 10 feet to a roomy 16 by 20 feet. The biggest tents have peaks almost 10 feet high. These aren't cheap consumer tents. The least expensive Outfitter, an eight by 10, is $300, and wood poles, snap-in floor and canopy/ fly are extra, bringing the total price to almost $600. If you need a 16- by 20-foot Guide, plan to shell out $1,142 if you want it made of 7.35-ounce fire-retardant camper cloth, $262 for wood poles, another $282 for snap-in floor and $396 for canopy/fly. Accessories include steel stakes, waterproofing compound, and telescopic steel upright poles. Two lean-to shelters are available, and if you want to try camping Indian-style, there's a tepee tent, complete except for poles. Another shelter is the Colorado Range Tent, a pyramid-shaped affair made in three sizes to 9½ feet square.

In addition to its own tents, Colorado Tent offers two models made by the Canadian company Woods. The 12- by nine-foot Lakeview lists for $416; the 12 by 10 Granview is priced at $550.

Other items include saddle bags, pack sacks, and pack saddles. For those campers who want to use a woodstove for heat and cooking there is an asbestos stove-pipe shield and a folding wood-burning stove. Six models of sleeping bags are offered, ranging from a $77 bag rated for comfort at a minimum temperature of 40 degrees to a $483 goose-down bag rated down to minus 20 degrees.

For foot travelers are three external-frame backpacks, four day packs and a fanny pack. Three canvas fish creels are designed to keep fish cool and fresh.

A specialty item is the Survivor 1, a one-man survival kit that contains enough supplies for one person for three or four days. Canvas water bags, long used by desert travelers because they keep water cool by evaporation, are available in two two-gallon styles.

PRODUCTS: Canvas tents, horsepacking gear, canvas creels, sleeping bags, backpacks, day packs, water bags.

COLUMBIA SPORTSWEAR COMPANY
P.O. Box 03239
Portland, OR 97203
503-286-3676
Full-color.

Gore-Tex and Thinsulate are names frequently encountered in the catalogs of outdoor equipment suppliers. Gore-Tex is a "miracle fabric" that is both waterproof and breathable. In other words, it will keep you dry in a rainstorm and at the same time it will allow sweat to evaporate so you don't get soaked from the inside out. To tell the truth, however, there have been quite a few miracle fabrics over the years that promised to do exactly this, but they never really lived up to their billing. Gore-Tex seems to be here to stay. Thousands of users agree that Gore-Tex actually works. First developed as an ultra-light-weight insulating material for copper wire, Gore-Tex fabric incorporates a layer of film with billions of tiny holes per square inch. The holes are larger than vaporized water molecules, but smaller than liquefied water molecules. Thus, the water vapor produced by your body can pass through, but liquid, such as rain, cannot.

Thinsulate is an insulating material developed by the 3M Company. It has the warmth of down or polyester with only half the thickness. Dead air—trapped air that is motionless—is a primary factor in insulation effectiveness. The traditional way to create a lot of dead air is to use a thick layer of insulation. Thinsulate achieves the same result by using ultra-thin fibers that are only 12 percent as thick as the fibers in polyester insulating materials. Molecular friction holds dead air to every one of these fibers, and because there are so many fibers in a given volume of Thinsulate, it provides more warmth than the same thickness of polyester.

Columbia Sportswear uses Thinsulate and Gore-Tex in their carefully designed garments. The Trinity Alps parka, for example, has a Thinsulate lining and a Gore-Tex outer shell. The parka also features two zippered upper pockets, two two-way cargo/insulated handwarmer lower pockets, a visored hood, raglan sleeves for freedom of movement, Velcro cuffs, and an inner storm skirt at the waist to keep out drafts.

Other Columbia Sportswear products include cold-weather jackets, insulated vests, rain garments, ski jackets, robes, and hats, as well as camera cases and day packs. Clothing for children uses Early Warning Cloth by the Arthur Kahn Company, a material that reflects car headlights but has a normal appearance during the day.

Columbia also manufactures a line of extremely high-quality hunting and fishing clothes. They make nine different models of fishing vests. The Yellowstone vest, a truly remarkable piece of equipment, has 36 pockets. Columbia's line of camouflage clothing will appeal to wildlife photographers as well as to duck hunters and bowhunters. Gore-Tex and Thinsulate are used where appropriate. The Stalker parka and pants are made of a special polyester mesh fabric that is designed to be extremely quiet.

Last but not least, Columbia's Crusher hat is something of a minor backwoods classic. This hat, made from 100 percent oiled wool felt, can be wadded up and put in a pocket without suffering in the slightest. Outdoorsmen have been wearing Crushers since 1902.

PRODUCTS: Outdoor clothing.

DAMART
1811 Woodbury Ave.
Portsmouth, NH 03805
603-431-4700 (800-258-7300)
Accepts AMEX, MC, VISA. Annual, four-color, free. Est. 1965. Linda S. Pawloski, Pres.

If you hunt or fish in cold weather you've likely heard the comment, "I'm cold even though I'm wearing longjohns." Damart promises to put an end to such comments. The company's Thermolactyl undergarments are said to be warmer by weight than cotton or wool. The patented fabric insulates the body, yet it wicks perspiration to outer garments, where outside air evaporates the moisture. Damart cold-weather underwear is used by the U.S. Olympic luge and bobsled teams as well as the New York Jets and several other National Football League teams. It has been used on expeditions to some of the world's highest mountains, including Mt. Everest and Annapurna.

Thermolactyl is made of Vinyon and acrylic. Originally made in France, the material is available in 10 styles of men's undergarments and nine women's styles. Thermolactyl socks and gloves also are available. Most styles are offered in brown, navy, and white. Some garments also are available in sky blue and champagne.

Sizes range from extra-large to small, and there are styles for tall men. A pair of long-legged pants cost from $13.50 to $36.50, depending on size, style, and color. Long-sleeved vests range from $18.25 to about $43.

PRODUCTS: Insulated underwear.

DANNER SHOE MANUFACTURING COMPANY
P. O. Box 22204
Portland, OR 97222
503-653-2920
Accepts MC, VISA. Color.

A long-time manufacturer of quality work boots, hunting boots, and logging boots, Danner offers six boot models of particular interest to backpackers.

The Mountain Trail is an all-around boot for weekend trips or longer hikes. It has full-grain leather uppers, leather lining, padded ankles and tongue, nickel D-rings and lacing hook, leather insoles, and Vibram Yellow Label outsoles. An average pair weighs four pounds, seven ounces.

The Salem Trail boot is quite similar to the Mountain Trail except for the use of a heavier grade of leather with the rough side turned out. This makes the Salem Trail a sturdier boot for scrambling across scree slopes or for bushwhacking.

The Pacific Crest is a boot for backpackers who want to carry heavy loads or attempt long-distance hikes. The tops are an inch higher than those on the Salem Trail or the Mountain Trail. An extra middlesole adds shock protection, and a removable innersole adds comfort. The average weight is five pounds, eight ounces per pair.

The Deschutes is a lightweight trail boot that can also be worn around town. If you plan to do most of your hiking in the summer and on well-maintained trails, there is no reason to buy more boot than you need. In fact, a too-heavy pair of boots are a definite nuisance that can substantially take away from the pleasure of a trip and may cause outright pain due to blisters. The Deschutes boot has 5½-ounce brown "Dynatan" uppers, a leather lining, padding at the tongue and ankle, eyelets and lacing hooks, steel shanks, and Vibram outsoles. The average weight per pair is three pounds, 14 ounces.

The Rogue River boot is quite similar to the Deschutes, but has suede leather uppers. Average weight per pair is three pounds, 14 ounces. The Mountain Trail, Salem Trail, Pacific Crest, Deschutes, and Rogue River all come in women's models that feature the same quality construction, but are specially sized for a woman's foot.

Danner's Everest boot is a heavy-duty boot for mountaineering and off-trail expeditionary backpacking. It has a hinged, one-piece, seven-ounce, rough-out leather upper, full leather lining, scree guard, padded tongue and ankle, steel shank, leather insole and midsole, and Vibram Yellow Label outsole. Average weight per pair is five pounds, 10 ounces.

Danner also makes two models of Gore-Tex hiking boots with Cordura uppers, leather reinforcing at critical wear points, steel shanks, cushion foam midsoles, chrome leather insoles, and Vibram Kletter Lift outsoles. The full Gore-Tex sock linings afford breathability that a leather boot simply cannot match. The weight of these boots is about one-third less than a comparable leather boot. The #8066 Danner Gore-Tex boot, with six-inch uppers, weighs about two pounds, 10 ounces per pair. The #8068, with eight-inch uppers, weighs about two pounds, 12 ounces.

In addition to the above items, Danner also makes a full line of hunting and work boots. Danner's calked logging boots, which have been on the market since 1932, are a true Pacific Northwest classic.

PRODUCTS: Hiking boots, hunting boots, work boots, logging boots.

DIAMOND BRAND CANVAS PRODUCTS
Naples, NC 28760
704-684-9848
Full-color.

With justifiable pride, some companies brag that they have been in the outdoor equipment business for 20 or 30 years. All well and good, but Diamond Brand has been making tents for an even century. They celebrated their 100th anniversary in 1981.

Diamond Brand's backpacking tents are fully contemporary. The Free Spirit series tents are freestanding shelters with A-frame poles front and rear that are linked together by a molded nylon connector bar that locks the entire structure of the tent into a solid unit. Tent construction features YKK nylon coil zippers, ripstop and taffeta nylon fabrics, large windows and doors, and a domed roof.

The Acorn tent is a two-person dome-style shelter with a rectangular floor and sectioned fiberglass poles. This tent weighs six pounds, four ounces. It does not require guy lines or stakes, although they can be used for added stability. The Acorn is extremely easy to set up.

The One Nite Stand tent has a modified hexagonal floor plan with a single A-frame in front. The tent slopes down gently to a rectangular panel in the rear. The One Nite Stand weighs five pounds with poles, stakes, and rain fly.

The Diamond Dome tent is a hexagonal, two-person, geodesic-style dome shelter that offers superb stability, roominess, and ventilation. The rain fly is fitted to maximize still air space so as to increase thermal insulation. The Diamond Dome weighs in at nine pounds, six ounces.

The Leader and the slightly larger Trail Leader tents are economical shelters with A-frame poles in front and single upright poles in the rear; their floor plans are rectangular. The Leader weighs six pounds, four ounces. The Trail Leader weighs seven pounds, eight ounces. These tents feature the same quality materials and construction as the rest of the Diamond Brand line.

Diamond Brand offers four different models of external-frame packs. The Catawba Compact is for younger hikers. The Blue Ridge 5 features adjustable frame combinations in three basic sizes. The pack bag, made of urethane-coated nylon, has five outside pockets, a divided main compartment, and a front entry in the lower compartment. The Pisgah pack is urethane-coated Cordura with a front-loading main compartment, outside tunnel pockets, and compression straps for stabilizing the load. The Great Smoky Mountain pack is a large-capacity expedition pack.

In addition to the external-frame packs, Diamond Brand makes four different day packs, a climbing pack, four sizes of nylon duffle bags, soft luggage in a wide range of styles, two sizes of nylon brief cases, and a well-designed 1,000 denier waterproof Cordura padded camera bag.

PRODUCTS: Tents, geodesic domes, backpacks.

DON GLEASON'S CAMPERS SUPPLY
9 Pearl St.
Northampton, MA 01060
413-584-4895
Accepts MC, VISA. Annual. Est. 1957. Don Gleason, Pres. Daniel J. Gleason, Cust. Svc.

Having been in the mail-order business for almost a quarter century, Don Gleason's Campers Supply has seen it all. They have lived through the revolution in lightweight outdoor equipment, from the era when it was virtually non-existent to the present day, when the choice of gear is frankly bewildering to the uninitiated consumer. The 80-page Don Gleason's catalog is a useful guide to some of the best products on the market.

The selection of packs is typical, with eternal-frame packs, internal-frame packs, day packs, rucksacks, and specialty packs by Wilderness Experience, Camp Trails, North Face, Jan Sport, Coleman Peak 1, and Kelty. Dog packs, kiddie seats, bicycle-touring packs, and soft luggage are available too. Sleeping bags by North Face, White Stag, and Don Gleason's own line feature a choice of sizes, temperature ratings and insulation materials including down, PolarGuard and Hollofil II. Backpacking tents are by Eureka!, Moss, North Face, White Stag, Diamond Brand, Sierra Designs, and Don Gleason's own brand. The Don Gleason Mt. Chesterfield two-man tent is an extraordinary value priced at $50.

Don Gleason's Campers Supply is particularly strong in the accessory department. The selection of plastic bottles, for example, is one of the best you are going to find anywhere. The cookware selection is extremely complete as well. Stoves, knives, compasses, flashlights, insect repellents, snakebite kits, tent stakes, air mattresses, foam pads, headlamps, canteens, lanterns, grills, axes, pot holders, etc., are of course available in abundance. Perhaps, however, you would not expect to find a camp stove toaster or a wind chill/wind speed indicator, but Don Gleason's has them. They have all that and more.

There is no getting away from the fact that in this day and age, parts of the outdoor equipment business have taken on a certain slickness. Refreshingly enough, Don Gleason's Campers Supply has resisted this trend. Their catalog is not fancy. It doesn't have the big four-color illustrations of alpine scenery or the slick Madison Avenue-style blurbs. It doesn't list a lot of high-fashion clothing. What it does have is good-quality gear described in a straightforward, informative manner. What else do you need?

PRODUCTS: Packs, sleeping bags, tents, camping accessories.

DOWN HOME
West Fork Rd.
Deadwood, OR 97430
503-946-3012
Catalog $3. Brochure available.

Down Home is a small company dedicated to making the best down sleeping bags available. Despite the recent advances in synthetic insulation, goose down remains unsurpassed in insulating efficiency. Nothing else is as warm that weighs so little and stuffs so small. With the use of Gore-Tex outer shells and vapor-barrier liners, down's traditional susceptibility to the detrimental effects of moisture can be greatly reduced. For extended camping in consistently wet and rainy climates, particularly if you cannot be sure of sleeping in a tent every night, synthetic bags may have an edge, but for most situations down is best. There is no getting away from the fact, however, that down is expensive, and it is this, as much as anything else, that accounts for the great popularity of synthetic-fill bags. The price of a really top-grade down bag can only be described as intimidating. On the other hand, a well-built bag should last for years and years.

Down Home bags are certainly well built. There are three bags in the Bird series, with a choice of hood styles, bottom loft options, girths, lengths, and shell fabrics offered for each model. The bags feature true differential cut, goose down with a fill power of 650 cubic inches per ounce, precision-cut baffles with each compartment filled to one-gram accuracy, No. 7 two-way YKK coil zippers with a zipper on both the inner and outer shell of the bag to maintain differential cut, and two down-filled tubes behind the zippers. Gore-Tex outer shells to prevent rain from getting in and vapor-barrier liners to prevent body moisture from passing into the down are available as options. Breathable liners are available too.

Down Home also makes a modular sleeping system which consists of a Zephyr sleeping bag, Zephyr sleeping pad, and Zephyr floating hood. A Zephyr bag may be combined with a Bird series bag for extremely cold weather.

The Misty Mountain Shelter is a Gore-Tex solo shelter that weighs 27 ounces. The hood of the shelter is supported by a fiberglass hoop and an inflatable tube. Fine mesh netting keeps out bugs and a rain closure keeps out weather. Down Home mukluks are deluxe down booties with Gore-Tex shells, Velcro closure, and EVA foam midsoles. These are some booties you can do some serious snow walking in.

PRODUCTS: Down sleeping bags, mukluks.

DUNN'S SUPPLY
Hwy. 57
Grand Junction, TN 38039
901-764-2193
Accepts AMEX, MC, VISA. Quarterly, four-color. Est. 1950. L. W. Dunn, Pres. Sam Jennings, Cust. Svc.

Most of the approximately 3,000 items stocked by Dunn's Supply are intended for duck hunters, dog owners, or horsemen, but other outdoorsmen will find some interesting things here too. Serious bird-watchers or wildlife photographers, for example, will like the extensive selection of camouflage clothing. Dunn's carries camouflage gloves, hats, insulated jackets, parkas, rain suits, coveralls, T-shirts, field shirts, flotation jackets, and shooting vests with a useful abundance of pockets. Camouflage tape from Dunn's can be used to mask shiny metal objects, and camouflage sticks tone down exposed skin. Camouflage cotton mosquito netting is just the thing for constructing a bug-proof photography blind.

The Baker tree stand allows you to climb rough or smooth bark trees five to eight inches in diameter and sit in comfort far above the ground. The whole set weighs 10 pounds and includes the stand, seat, hand climber, and safety belt. This is a superb device for photographers. With a telephoto lens you can look right into a bird's nest in a neighboring tree.

Dunn's carries a complete line of animal calls. These are wonderful little devices for passing spare time around camp or on the trail. They weigh practically nothing and are priced under $10 each. Different models are available for wild turkeys, ducks, geese, crows, hawks, bobwhites, coyotes, coons, squirrels, and deer. With a little practice you can become a virtuoso.

Dunn's offers an extensive line of outdoor clothing, some of which is too heavy or too specialized for backpackers, but other items may be just what you are looking for. The selection includes shirts, jeans, overalls, sweaters, vests, jackets, leather boots, rubber boots, waders, socks, and underwear. The wide choice of Stetson hats is intriguing, as are the various types of leather chaps. Speaking of horses, Dunn's has its own brand of saddles that are made with a wooden tree in the traditional fashion.

Of more interest to hikers, perhaps, is a complete line of knives. Buck, Case, Puma, and Victorinox (the original Swiss Army knife) are offered in a wide array of models.

If you need a pair of the best waterproof, shock-proof field glasses available, Dunn's carries Zeiss armored binoculars. Zeiss is a German firm that makes the lenses for Hassleblad cameras.

These glasses deliver a clear, sharp image in absolutely minimal light. They are totally waterproof and are coated with rubber to insure noiselessness, an important consideration in observing nervous animals. At about $595 a pair they are a good bargain.

PRODUCTS: Outdoor clothing, knives.

EAGLE CREEK PRODUCTS

P.O. Box 744
143 S. Cedros
Solana Beach, CA 92075
714-755-8931
Accepts MC, VISA. Est. 1976. Steve Barker, Pres. Connie McDonald, Cust. Svc.

Eagle Creek specializes in the manufacture of packs. The Saker is an internal-frame pack designed for mountaineers and backpackers. With a capacity of 3,800 cubic inches, it has a full-grain leather bottom, three external pockets, an internal compression compartment, and a removable harness for easy handling when traveling by plane or bus. The Saker II, with a capacity of 4,300 cubic inches in the large size and 3,900 cubic inches in the regular size, is an internal-frame pack for extended backpacking trips. It has three external pockets, an internal compression compartment, and a breakaway compartment divider.

Both the Saker and the Saker II feature a harness system that is designed to ease shoulder strain through the use of a sterum strap, top load adjustment straps, lateral adjustment straps, and a harness adjustment patch on the back of the pack. Strap materials are wool felt and latigo leather for superior comfort and durability. The Eagle Creek contour hip-belt with quick-release buckle also contributes to load-carrying comfort, as does the free-floating internal frame, which flows and flexes with the natural rhythm of the stride of the person who is wearing the pack.

Pack bag material is nylon ballistic cloth, one of the sturdiest fabrics ever made. Internal seams are bound with nylon tape to reduce wear. The back panel of the pack bag is Cordura. Major zippers are #10 YKK nylon coil with #5 YKK used on side pockets. All zippers are sewn with double stitching on both sides. All grommet-clevis pin assemblies are set in leather for added strength.

Eagle Creek offers Convertible Travel packs in three sizes,

with capacities of 1,400, 2,600 and 3,400 cubic inches. The 1,400-cubic-inch model can be used as an overnight bag or a day pack. The 2,600- and 3,400-cubic-inch models function as suitcases and as internal-frame backpacks with padded hip-belts, external compression straps, leather lash points, and optional external pockets. The harness system folds away behind a zippered back panel.

The Kestral is a pack with a capacity of 1,800 cubic inches for all-day hikes. It has a leather bottom, leather/felt shoulder straps, a bivouac extension skirt, and optional side pockets. The Peregrine is a 2,750-cubic-inch internal-frame pack for shorter trips. It has three external pockets and a double-layer foam bottom. The Sparrow Hawk is a teardrop-shaped day pack with a foam-padded back panel, felt/leather shoulder straps, and a removable waist strap. Eagle Creek also makes a complete line of soft luggage.

PRODUCTS: Backpacks, daypacks.

EARLY WINTERS
110-XT Prefontaine Pl. S.
Seattle, WA 98104
206-622-5203
Accepts AMEX, MC, VISA. Four-color, free. Bill Nicolai, Pres.

Among mountaineers, Early Winters enjoys a reputation as a manufacturer of high-quality expedition tents. Fair enough, but Early Winters offers much more, as a quick look through their 76-page catalog shows. Have you ever felt a hankering for a drinking cup that folds flat or a notebook with waterproof paper? Then Early Winters is your store. What about a compass that doubles as a sundial? Or a pair of socks that last 1,000 miles? Or a stove that fits into the palm of your hand? Early Winters has it. This is a store for people who want the unusual. In fact, if there is some obscure piece of gear you cannot find in the catalog, or anywhere else, Early Winters offers a unique (and free) "seeker service" that can probably track it down.

But Early Winters' merchandise is not just unusual; it's practical. The Lightning Bug, for example, a tiny flashlight the size of a walnut, glows in the dark when not turned on so you can find it instantly. The Gore-Tex hiking boots are among the lightest and most comfortable trail shoes ever made. The "Silver Lining" PolarGuard-filled sleeping bag features a thin layer of space-age material (the silver lining) sandwiched in between the PolarGuard layers to prevent radiant-heat loss. The result is a synthetic bag that performs as well as a goose-down bag without extra weight or bulk.

Early Winters' complete line of bicycling accessories exhibits the same sort of practicality. Panniers and windbreakers are made of "Early Warning" material by Arthur Kahn, a fabric that reflects car headlights at night but appears perfectly normal in the daytime. The Gore-Tex cycling jacket has a seat flap for wet-weather riding that folds up when not in use. Early Winters' knicker-length Gore-Tex rain chaps weigh just five ounces.

Early Winters also makes Gore-Tex running suits, mountain parkas, and rain pants that are waterproof, windproof, and breathable. And then, of course, there are the Early Winters tents, ranging in size from the two-pound, one-man Pocket Hotel to the famous Omnipotent expedition tent to the luxurious Starship dome tent. Early Winters also carries packs, cross-country skis, snowshoes, clothing, and a good many other items that utterly resist classification.

PRODUCTS: Backpacking equipment—sleeping bags, tents, packs, protective clothing, boots, cooking gear. Cross-country skis, bicycle accessories, running gear.

EASTERN MOUNTAIN SPORTS
Vose Farm Rd.
Peterborough, NH 03458
603-924-9212
Accepts AMEX, MC, VISA. Color, on request.

After a very modest beginning in Boston, EMS has grown into one of the largest retailers of backpacking and related outdoor sports equipment in the United States. From the size of the catalog (90 pages) and the number of retail outlets (20) it is tempting to categorize EMS as the Sears of backpacking, and in a way that is true. On the other hand, EMS is still a specialty store, despite its size. Wilderness sports, after all, are extremely popular; a tremendous variety of products is available and a single retailer, no matter how big, can only stock a fraction of them. EMS carries some of the best. It would not have grown the way it has if it didn't.

In the pack department, for example, EMS offers packs by Jan Sport, Lowe, North Face, and Kelty, as well as packs with the EMS label. The packs fall into the expected categories of external-frame packs, internal-frame packs, rucksacks, day packs, and specialty packs. The EMS label external-frame packs are noteworthy for a good combination of features, quality, and economical price. The EMS Green Mountain pack has a heliarc welded frame, wraparound waist belt, panel-loading pack bag, compression straps, and side pockets with ski slots. It is priced well under $100. The top of the line, the EMS Appachian pack, is more expensive (about $115), but is still significantly less costly than many other premium packs on the market.

Other packs in the EMS catalog include the classic Lowe Expedition pack, the innovative North Face Bergschrund internal-frame pack, the Jan Sport Super Sack, the EMS line of internal-frame packs (including the new Katahdin pack with a stressed X frame that draws the pack away from the hiker's back while still transfering weight to his hips), the Kelty Tioga frame pack, the Jan Sport D-3, D-5, Cascade 1, and Cascade 2 frame packs, the EMS Simple Sack frame pack, the EMS junior pack frames, the EMS guide pack for climbers and skiers, EMS day packs, book bags, dog packs, fanny packs and, finally, the unusual Rec Pack, a pack frame with a high-density polyethylene pack box instead of a pack bag.

In this small space it is impossible to detail the rest of the EMS line, but the selection of packs described above is typical of the choice offered in other departments. As you would expect, EMS offers a full range of sleeping bags, tents, climbing gear, boots, cookware, knives, compasses, parkas, vests, jackets, etc. They also have a good selection of running shoes and gear, bicycle touring equipment, fishing gear, soft luggage, outdoor clothing, and books.

PRODUCTS: Backpacking equipment, outdoor clothing and equipment.

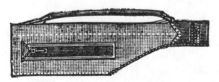

EDDIE BAUER
P. O. Box 3700
Seattle, WA 98124
800-426-8020 for credit card orders
Accepts AMEX, MC, VISA. Color.

Although Eddie Bauer carries a broad range of outdoor products and clothing, a good deal of which has little or nothing to do with backpacking, this world-famous company was one of the very first in the United States to manufacture high-quality goose-down-filled sleeping bags. It is hardly an exaggeration to say that the reputation of Eddie Bauer down bags is legendary. Eddie Bauer's cold-weather goose-down clothing is scarcely less well known.

Today Eddie Bauer offers 19 different sleeping bag models for virtually every use from car camping to high-altitude mountaineering expeditions. Some of these bags are insulated with goose down, others with PolarGuard or Hollofil. One bag, the Combo Mummy, combines all three types of insulation with down on top and PolarGuard and Hollofil on the bottom.

The down bags range from the ultra-lightweight (two-pound, six-ounce) Touring Mummy (with sewn-through seam construction and a very economical price—$125) to the top-of-the-line Skyliner, a slant box baffled bag good to minus 30 degrees. The Kara Koram Expedition bag uses a V tube baffling system and is a bit lighter (six pounds, six ounces, compared to seven pounds, 12 ounces) although it only has two ounces less fill and is good down to the same temperature.

In between the lightweight bags and the expedition bags there are a host of different models in rectangular and mummy shapes. When you come right down to it, no company really offers a broader selection of bags.

Eddie Bauer down parkas and vests feature the same quality as the sleeping bags. Here again, the choice is very extensive. Other products for backpackers include tents, packs, hiking pants, hiking boots, shell clothing (Gore-Tex and others), rain suits, knives, foam pads, cookware, and headlamps. Some of these items bear the Eddie Bauer label; others are by well-known manufacturers such as Lowe Alpine Systems and Eureka! Tent. It is also worth pointing out that although Eddie Bauer has had a reputation for expensive merchandise, most of their backpacking equipment is actually priced quite competitively. Some items are rare bargains. The Carbon River external-frame pack, for example, has all the features of a good pack (heliarc welded frame, urethane-coated nylon pack cloth bag, fully padded straps, and free-floating waist belt, extender bar on top, etc.), but goes for $79.50 (as of summer 1981).

Other interesting things in the Bauer catalog include bicycle-touring gear, inflatable kayaks, waterproof gear bags, a wide selection of hats, internationally famous Atlantis foul-weather gear, and fishing equipment—including a deluxe float tube.

PRODUCTS: Sleeping bags, down-wear, backpacking equipment, bicycle-touring gear, inflatable kayaks, hats, foul weather gear, fishing equipment.

ESMAN'S
560 Broadway
Pitcairn, PA 15140
412-243-7515
Accepts MC, VISA. Est. 1936. Saul Esman, Pres. Dave Inko, Cust. Svc.

The Esman's 96-page catalog is heavy on shooting supplies (it seems highly unlikely they've left anything out), but also lists an extremely complete selection of binoculars, spotting scopes, and telescopes, plus other items of interest to backpackers.

Major brands of binoculars carried by Esman's include Nikon, Bausch & Lomb, Leitz, Swift, Zeiss, and Bushnell. Compact, waterproof, armored, lightweight, roof prism, wide angle, and standard models are listed in great variety. These binoculars are among the best in the world; it's hard to imagine that you can't find something here to fill your needs. The prices, moreover, are very competitive.

The Celestron spotting scopes and telescopes are of particular interest. These remarkable devices seemingly do the impossible. Despite their compact size and light weight, they offer great magnification, simple focusing, and a crystal-clear image. They can also be used on 35-mm cameras as high-power telephoto lenses. For observing or photographing wildlife, or for serious stargazing, a Celestron is hard to beat.

Wildlife photographers will also be interested in the Esman's selection of tree stands, hand climbers, bird calls and camouflage material (for making photography blinds). The catalog also lists a good selection of knives, boots, and outdoor clothing.

PRODUCTS: Hunting equipment, binoculars, spotting scopes, telescopes, outdoor clothing.

EUREKA! TENT (Division of Johnson Camping)
1 Marine Midland Plaza
P. O. Box 966
Binghamton, NY 13902
607-723-7546
50¢. Est. 1895. James R. Reyen, Pres. Kris Hubschmidtt, Cust. Svc.

Eureka! began making tents and Conestoga wagon covers in 1895. Today they manufacture a complete line of tents ranging from lightweight backpacking models and car-camping tents to commercial tents for fairs and expositions.

The Eureka Timberline tents are freestanding external-frame tents that come in three sizes: the two-person Timberline (six pounds, 14 ounces), the four-person Timberline (nine pounds, five ounces), and the Timberline Base Camp (17 pounds, 10 ounces). The two- and four-person models are made of 1.9-ounce ripstop with a 1.9-ounce K-Kote bathtub floor. The Base Camp model has a four-ounce Super K-Kote oxford nylon floor. Optional vestibules are available for all three of these tents. The Timberline series is patterned after the famous Draw-Tite expedition tents that were used on the 1963 American Mount Everest Expedition.

The Saranac, the Catskill 2, 3, and 4, and the Mojave are A-frame tents for backpackers. The Saranac weighs six pounds, five ounces. The two-person Catskill weighs six pounds. The three-person Catskill weighs eight pounds, nine ounces and the four-person Catskill weighs 10 pounds, six ounces. The Mojave is similar in design to the two-person Catskill but has insect-netting walls for cool summer sleeping. A rain fly is provided for wet-weather use. The Mojave weighs four pounds, 15 ounces.

The Domension and the 6th Domension are economical dome tents with fiberglass rods, Eureka's twin-track door, and rain flies. The Domension has a rectangular floor plan and weighs six pounds, one ounce. The 6th Domension has a hexagonal floor plan and weighs six pounds, 11 ounces.

The Back Country is a two-person tent with plenty of space for gear and excellent head and shoulder room. It is supported by a single A-frame pole assembly in front. The walls are 1.9-ounce ripstop nylon, and the floor and fly are 1.9 ounce K-Kote FR ripstop. The Back Country weighs five pounds, four ounces.

The Caddis and Mushroom models are advanced-design backpacking and mountaineering tents that feature 7000 series anodized frames, catenary cut to reduce wind flapping, oxford nylon reinforcements at stress points, lock-stitch construction, cotton-wrapped polyester thread, and freeze-resistant self-healing nylon zippers. The Caddis tents have hexagonal floor plans. The one-person Caddis weighs four pounds, 12 ounces. The two-person Caddis weighs seven pounds. The four person Caddis weighs eight pounds, 13 ounces. The Mushroom tents have a square floor plan. The two-person Mushroom weighs eight pounds, four ounces, and the four-person model weighs 11 pounds, two ounces.

The Eureka Sentinel is a two-person, four-season back-packing and mountaineering tent that weighs seven pounds, six ounces. Like the Caddis, it has a hexagonal floor plan and the tent is supported by three sets of hoops that break down into rods no longer than 20 inches. An optional vestibule is available.

Other Eureka! tents include the Portage, the Mt. March, and the ultra-light (three-pound, 12-ounce) Nulite.

PRODUCTS: Tents.

FABIANO SHOE COMPANY
850 Summer St. S.
Boston, MA 02127
617-268-5625
Illustrated.

Italian-made Fabiano hiking and mountaineering boots are long-time favorites of American outdoorsmen. Most of us who've been around the sport for a few years have owned at least one pair of Fabianos, and for dependability and common-sense practicality it's hard to do any better.

The lightest hiking boot in the Fabiano line is the #501, which weighs in at 28 ounces. It features uppers of split leather and tight-weave nylon, plus a padded scree collar, a bellows tongue, and full leather lining. #501 is blue and red. #502 is brown and beige.

The Il Padre, #360, is a more conventional lightweight leather hiking boot with one-piece chrome-tanned leather uppers, steel shanks, and padded tongue and ankles. The #90 Il Madre is a bit heavier than the Padre and has a scuff-resistant toe guard.

Numbers 63, 791, 36 and 366, the Lisa, Tisha, Ria, and A. F. F., are top-quality medium-weight backpacking boots that work well on or off the trail, in spring mud, above timberline, and for non-technical peak-bagging. All have Norwegian welt construction, the hallmark of a durable mountain boot. The Lisa features one-piece vegetable-tanned uppers, full leather lining, padded ankles, and bellows tongue with scree guard. On the market for 20 years, it comes as close as anything to being the standard, all-purpose back-packing boot. The Tisha resembles the Lisa but has reverse chrome-tanned one-piece uppers and a cushioned innersole. The Ria, which has a slightly lower top, features one-piece oil-tanned uppers. The A. F. F. has one-piece waxed-hide leather uppers.

The Edwardo, #774, is a boot suited for hiking in the most difficult conditions, for alpine scrambling and for occasional mountaineering. It has Norwegian welt construction, a bellows opening over the thick padded tongue, leather lining, ankle padding, steel shank, and scree guards. Average weight per pair is 4½ pounds.

The Mountain Master, #7720, is heavier (6¾ pounds), and comes up a bit higher on the ankle. It features Norwegian welt, one-piece Gallusser waxed-hide uppers, leather lining, Velcro contour enclosed tongue, recessed self-locking lacing hooks, heavy steel shanks, and double-action hinged scree guards.

The #773, the Cragman Leader, is a mountaineering boot for difficult alpine rock or ice climbing. It features a hinged back for freedom of movement, one-piece waxed-hide uppers, waterproof gusset tongue, elastic leather scree collar, and heavy steel shanks. This boot is stiff enough for crampons and trim enough for delicate rock moves.

The #838 is a deluxe expedition double boot for high-altitude and winter mountaineering. It has hinged backstays, gusset double tongue, full steel shank, heavy leather innersoles and midsoles, and a built-in fur-lined gaiter around the top.

Fabiano also carries ski-touring boots, walking shoes, and an advanced-design alpine touring/ski mountaineering boot with a polyurethane shell and a built-in inner boot.

PRODUCTS: Hiking boots, mountaineering boots, ski-touring boots, multi-purpose boots.

FAMOUS TRAILS
5232 Lovelock St.
San Diego, CA 92110
714-299-8555
Accepts MC, VISA. Est. 1967. Oscar Davila, Pres. Beverly Lupek, Cust. Svc.

Famous Trails offers a full line of imported items and domestic products of their own manufacture, including tents, packs, and soft luggage.

Famous Trails dome tents come in various models with hexagonal and rectangular floor plans. They have all the features you would expect in state-of-the-art backpacking tents. Heavy-duty waterproof floors, rain flies, shock-corded poles, self-healing zippers, and insect netting are standard.

The Trail Tunnel tent looks something like a Quonset hut and provides great wind stability and sleeping comfort for two people without an ounce of excess tent weight. The two-person and four-person Trail Lodge tents are traditional A-frame designs that also have light weight for easy carrying. The Octadome is an exceptionally lightweight dome-style tent for four people.

Famous Trails heliarc-welded aluminum pack frames come in two designs: the "H" frame and the "Stand-Up" frame. Both the H and the Stand-Up are available in large and medium sizes. Famous Trails pack bags all feature a basic two-compartment design, and offer a variety of features and external pocket configurations. Bag capacities range from 2,300 cubic inches for the Wolverine to 3,850 cubic inches for the McKinley (with bag extension in use).

Famous Trails also carries a wide range of soft packs, some with internal frames. The packs come in sizes and designs appropriate to day hikes, rock climbing, cross-country skiing, and everyday use around town. A special Tennis Tote pack has a hidden tuck pocket for a tennis racquet. The Deluxe Cordura pack features a leather bottom.

The Famous Trails Sportsman bag—a cylinder-like design—comes in a wide range of sizes and colors. The Tourister Luggage Carry-Alls and the Cordura Traveler packs and bags are suitcase-style soft luggage that can be converted into backpacks. Famous Trails also carries fanny packs, stuff bags, ditty bags, bicycle touring gear, ski-boot bags, ski bags, gaiters and ponchos.

In addition, Famous Trails handles a line of inflatable boats; a wide range of cook sets, mess kits and canteens; two types of gasoline backpacking stoves; air mattresses; rain suits; waders; and hiking boots.

PRODUCTS: Tents, packs, soft luggage, backpacking equipment.

FISHERMAN'S PARADISE
2727 N.W. 38th St.
Miami, FL 33142
800-327-2507 or 800-432-5404 (in Florida)
Accepts AMEX, DC, VISA, MC. Quarterly, B&W, free. Est. 1960.

A saltwater fisherman couldn't need much more than the products listed in the 75-page Fisherman's Paradise catalog. Available to mail-order customers are boats, outboard motors, reels, rods, lures, boat electronics, and dozens of other accessories.

The catalog seems to be geared chiefly toward the saltwater angler who owns his own boat and who fishes for such big-game species as sailfish and wahoo.

The company calls itself Mako Marine's largest representative. Listed in the latest catalog are seven models of Mako sport-fishing boats from 17 to 25 feet long.

Other boats include an eight-foot Warrencraft dinghy for about $400 plus freight and sales tax, nine Warrencraft fishing boats up to 21 feet long and costing from about $800 on up, three Zodiac inflatable boats, a Zodiac life raft, a two-person canoe, a four-person paddle boat, a 15-foot sailboat, five johnboats, and four 12- to 14-foot semi-V boats costing from $500 to $725 plus freight and tax.

If you want to mail-order an Evinrude outboard motor, Fisherman's Paradise can accommodate you. Eight models are listed. They range from a $350 two-horsepower motor to a $4,400 200-horsepower one. Two electric trolling motors are available.

There is a wide variety of electronic gear, including VHP marine radios, graph-type depth recorders, direction finders, flashing depth-finders, Loran receivers, digital depth computers, a power hailer, battery guards, transducers, antennas, and accessories.

The company offers five brands of reels. Penn is featured with 36 different models. The largest and most expensive is the Penn International 130H, which is priced at about $630 and has a shipping weight of 16 pounds. About 20 Diawa reels are available.

Rods are by Fenwick, Pflueger, Daiwa and Fisherman's Paradise. Prices range from less than $20 for a 6½-foot spinning rod to about $330 for a 130-pound-class big-game rod.

Other offerings include two downriggers, electric reel drives, big-game-trolling lures, Mann's Jelly Worms, plugs, jigs, weedless spoons, fishing lines, hooks, knives, gaffs, ice chests, spotlights, and much more.

PRODUCTS: Boats, outboard motors, fishing tackle, boating accessories.

FOLBOT CORPORATION
Stark Industrial Park
Box 70877
Charleston, SC 29405
803-744-3483
Accepts MC, VISA. Annual, four-color, $2. Est. 1935. J. Kissner, Pres.

A Folbot, as the name suggests, is a small boat that folds into portable packages. Not all Folbots are folding models, however. Some are made of plywood, others of rigid plastic. Founded in 1935, Folbot Corporation offers 14 models ranging in length from 10 to 17½ feet. Most are similar to kayaks in that they have raised cockpits and pointed, covered bows and sterns. Sailing rigs are made for some models.

The hull material for folding Folbots is a tough vinyl fiber-plastic. Folding and rigid types are said to be comparable in performance. While folding boats come only factory-finished, portable rigid boats are sold in finished or in pre-fabricated kits. Most folding types are in the $600-to-$800 range. Portable rigid Folbots cost $350 to about $800, and pre-fabricated kits range from about $185 to about $470.

Two models can accommodate outboard motors—the 13½-foot Square Stern and the 14½-foot Sportaboat. The Square Stern can accept 1½- to 7½-horsepower outboards; the Sportaboat operates with an outboard as powerful as 10 horsepower.

The company recommends bright deck colors on boats that will be used in crowded waterways, since Folbots have low profiles and can be hard to see. Most fishermen choose hulls in blue, green, or aqua hues. Drab finishes are available for duck-hunters and wildlife observers.

Folbot offers a good selection of such accessories as double and single paddles, safety bladders, Coast Guard-approved seat cushions, carrying bags, life vests, spray covers, and car-top racks.

PRODUCTS: Folding and rigid kayaklike boats.

FORREST MOUNTAINEERING
1517 Platte St.
Denver, CO 80202
303-433-3372
Accepts MC, VISA. Est. 1968. Bill Forrest, Pres.

Forrest Mountaineering specializes in the manufacture of technical rock- and ice-climbing tools and mountain clothing.

This is a company run for climbers by climbers and it enjoys an outstanding reputation for quality and innovative products. A completely equipped quality-control laboratory insures adherence to the highest standards. The tensile testing facility can measure to plus or minus 25 pounds in the 10,000-pound range.

Forrest ice axes have been to the summits of high peaks all over the world. Extreme durability and sophisticated design are the prime features. The Neve ice axe is a good choice for general mountaineering. The Verglas ice axe is designed both for general mountaineering and technical ice climbing. The North Wall hammer is for use in technical ice climbing and for setting ice screws. The Serac Saber ice tools come in hammer and axe models for difficult ice climbing.

The Forrest Mjollnir hammers are available with either straight or hatchet-type handles and feature four interchangeable picks. Like the ice axes, the Mjollnir hammers have a five-year guarantee against breakage.

Forrest climbing nuts come in a wide range of sizes in four models: Titons, Copperheads, Arrowheads, and Foxheads. Forrest offers a broad range of nylon webbing and cordage along with gear slings, daisy chains, etiers, rabbit runners, sit harnesses, and swami belts.

Forrest knee-high gaiters have a Velcro-and-snap rear closure with waterproof nylon on the lower portion of the gaiter and breathable nylon on the top. Nylon elastic around the bottom of the gaiter keeps it snug against the boot. A neoprene-coated strap goes under the foot.

Ulti-Mitts feature nine-ounce urethane-coated Cordura with four-ounce oxford Gore-Tex on the back of the hand. The Ulti-Mitts fit over regular gloves and have elasticized wrists and quick-release buckles at the cuffs. Expedition Ulti-Mitts are lined with eight-ounce PolarGuard insulation.

The Forrest snow mitt is an overmitt made of four-ounce coated nylon oxford cloth. It is also available in an expedition model lined with PolarGuard.

Other Forrest Products include PolarGuard booties, expedition overboots, pile garments, wool hats and socks, haul bags, Wall Womb single-anchor hammocks, and Gore-Tex bivouac sacks.

PRODUCTS: Mountain clothing, ice-climbing tools, rock climbing tools.

FREEFORM R&D
1539 Monrovia Ave.
Newport Beach, CA 92663
714-646-3217
Accepts MC, VISA. Illustrated brochure. Est. 1975. Stephen B.
Wheeler, Pres.

A portable chair is probably not on anyone's list of the 10 most essential items to take on a wilderness camping trip—unless, that is, you happen to have a bad back. In fact it was a bad back that inspired Stephen Wheeler, president of Freeform R&D, to invent the Sling-Light camp chair. For those of us without such an infirmity, the Sling-Light can add an amazing amount of pleasure, and downright luxury, to the wilderness experience. It's as simple as this: After a few days you get extremely tired of sitting on rocks or logs or squatting on the ground. Your friends may laugh at you at first for carrying a chair around in the woods, but before long they will be lining up to sit in it.

The Sling-Light, moreover, is easy to carry. It weighs 18 ounces, the same as a can of beer. It folds flat so you can strap it onto the back of your pack. It is guaranteed to support 250 pounds and has successfully supported 545 pounds in tests. The frame is heat-treated aluminum tubing. The seat is a double layer of waterproof ripstop nylon insulated with closed-cell foam. It floats. The chair comes in three colors: blue, forest green, and red.

If you are having some difficulty imagining what the Sling-Light looks like, picture an aluminum V with one arm about twice as long as the other. This is the chair in profile. The nylon seat is slung between the two arms of the V with your fanny positioned several inches above the point where the two arms join at ground level. A brace attached to the top of the chair keeps it upright. You sit in a semi-reclining attitude with your knees elevated to mid-chest level. This should be great for catching rays or dozing, especially with the optional headrest attached.

PRODUCTS: Portable chairs.

FROSTLINE
Frostline Circle
Denver, CO 80241
303-451-5600
Accepts AMEX, MC, VISA. Color. Est. 1966.

Kits are an excellent way to fight the rising cost of outdoor equipment. At Frostline, the best-known kit maker in the country, the kits include everything necessary to produce a finished item. All fabric is pre-cut, and the instructions are designed for people who have no sewing experience. In addition to saving money (30-50 percent off the cost of ready-made items) putting together your own kit allows you to do the kind of quality detail work that simply is not possible on an assembly line. Custom modifications are also possible. For those people who don't have the time or the inclination to take up needle and thread, no matter how cost-efficient it might be, Frostline offers custom-sewn versions of many of their kits, as well as a selection of brand-name clothing and accessories.

Frostline goose down has 550 cubic inches of fill power per ounce. It is used in vest, parka, ski-jacket, comforter and sleeping-bag kits. The **Big Horn** sleeping-bag kit features overlapping V-tube construction, 1.9-ounce ripstop nylon fabric, two-way nylon zipper and draft flap. It is available in standard or winter models. The **Puma** sleeping-bag kit is a lightweight bag with goose-down insulation on top and shredded polyurethane foam insulation on the bottom. The Northwoods sleeping-bag kit has PolarGuard insulation. This is a good bag for wet-weather camping. The Frostline down-liner kit is an inexpensive way to add extra warmth to one of the other bags. The Frostline foam-pad kit is another indispensable sleeping bag accessory.

The Classic High Country vest kit features a stand-up convertible collar, extended back panel, front zipper with snap flap, cargo/handwarmer pockets, and an optional yoke. The fabric is either nylon taffeta or mountain cloth. The fill is goose down or polyester Hollofil II. The Classic High Country jacket kit has many of the same features as the vest and a number of customized styling possibilities. The down ski jacket kits feature an Antron nylon outer shell, a layer of insulated polyester, and prime goose down quilted to a nylon lining.

The Classic High Country Mountain parka kit has a water-repellent mountain cloth outer shell and a polyester/cotton lining, plus drawstring hood, gusseted cuffs, drawstring waist, two-way front zipper, four outside pockets, an inside zippered security pocket, and a full-width pocket across the back. The Thinsulate Mountain parka kit features the durability of a windproof mountain parka and the low-bulk warmth of Thinsulate insulation. Vests and jackets are also available with Thinsulate insulation. The Pullover parka kit is a mountain cloth parka designed especially for cross-country skiers.

The Zephyr Gore-Tex parka kit combines the features of a classic mountain parka with the breathability and the waterproof protection of Gore-Tex. The Wool-Lined Mountain parka kit has an attractive wool plaid lining with nylon added for durability.

Frostline tent kits feature advanced design, quality materials, poles, pegs, carrying bags, and seam sealer. At three pounds, two ounces, the Explorer tent kit is exceptionally lightweight. The Hatchback Sack kit is a pack bag designed to fit on the Alpenlite frame. Kits for day packs, belt packs, and soft luggage are available too. Other items in the Frostline catalog include warm-up suits, bicycle-touring gear, wool sweaters, ski accessories, kites, polypropylene underwear, knickers, turtlenecks, skirts, robes, shoes, foul-weather gear, wool pants, and much more.

PRODUCTS: Kits for outdoor clothing and equipment.

GIBBS PRODUCTS
202 Hampton Ave.
Salt Lake City, UT 84111
801-466-2530
Annual. Est. 1968. Peter Gibbs, Pres.

A prussik knot is a mountain climber's knot of remarkable usefulness. One rope is wrapped around another (usually larger diameter) rope in such a way that the smaller rope will slide freely along the larger rope until weight is placed on the smaller rope. Then it locks firmly in place. The main application of prussik knots is in self-rescue from crevasses. Assuming the climber's fall has been arrested by a belay from above, he attaches two foot loops to the climbing rope by means of prussik knots and then climbs out of the crevasse by sliding first one loop and then the other up the climbing rope.

Prussik knots are also useful for climbing fixed ropes during the ascent of a sheer face, for hauling packs up a face, for rescue work, and a number of other technical applications. If contemplating extensive use of these techniques, however, most climbers prefer to substitute mechanical ascending devices for the prussik knot. A number of such devices are available, but the Gibbs ascender is one of the simplest and safest.

The Gibbs ascender is offered in a spring-loaded model and a free-running model. The free-running model is designed for use with the foot-and-knee method of climbing fixed ropes in which the legs rather than the arms do the work. In a special competition held in 1971, one individual climbed 100 feet in 35.5 seconds using the foot-and-knee method.

Gibbs ascenders can be used on ropes one-half inch or less in diameter. The teeth are designed so that they cause little or no rope damage but hold well on muddy or icy ropes. Each ascender is pull tested to 1,000 pounds.

Mechanical ascenders are also extremely useful for caving. In fact, it was caving that inspired the original design of the Gibbs ascender. Sailboat owners find the Gibbs ascender to be a practical method for climbing up the rigging or attaching themselves to safety lines.

In addition to ascenders, Gibbs makes a combination snow anchor and snow shovel. An ice axe functions as the nadle for this shovel. Gibbs also sells Mammut, Plymouth Goldline, and Gladding Mountain climbing rope, SMC carabiners, nylon webbing, marking stamps for metal objects (such as ascenders), water bottles, and Wet Socks, a lightweight replacement for wetsuit booties that can be worn inside a pair of sneakers.

PRODUCTS: Mountaineering equipment.

GLEN-L MARINE
9152 Rosecrans
Bellflower, CA 90706
216-630-6258
Accepts MC, VISA. Annual, B&W, $2. Est. 1953. Glen-L. Witt, Pres.

Glen-L Marine says it is the largest company to design and sell its own boat plans. Based in Bellflower, California, the company offers plans for 150 different boats. To make construction easier, many frame kits are available. Some of the boats are designed to be made of steel, but most are wood or fiberglass models. Plans and patterns range in price from $15 to $325; the average is less than $50. Patterns are full size, eliminating the need to redraw from reduced patterns.

All designs are said to be suitable for typical amateurs, and no experience in reading blueprints is required. A company spokesman says no boat design is released until it is thoroughly researched and prototypes are tested.

Designs vary greatly—from an eight-foot dinghy to a 49-foot yacht. Several boats are designed for hunting and fishing. Examples include 12- and 14-foot duck boats, 12- and 14-foot johnboats, 13-, 15-, and 17-foot canoes, 14-, 16-, and 18-foot river driftboats, a 15-foot bass boat, a 23-foot fishing dory, a 23-foot sport-fisherman, and several 33- to 42-foot workboats.

Glen-L Marine distributes a 24-page catalog of boat-building supplies. It lists such materials as fiberglass cloth, polyester resins, PVC foam, glues, bronze and galvanized nails and screws, steering systems, drain plugs, port lights, and sailboat hardware. Listed are about 30 boat-building books selected by the company's staff of naval architects and boating experts. Also offered is a consulting service. All letters from customers are said to be answered expertly.

PRODUCTS: Boat-building plans, patterns, frames, accessories, supplies, and books.

GREAT CANADIAN

45 Water St.
Worcester, MA 01604
617-755-5237
Accepts MC, VISA. Annual, B&W, free. Est. 1882. John Gunnar Berg, Pres.

Great Canadian specializes in canoes, but it also sells six different small boats and a large variety of snowshoes. The company's motto is "Quality and money talk, and we listen." Each canoe is sold with a written guarantee that any parts broken under normal use will be replaced free for the life of the canoe.

There are 38 canoe models and sizes ranging from a 13-foot, two-inch fiberglass craft to a 24-foot Indian-made birch-bark canoe. Prices range from $289 to $4,800. Besides birch bark and fiberglass, Great Canadian makes canoes of aluminum, cedar, and canvas and wood. The canvas-and-wood models are remarkably light. A 16-footer, for example, weighs 67 pounds, a pound lighter than the company's lightest 16-foot fiberglass model and seven pounds less than the lightest 16-foot aluminum model. Prices for 16-footers are about $470 for the wood-and-canvas, $339 for fiberglass, and $489 for aluminum.

A cedar 16-footer, made by "two old canoe masters," sells for about $690.

A classic Nantucket dory has lapstrake construction and oak gunwales. A 14-footer weighs 295 pounds, accepts a 20-horsepower outboard, and costs about $1,150. A 16-footer weighs 348 pounds, accepts a 25-horse outboard, and costs $1,450. There are two New Bedford whaling prams. A seven-footer costs $350, and an eight-footer $390.

Great Canadian offers two fiberglass boats, an 11-foot, six-inch Andrea Dory for about $340 and a 13-foot, 1-inch Lord Nelson (no price listed). They are rated for three- and five-horsepower motors, respectively.

Other products include canoe paddles, life vests, car-top canoe carriers, canoe sail rigs, river bags, side motor mounts, kayak paddles, spray skirts, canoe seats, teak gunwales, oars, and birch-bark moose calls.

PRODUCTS: Canoes, kayaks, dories, accessories.

GREAT PACIFIC IRON WORKS
P.O. Box 150
235 W. Santa Clara
Ventura, CA 93002
805-646-3386
Accepts MC, VISA. $1. Est. 1957. Yvon Chouinard, Pres. Shirley Aitchison, Cust. Svc.

Of all the climbers who made their reputation during the golden age of Yosemite big-wall climbing, Yvon Chouinard was the most intriguing. Perhaps the exotic sound of his name had something to do with it, but it was his high sense of style that really caught your attention. Chouinard was an artist. He made climbing seem like a mystical experience. Chouinard also displayed true genius when it came to designing equipment. His pitons—Lost Arrows, Angles, Knifeblades, Bugaboos, Bongs, and the famous RURP, the Realized Ultimate Reality Piton—quickly became the standard against which others were judged. They still are. The same goes for the Chouinard carabiner. Somewhat later, Chouinard turned his creative attention to ice climbing and developed his ice axe, north-wall hammer, and rigid adjustable crampons. Chouinard was also in the vanguard of the clean climbing revolution with his hexentrics and stoppers (climbing nuts). Never content with simply being a businessman or a designer, Chouinard offered liberal doses of philosophy and climbing ethics along with his equipment. From someone else it might have seemed preachy, but Chouinard's own record as a climber was always there to back up his rhetoric.

Over the years, Chouinard's equipment business evolved from a part-time backyard operation into the present-day Great Pacific Iron Works, which offers a wide range of gear from clothing to packs to pitons to mountain footwear. Chouinard's line of Patagonia pile garments deserve special attention. Unlike goose down, pile retains warmth when wet, and unlike wool, pile dries out quickly. Pile garments are ideal for kayakers and canoeists, and are becoming standard equipment for winter and high-altitude mountaineering. A pile jacket worn with a windshell is more versatile over a wider range of weather conditions than a bulky parka insulated with down or synthetic. Great Pacific Iron Works Patagonia Pile garments come in a variety of configurations—jackets, vests, sweaters, pants, hats, mitts, etc.—that will fill just about any need.

Patagonia polypropylene underwear is outstanding for its ability to wick moisture away from the skin while at the same time providing a substantial measure of insulation. Polypropylene gloves are also offered. Other Patagonia software items include plaid shirts, corduroy trousers, wool T-necks, wool sweaters, cotton sweaters, canvas trousers, canvas shirts, twill trousers, stand-up shorts, climbing pants, and knickers. Chouinard boots, including a technical rock shoe, a hiking boot, and a ski-touring boot, are made in Italy by Asolo. Chouinard packs, made with climbers in mind, come in three models.

PRODUCTS: Outdoor wear, packs, climbing gear, mountain footwear.

HANS KLEPPER CORPORATION
35 Union Square W.
New York, NY 10003
212-243-3428
Est. 1885.

Anyone involved in the planning of a canoe or kayak trip to a remote wilderness area has to answer this question: How do you get the boats to the water? It's no problem if you can drive, but wilderness areas, by definition, have no roads. And what if you're running a river in Alaska or the Canadian Arctic? How do you get a boat up there? The round-trip air-freight charge on a 17-foot canoe (if the airline will agree to take it at all) can equal the boat's purchase price.

One answer to this problem is a boat that you can take apart. There are several of these on the market, but the one-man and two-man folding kayaks by Hans Klepper Corporation have become the world standard for demanding adventurers. Basically, a Klepper kayak consists of a wooden frame and a canvas/Hypalon rubber hull. The parts fit into two duffle bags. When assembled, they make a two-man kayak 17 feet long or a one-man kayak 15 feet long. Assembly time is about 20 minutes. The two-man kayak weighs 70 pounds, the one-man kayak, 59 pounds. Inflatable airsponsons built into the gunwales provide emergency flotation. The wood parts are mountain ash or nine-layer, cross laminated Finnish birch. Metal fittings are rust-proof Dural alloy. The deck material is long-staple cotton canvas, and the lower hull material is Hypalon rubber with a Trevira polyester cord core. The hull is repairable in the field.

The design of Klepper kayaks make them suitable for flat water, whitewater and ocean cruising. These are exceptionally stable boats. A foot-operated rudder can be used if desired. Cargo capacity is excellent, especially for a kayak. Additional duffle can be strapped on top of the deck. A spray skirt is available for rough water.

The best testimony to the versatility and dependability of Klepper boats comes from their owners. Kleppers have been used in remote areas all over the world, from the Arctic to the tropics. If a body of water is hard to get to, Kleppers have probably been there. The Klepper Corporation also manufactures a line of fiberglass kayaks and a line of spare parts and accessories for the folding boats, including a sailing rig.

PRODUCTS: Kayaks.

HARRISON HOGE INDUSTRIES/LEISURE IMPORTS DIVISION
14 Arlington Ave.
St. James, NY 11780
516-724-8900

The ultimate advantage of inflatable boats is their portability. Even a large whitewater raft will fit inside a duffle bag. A rigid

canoe or kayak, on the other hand, is unavoidably bulky. A canoe's dimensions are not a problem if you are planning to car-top your boat to the water, but this is not always possible. A journey to a wilderness river may involve traveling thousands of miles, perhaps by commercial aircraft, and the river itself may only be reachable by private charter flight. Air freight is expensive, and bush pilots are not always thrilled about lashing two or three canoes to the floats. It all adds up to a hassle. Thus the popularity of inflatables. On a more mundane level, there is the question of storing your boat between trips. Apartment dwellers may have no place to keep a 17-foot canoe. Once again, inflatables have an obvious advantage.

But the word "inflatable" calls to mind an image of a rubber raft, and rafts are not to everyone's taste. While a heavy-duty raft is fine for big whitewater, it definitely lacks the maneuverability, grace, and paddling ease of a canoe or kayak. Sea Eagle inflatable canoes, distributed by Leisure Imports, offer the best of both worlds.

The Sea Eagle Heavyweight 290 canoe has a 24-gauge PVC hull, built-in back seat, removable front seat, pressure gauge, repair kit, drain valve, nine air compartments, and a carrying bag. Although the boat is called a "heavyweight"—for its durability—it weighs just 21 pounds. It is nine feet, eight inches long. The Sea Eagle 330 Heavyweight canoe is 11 feet, two inches long, weighs 29 pounds and has 30-gauge PVC hull material.

Sea Eagle Explorer Series inflatable canoes come in three sizes (nine feet, six inches; 11 feet; and 12 feet, five inches) and range in weight from 27 to 36 pounds. The hull material is DynaWeb, which features a layer of ripstop polyester threads between layers of modified PVC. With electronically welded overlap seam construction and a double floor system, these boats are as rigid as an aluminum canoe (rigidity is an important performance factor) and very durable. The Explorer canoes are designed for serious whitewater and expedition use, and they have won considerable praise from experienced river-runners.

The Sea Eagle Sport canoes, while not as rigid or strong as the Explorer canoes, are very economically priced and lightweight. The nine-foot, eight-inch model, for instance, weighs just 21 pounds.

Even lighter are the Sea Eagle pack boats. The SE measuring five feet, eight inches by three feet, three inches weighs eight pounds. Yet it has a 250-pound capacity. The SE4 weighs 12 pounds, and the seven-foot, four-inch SE5 weighs 14 pounds. These boats are ideal for fishermen who want to pack into roadless lakes or beaver ponds, or for backpackers who want to camp on some otherwise inaccessible wilderness island.

The possibilities for a boat that takes up little more space in your pack than a sleeping bag are nearly endless.

Sea Eagle also offers a complete line of rafts, dinghys, and portboats, plus a line of accessories.

PRODUCTS: Inflatable canoes, rafts, dinghys, portboats, accessories.

HAVLICK SNOWSHOE COMPANY
P.O. Box 508
Gloversville, NY 12078
518-725-6175
Annual, B&W, free. Est. 1969. Richard S. Havlick, Cust. Svc.

Havlick Snowshoe manufactures and sells two styles of ash-frame snowshoes, one style of aluminum-frame showshoes, a snowshoe kit, and three sizes of pack baskets.

The company is best known for its modified bear-paw model, also known as the Adirondack model. Fairly stubby, this snowshoe is designed for maneuvering and is therefore ideal for snowshoeing in rough terrain. Its frame is made of white ash, and the lacings and bindings are made from tough neoprene-coated nylon scrim. The nylon does not absorb water or collect ice and snow as rawhide does. The ash frames are doubly coated with marine spar varnish. All rivets are made of copper, which does not corrode or rust as some other metals do. There are five sizes, ranging from 10-inch by 30-inch for children weighing as much as 90 pounds to 14-inch by 36-inch for adults to 225 pounds.

A cross-country model is 10 inches wide and 46 inches long, and has a tail that acts as a stabilizer. This model is also made of ash and nylon. It is rugged and suitable for all-around use and will support hikers weighing as much as 250 pounds.

Havlick's Green Mountain bear paw is made from high-strength aluminum tubing and neoprene-coated nylon, making it easy to maintain. The aluminum tubing never needs varnishing, and is coated with a baked-on polyester coating, which prevents snow from collecting on it.

For the do-it-yourselfer, there is a modified bear-paw kit. The frames are assembled and varnished. The kit contains all materials and an instruction booklet.

Havlick's pack baskets are available in three sizes: a four-peck, a three-peck, and a two-peck. The largest basket weighs three pounds and the lightest, half as much.

Other products include a neoprene snowshoe binding, aluminum crampons for improved traction on ice and hard snow, and a 42-inch ash walking stick.

PRODUCTS: Snowshoes, pack baskets, accessories.

HIDALGO SUPPLY COMPANY
P.O. Box 35339
Houston, TX 77035
713-729-6940
Accepts AMEX, DC, MC, VISA. Catalog. Est. 1967. James Hidalgo, Pres.

Perhaps sunglasses are not thought of as part of a traditional outdoorsman's kit, but experienced backcountry travelers know that eye protection is important. In the winter, or at high altitudes, the glare off snow can be a painful hazard. Snow blindness aside, however, continual eyestrain may not actually ruin a trip, but it can certainly reduce your pleasure. When you think about it, a good deal of wilderness enjoyment comes from looking at your surroundings. It pays to take care of your eyes.

Hidalgo Supply offers one of the world's largest selections of sunglasses with models by Ray-Ban, Porsche and Zeiss. The glasses are available in prescription and non-prescription lenses. For most models, Hidalgo offers substantial savings over normal prices.

Bausch & Lomb Ray-Ban sunglasses are available with a variety of lenses. The G-15 gray-green lens is the darkest uncoated lens. It reduces light intensity without changing colors. The Photochromic Gray lens admits varying amounts of light, depending on how much ultraviolet light strikes the lens. In other words, this lens darkens outdoors and lightens indoors. The AmberMatic lens is made of light-sensitive glass that changes color and density. On overcast days, this lens has a light yellow color. It becomes dark gray in bright sunlight. The AmberMatic Mirror lens has a mirror coating for extra protection. The G-31 Mirrored lens is designed for extreme glare conditions. The Changeable Green lens features rapid reaction times to changing light conditions. In addition, Ray-Ban makes yellow and clear lenses. Frames are available in numerous styles in either metal or plastic.

Hidalgo carries glasses by the world-famous optical firm of Zeiss with three different lenses: gray/green, yellow, and vermillion. In addition, Hidalgo has Porsche-Carrera sunglasses made by the Porsche Design Company, a firm founded by Ferdinand Porsche, the automotive designer.

Hidalgo also carries a number of other products, including binoculars, hand lenses, altimeters, pocket telescopes, emergency whistles, and Victorinox Swiss Army knives in six models that feature 36 different specialty blades.

PRODUCTS: Sunglasses, binoculars, hand lenses, altimeters, pocket telescopes, emergency whistles, Swiss Army knives.

HIMALAYAN INDUSTRIES
P.O. Box 5668
Pine Bluff, AR 71611
501-534-6411

Himalayan Industries offers a line of clothing and equipment oriented toward hunters that is also of interest to wildlife photographers and backpackers.

The Himalayan #1014 Field coat is a hip-length Thinsulate-insulated garment with an extra-long tail in back, front cargo pockets, bellowed sleeves with zippers, and a vertical, zipper-closed breast pocket. The shell material is a polyester/cotton blend. The Field coat is available in green camouflage, brown camouflage, and taupe with a brown yoke.

The Mountaineer parka is a Thinsulate-insulated garment with two-way cargo pockets, waist drawstring, Velcro cuffs, outside patch breast pocket, outside slit breast pocket, and a snap-closed weather flap that covers the two-way front zipper. A detachable hood is included. The colors are taupe or green camouflage.

The #6418 Chillfighter is a hooded, hip-length cotton/polyester blend windbreaker with slash pockets and a drawstring. It comes in either green camouflage or blaze orange.

The Cherokee hunting jacket features Hollofil II insulation, stand-up collar, elastic band cuffs, and slash pockets. This is a reversible jacket with green camouflage on one side and blaze orange on the other.

The #8005 Alaskan is a down-filled waist-length jacket with zipper front, stand-up collar, knit cuffs, and insulated slash pockets with flaps. The color is taupe.

The #1025 Summit is a hip-length Thinsulate-insulated coat with concealed knit cuffs, stand-up collar, slash pockets and a snap front closure with a zipper underneath. The colors are green camouflage or mahogany.

The High Country is a vest that is filled with 4½ ounces of prime goose down. The Mohawk is a Thinsulate vest that comes in two reversible combinations: green camouflage/taupe or green camouflage/blaze.

Himalayan Deluxe overalls have a bib arrangement on top and long zippers at the cuffs. They are insulated with Thinsulate and feature a special polyester/cotton blend that reduces fabric noise while walking—an important consideration when you are trying to approach wildlife. The overalls are available in green camouflage, brown camouflage, or blaze orange. The camouflage bush pants have the same quiet fabric plus six pockets, extra-wide belt loops, and bellowed zippered legs. They are available in a Thinsulate-insulated model, too.

The Hunter frame pack has a 400 denier coated nylon camouflage pack bag, four side pockets, two main inner compartments, a free-floating suspension system, padded hip-belt, and a black frame available in stand-up or recurve models. Himalayan also offers a wide range of rucksacks, day packs and belt packs with camouflage fabric.

The Packer is a special-purpose frame without a bag that is designed for carrying heavy and bulky objects. A supported platform, mounted D-rings, and five cinch straps aid in lashing down oddly shaped objects.

The #9950 sleeping bag is insulated with Hollofil 808 for three-season use. It has a cotton/polyester shell and a nylon lining. The outside color is green camouflage.

PRODUCTS: Outdoor clothing, sleeping bags, hunting packs.

HINE/SNOWBRIDGE
P. O. Box 4059
Boulder, CO 80306
303-530-1530
Color.

The mushrooming popularity of internal-frame packs has proved to be one of the major developments in the backpacking equipment industry during the 1970s and 1980s. While external-frame packs are not about to disappear, not now or in the distant future, rock climbers and cross-country skiers on multi-day trips have found internal-frame packs to be almost indispensable, because of the trim shape, which does not interfere with arm movements, and the improved center of gravity, which does not cause you to lose your balance. Trail hikers who do not plan to carry extremely heavy loads also like internal-frame packs because they are just plain easier to live with. They are compact and easy to load. Moreover, internal-frame packs are definitely superior when it comes to traveling with your pack by train or airplane. They are the packs for all seasons.

Hine/Snowbridge is a pack specialist that offers eight models of internal-frame packs. They feature independent aluminum X stays in the back of the pack that flex with light loads and become rigid with heavier loads. The modified yoke suspension system can be custom fitted to your own comfort requirements. Shoulder straps go all the way around the shoulders—not just across the front and top—and the padded waist-belt forms a complete circle around the hips. Compression straps allow the size of the pack to be reduced so the contents don't rattle around even when the pack is half full. External add-on pockets provide additional pack capacity. Pack bag fabric is 11-ounce Cordura for abrasion-resistant durability.

The Serex is a large-capacity (4,500-cubic-inch) pack for long trips and expeditions. The Lite Serex is the same size, but has fewer features such as external tie down points, etc.

The Omega is a large-capacity (4,200-cubic-inch) pack that also works well as luggage. The Alpha is a slightly smaller pack that has three main compartments instead of one. The Alpha Special is like the Alpha with more features. The Tararak is a 3,000-cubic-inch-capacity pack for shorter hikes. The Apogee and Perigee are designed for smaller individuals. The Apogee is a top-loading model while the Perigee has a "hatchback" opening.

Hine/Snowbridge also manufactures a complete line of day packs, fanny packs, climber's rucksacks and nylon cargo bags.

PRODUCTS: Backpacks, daypacks, fanny packs, climber's rucksacks, nylon cargo bags.

HUBBARD
Box 104
Northbrook, IL 60062
312-272-7810
Accepts AMEX, MC. Est. 1960. Pat McKeon, Pres.

Most backpackers are familiar with USGS topographic maps, and if they aren't they should be. These accurate, easy-to-read government survey maps show land forms, watercourses, vegetation, trails, roads, and buildings in amazing detail. They are well-nigh indispensible for finding your way in the wilderness.

But while the contour lines on USGS maps give you a pretty good idea of what a strange piece of terrain is going to look like, Hubbard raised-relief maps are even better. Molded in plastic, Hubbard maps are virtual scale models of the outdoors. It's like looking at the ground from an airplane, except that you can study everything in detail.

Hubbard raised-relief maps are based on the USGS 1:250,000 scale topo maps and contain all the information shown on a regular flat map sheet. Each map covers an area approximately 110 by 70 miles. The map itself is 22 by 33 inches.

Hubbard offers maps for the entire Appalachian Mountain Range, from Maine to Alabama, and for all of California, Oregon, Washington, Idaho, Nevada, Arizona, Wyoming, Utah, and the western portions of Montana, Colorado, and New Mexico, plus part of Hawaii. (There is not much point, of course, for a raised-relief map of the Great Plains or the Atlantic coastal plain.)

Because Hubbard maps cannot be folded, they are of limited use in the field. Nevertheless, they can be extraordinarily helpful in planning trips. They also make fine decorative items. Short of being there yourself, there is no better way to visualize a piece of landscape than with one of these maps.

PRODUCTS: Raised-relief maps.

HUDSON'S
97 Third Ave.
New York, NY 10003
212-473-8869
Accepts AMEX, MC, VISA. Color.

Along with a complete line of jeans, shoes, shirts, sweaters, jackets, and general-purpose outdoor clothing, Hudson's carries a full selection of brand-name backpacking equipment.

The Camp 7 down sleeping bags offered by Hudson's feature precision-injected goose down with a fill power of 550 cubic inches, differential cut, segmented draft tubes, and omnidirectional polyester knit baffles. The Red Scooter is a super-light mummy, the Frontier is an economical three-season bag, the Cirque is a year-round mummy, and the Arete is a three-season mummy that weighs only two pounds, 11 ounces in the regular size.

Camp 7 synthetic-fill sleeping bags feature PolarGuard insulation, two-way self-healing Talon zippers, double stitching, cross-block baffles, and full-length draft tubes. Four models are available to cover a wide range of temperatures. Hudson's also offers the Camp 7 vapor-barrier liner, a polymer-coated six-ounce nylon liner that fits inside a sleeping bag to increase thermal efficiency by controlling dehydration.

Coleman Peak 1 sleeping bags available from Hudson's feature high-loft Hollofil II synthetic insulation, double quilt stagger seam construction, oversized draft tubes, and coil zippers with double sliders. Hudson's carries three basic models.

Hudson's own-brand sleeping bags feature Hollofil 808 or Hollofil II insulation, a rectangular bag shape, and careful attention to construction details. Ensolite pads, Volarafoam pads, Sierra Pads, and Therm-a-Rest mattresses are available for use with the sleeping bags.

Hudson's carries a wide variety of tents by Eureka!, Moss, and Wilderness Experience, plus a lightweight bivouac sack by Camp 7. The Eureka! tents come in A-frame, freestanding external-frame, and dome models. They feature sturdy construction, light weight and a range of tent sizes that will accommodate anywhere from two to six people.

Moss tents are well known for their innovative design. The Star Gazer, for example, is a freestanding design with a screened top window. The Solus II tent carries the stargazing concept one step further with a shell made entirely of insect netting. A full rain fly is provided for inclement weather. The Eave III is an unusual-looking tent that is designed to withstand strong winds without sacrificing interior space. It features lap-felled structural seams and weighs six pounds, four ounces. The Moss Trillium is a tent that seems to do the impossible: It has a beautiful, freestanding aerodynamic design, three separate entrances, ample room for six sleepers, and it weighs only 12 pounds, five ounces complete.

The selection of packs available from Hudson's includes models from Lowe Alpine Systems, Wilderness Experience, Coleman Peak 1, Renegade, Cannondale, and Kelty. Internal-frame, external-frame, day packs and climbing models are offered. Hudson's also carries a good range of accessory items including Swiss Army knives, Buck knives, Coleman Peak 1 stoves and lanterns, Optimus stoves, butane stoves, air mattresses, flashlights, and hammocks.

PRODUCTS: Sleeping bags, pads, tents, packs, accessory items.

INDIANA CAMP SUPPLY
P. O. Box 344
Pittsboro, IN 46167
317-892-3310
Accepts AMEX, MC, VISA. Est. 1973. William W. Forgey, Pres.

Many retailers catalog equipment for backpackers and wilderness travelers, but Indiana Camp Supply stands out from the crowd because of the variety and selection it offers in two product areas—food and medical supplies.

Indiana Camp Supply stocks one of the largest selections of freeze-dried and dehydrated trail food in the world. Their food list is mind-boggling, with everything from shrimp creole to Mexican omelettes to cheesecake. They carry products by Tea Kettle, Chuck Wagon, Rich Moor, Dri Lite and Mountain House. Discounts are available on large orders. An order of $50 or more, for example, earns a discount of five percent. Orders of $100 or more earn a 10 percent discount, and so on up to orders of $250 or more, which earn a 25 percent discount. As a service to backpackers who are planning long trips, Indiana Camp Supply will send food packages to post offices along the proposed route.

Medical equipment available from Indiana Camp Supply includes immobilization air splints, tourniquets, forceps, stethoscopes, blood-pressure cuffs, and much more. A large variety of medications, ointments, and vitamins are available, as are comprehensive wilderness medical kits, including a temporary dental-filling kit. This last item can be worth much more than its weight (two ounces) in gold if you need it when you're out in the backcountry, miles from a dentist's chair.

In view of the above items, which are listed here only in small part, it should not be surprising to learn that the president of Indiana Camp Supply, William Forgey, is a medical doctor. In fact, he has written a book about wilderness medicine, and of course it is carried by his company. Other titles published by Indiana Camp Supply include *Woman in the Woods* by Kathleen Farmer, and *Hiking Back to Health* by Calvin Rustrum. ICS carries a good selection of outdoor books by other publishers as well.

Along with books, medical supplies and food, ICS offers Gore-Tex parkas, rainwear, wool socks and mittens, gaiters and overmitts, emergency signaling systems, Snow Lion and Peak 1 sleeping bags, Therma-Rest sleeping pads, Eureka! tents, compasses, knives, stoves, cookware, axes, duffle bags, Wilderness Experience and Peak 1 packs, and many other items.

Canoeists will be interested in the line of Duluth Packs, heavy-duty canvas cargo bag/packs with tump lines that have been used by North Woods wilderness travelers for generations. Tradition-minded outdoorsmen will also be interested by ICS's ash-framed Canadian snowshoes that are expertly laced by Huron Indians. ICS also carries state-of-the-art aluminum/ neoprene snowshoes by Sherpa.

PRODUCTS: Food, medical supplies.

INTERNATIONAL MOUNTAIN EQUIPMENT
Box 494
North Conway, NH 03860
603-356-6316
Accepts AMEX, MC, VISA. Illustrated.

The name suggests climbing equipment and, indeed, International Mountain Equipment carries a broad selection, with ropes by Edelweiss and Beal; hardware by Chouinard, Leeper, Forrest, Clog, SMC, and CMI; harnesses by Chouinard and Whillans; ascenders by CMI; ice axes by Chouinard and Forrest; Joe Brown helmets; crampons by Chouinard and SMC; and Sherpa snowshoes. The boot selection includes specialized rock-climbing shoes, hiking boots, mountaineering boots, and double boots for high altitude or winter conditions.

Tents include various models by Trailwise, North Face, and Diamond Brand. The Trailwise Great Arc tent is a bizarre-looking structure that in fact has one of the best wind profiles of any dome tent on the market. The North Face Westwind tent is, if anything, stranger looking. It resembles a distorted Quonset hut, but the peculiar shape is intentional. This tent is small where it can afford to be small and large where the occupants need space to move around. With a total floor space of 32 square feet, it weighs just five pounds, five ounces. The Trailwise Fitzroy III has a traditional A-frame design, but is built for maximum stability in the most hostile of high mountain environments.

International Mountain Equipment offers down sleeping bags by Camp 7 and Marmot Mountain Works, and PolarGuard bags by North Face and Twin Peaks. The pack selection covers a full range from day packs to internal-frame packs to external-frame packs to heavy-duty expedition packs. The line includes such classic models as the North Face Ruthsac, the Kelty frame pack, and the Lowe Alpine Systems expedition pack, one which has set the standards in internal-frame pack design. The

Bouchard Extreme Expedition pack will be of interest to serious climbers.

The clothing line includes chamois shirts, canvas shirts, rugby shirts, various styles of shorts, painter's pants (popular with rock climbers), iron worker's pants, ponchos, cagoules, anoracks, rain pants, Gore-Tex pants, Gore-Tex parkas, mountain parkas, sweaters, pile garments, hats, goose-down parkas (including a $265 expedition parka), mittens, gaiters, and super gaiters.

International Mountain Equipment runs a climbing school that works out of their North Conway store in the heart of New Hampshire's White Mountains. The school is now in its seventh year of operation. Expedition gear is another specialty of International Mountain Equipment. The staff has first-hand experience in major—and minor—ranges all over the world, and can help plan equipment lists for specific areas. They also carry many specialized items not listed in the catalog and can obtain many other items if there is enough lead time. Discounts are available for group orders.

PRODUCTS: Climbing equipment, climbing/hiking boots and shoes, tents, sleeping bags, back packs, outdoor wear.

IVERSON SNOWSHOES
Box 85
Shingleton, MI 49884
906-452-6370
Illustrated brochure.

The snowshoe is the classic North American device for moving across a winter landscape. The popularity of snowshoes has diminished somewhat in recent years with the phenomenal explosion of interest in cross-country skiing, but loggers, trappers and other woods workers still find snowshoes to be indispensible. The cross-country skier can glide silently across an open field where the man on showshoes has to trudge, but in thick brush, in timber, on steep terrain, or in deep powdery snow, a skier gets into trouble. Those skinny little cross-country boards don't have much flotation, and when it comes to clambering over fallen logs or making frequent changes of direction in close quarters, skis are a source of much frustration. They are fine for an afternoon workout on the golf course or for a climbing trip above the timberline, but a backpacker who

plans to carry a heavy load in the woods is better off with snowshoes. The truth of this statement is easily demonstrated by walking a mile or two on just about any woods trail. Notice how narrow the trail is. Notice how steep it is. Try to imagine that trail under three feet of snow. Could you handle it on skis?

This is not to say that snowshoes turn all winter travel into a piece of cake. Snowshoes have their drawbacks. They don't work very well on ice, for one thing. And while old-fashioned wood and rawhide snowshoes look great hanging up over the fireplace, they demand a lot of maintenance. Iverson snowshoes have solved this problem, in large part, by using neoprene instead of rawhide for the laces. The neoprene not only never has to be varnished, but it also is much stronger than rawhide. It has, in fact, a breaking strength of 700 pounds per square inch. Moreover, neoprene does not pick up water; it won't sag, stretch or ice up like conventional lacing.

The frames of Iverson snowshoes are selected quarter-sawed northern white ash. The ash does need yearly varnishing, but this is a far cry from the old days when the whole shoe had to be varnished and, like as not, sections of the lacing had to be replaced as well. The Iverson snowshoe harness is made of waterproof material, designed for positive foot control, and equipped with slide fasteners and buckles to fit any kind of boot.

The Modified Bearpaw snowshoe is a short, oval-shaped shoe with short tails and a slightly turned-up toe. It is the best shoe for all-around use. It comes in four sizes to support individuals weighing from 100 to 210 pounds. The Modified Bear Paw weighs about five pounds, with harness. The Alaska Trail model snowshoe is long and thin for fast travel across open country. The pair weighs about 6½ pounds. Iverson also makes a Cross-Country model, a Michigan model, and a Snow-Mate model for children weighing up to 90 pounds.

PRODUCTS: Snowshoes.

JAN SPORT
Paine Field Industrial Park
Everett, WA 98204

Jan Sport is larger than many manufacturers of outdoor equipment. Nevertheless, it specializes in just three product lines: packs, tents, and soft luggage.

Going on the principle that a flexible load (such as a 50-pound child) is easier to carry than a static load (such as a 50-pound bag of cement), Jan Sport pack frames are designed to flex and bend according to the movements of the people who are wearing them. Because Jan Sport frames do not have rigid or welded joints, the frame can twist diagonally and flex forward. Rather than resisting weight shifts, the load conforms to the movements of the hiker.

The large-capacity Dhaulagiri series of frame packs are for heavy loads on extended trips. The pack sack (5,520-cubic-inch capacity in the D2 model) is compartmentalized, and features large side pockets, accessory straps, and a pair of external load compression straps to stabilize items inside the main bag. A multi-use pocket on the D2 model completely detaches from the main sack by means of a zipper. D3 and D5 models are smaller than the D2.

The Alpine Phantom is a large-capacity (6,980-cubic-inch) pack suitable to expedition use. The suspension system incorporates lightweight, high-strength titanium parts. A hinge mechanism allows the lower portion of the frame to follow the motion of the wearer's lower spine. The upper portion of the frame uses four flexible joints and Jan Sport's patented adjustable shoulder bar. Jim Wickwire, the first American to stand on the summit of K2, used an Alpine Phantom pack on the climb.

Jan Sport's three internal-frame packs, the Rock Standard, the Spire and the Route 1, feature pack sacks made of DuPont nylon ballistic cloth, a fabric developed for use in bullet-proof vests. Load compression straps give these packs versatility. The packs themselves are designed to permit active uses such as rock climbing or cross-country skiing.

Jan Sport also offers the Framesack and Rover series of frame packs, and soft packs such as the Boomer, St. Helens, Bravado and Nomad. Jan Sport soft lugguage comes in all the usual styles and shapes.

Jan Sport tents, which look a little like igloos, are designed to reduce wind noise, increase stability, and provide easy entrance and exit, proper ventilation, and maximum interior space. Durability is a major feature. Poles are hollow fiberglass for strength and flexibility. The Trail Wedge tent is a two-person shelter. The Trail Dome accomodates two people plus packs. The Mountain Dome sleeps three persons. The Isodome 2 and Isodome 3 tents are similar to the Dome series tents, but have added features for winter use.

PRODUCTS: Tents, packs, soft luggage.

KANCAMAGUS SNOWSHOE CENTER
Conway, NH 03818
603-447-5287
Illustrated brochure.

The Kancamagus Snowshoe Center turns out high-quality shoes made the Indian way, by hand. All Kancamagus snowshoes use white ash frames. The webbing is either rawhide, neoprene, or nylon. Rawhide is the traditional webbing material, but nylon or neoprene are usually preferred because they are stronger, rodent-proof, and water resistant.

The Beaver Tail snowshoe looks something like a tennis racket. It is bluntly pointed in front, oval in the middle and tapers off to a thin tail. This easy-handling shoe is the most popular in the Kancamagus line. The Beaver Tail is available in eight different sizes for people weighing from 60 pounds to 270 pounds. The smallest size is 29 inches long, the largest, 42 inches long.

The Yukon is a snowshoe for fast travel in open country. It is narrower than the Beaver Tail and longer. The Otter is a 36-inch tailless snowshoe popular with climbers and snowmobilers. The sides of this shoe are straight with curved ends, front and rear. Otters are easy to maneuver in close quarters.

Snowshoes are a necessity for people who live and work in the north country. With the growing popularity of winter camping, more and more recreationists are using them as well. The relative merits of snowshoes and cross-country skis are often debated, but the serious winter wilderness traveler knows there is a place for both. In fact, some people carry snowshoes on their packs while cruising along on their cross-country skis.

PRODUCTS: Snowshoes.

KELTY PACK
9281 Borden Ave.
Sun Valley, CA 91352
213-768-1922
Full-color.

Kelty pioneered the lightweight aluminum pack frame almost thirty years ago, and for many years after that, the terms "Kelty" and "pack" were interchangeable. One meant the same as the other. An astonishing variety of external-frame packs by

different manufacturers are on the market today, but they all owe something to the original Kelty design. Kelty, in other words, set the standard.

The current generation of Kelty frame packs is fully abreast of contemporary pack technology. The pack bags are made of four-ply coated 7½-ounce pack cloth with reinforced stitching in stress areas and heavy-duty nylon thread used throughout. The bags and frames come in a wide variety of sizes (including an adjustable model for growing hikers). Nine different models offer pack bags with various outside-pocket and main-compartment divider systems. Other features include ice-axe loops, Cordura crampon patches, nickel-plated grommets, and cam-lock buckles. When all is said and done, however, this one fact remains: Few companies have as much experience making frame packs as Kelty.

Kelty also makes an outstanding line of internal-frame packs. Five models are offered, all with fairly large main-bag capacities (up to 4,500 cubic inches), and they are suitable for backpacking, skiing and active mountaineering. The bag material is Cordura and polyurethane-coated nylon, except for the El Capitan pack, which is made of ballistics cloth. The suspension system has a wraparound waistband, a leather yoke shoulder harness, and a breathable lumbar support pad. All the packs have ice-axe abundant external tie-down points and vertical and horizontal load compression straps.

Kelty's Mockingbird series of packs are designed for all-day hikes, overnight trips, rock climbs, and ski tours. They resemble the classic rock climber's rucksack, updated with contemporary materials. The Mockingbird H/D has a leather bottom (all real climbing packs used to have this feature, but few do now) and a bag made of ballistics cloth for rough use.

Kelty makes day packs in square and teardrop shapes. A belt pack and a fanny pack are available too, along with a convertible pack that fuctions as a fanny pack or as a regular day pack. The Night Hawk and Night Owl packs are made of reflective Early Warning cloth for safety. Kelty's soft luggage comes in flight bag, garment bag, and duffle bag styles.

In the clothing department, Kelty offers flannel, poplin, and chamois shirts, poplin and corduroy pants, as well as T-shirts and shorts. Rainwear includes ponchos, bib overalls, jackets, and complete rain suits. A variety of jackets and pants are available in breathable/waterproof Gore-Tex fabric. Stuff sacks, accessory straps, rain covers, down booties, air mattresses, and ground sheets round out the line.

PRODUCTS: Packs, outdoor clothing, rainwear, air mattresses.

KERSHAW CUTLERY COMPANY/KAI CUTLERY USA
6024 Jean Rd.
Lake Oswego, OR 97934
503-636-0111
Accepts MC, VISA. Color. Est. 1974. Peter Kershaw, Pres. Kevin Anderson, Cust. Svc.

Kershaw knives are manufactured by Kai Cutlery of Seki, Japan, a leading knife maker for more than 70 years. Every Kershaw blade is AUS 8A or 6A Kai stainless steel with a hardness range of Rockwell C57-59. An advanced sub-zero quench heat-treating process insures a durable, razor-sharp edge. The metal parts of all Kershaw knives are mirror polished to prevent corrosion.

Kershaw pocketknives, which come in 11 different models, will be of particular interest to backpackers. All have stainless steel cases with rosewood inlays and most have locking blades. Various models have accessories such as folding scissors, screwdrivers or files.

The Kershaw Blade-Trader knife has six interchangeable blades: a carving blade, a saw blade, a bread knife, a frozen-food knife, a boning knife, and a cook knife.

Kershaw hunting knives come in folding and fixed models, and are designed for a variety of uses. All of them are rugged, hefty knives built for years of service in the field.

Kershaw limited-edition folding knives feature handles made of Oregon petrified wood or water buffalo bone. The bone-handle knives, which come in sets of three, have scrimshaw scenes of big-game animals.

Serious outdoorsmen have always wanted something more than just the bare necessities from a knife. It has to perform well, of course, but aesthetic considerations are important, too. A good knife will outlast almost any other piece of equipment that you carry, so you want something that you are comfortable with. It has to look good, feel right in your hand and work properly. Kershaw knives are definitely worth examining.

PRODUCTS: Knives.

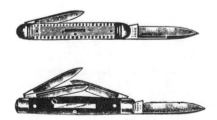

K.I.M. INDUSTRIES
9933 W. 151st St.
Orland Park, IL 60462
800-323-7673
Brochure, four-color, free. Est. 1962. James Vos, Pres.

Until I went on a walleye and pike fishing trip in Quebec one spring, I'd never heard of Muskol. But I soon got to know it intimately. Muskol is an excellent insect repellent—my French Canadian guide told me it was the only repellent he'd used that could keep Canada's bloodthirsty little blackflies away. And that it did. By far it was the most effective insect repellent I'd ever used.

After I returned home I found a magazine article about the wonder liquid. Muskol is 95 percent DEET, the active ingredient in most insect repellents. Few others contain more than 30 percent.

Since my trip, K.I.M. Industries in Orland Park, Illinois, has started heavily advertising Muskol in the United States. Now the stuff is sold at many backpacking and sporting-goods outlets, and a few mail-order dealers sell it, too.

Muskol comes in two-ounce and 1.06-ounce bottles, more than enough for most expeditions. If you fish or hunt in a place infested by mosquitoes, blackflies, chiggers, gnats, or ticks, take some Muskol with you. I heartily recommend it.

K.I.M. also sells Muskol Deer Scent and Muskol Fish Lure Paste. I've used neither, but if they're half as effective as Muskol bug juice, my troubles are over.

PRODUCTS: Insect repellent, deer scent, fish lure paste.

KIRKHAM'S OUTDOOR PRODUCTS
3125 S. State St.
Salt Lake City, UT 84115
801-486-4161
Accepts AMEX, MC, VISA. Illustrated. Est. 1945. Jack Kirkam, Pres. Judy Jensen, Cust. Rel.

It has been over 35 years now since Jack Kirkam bought the AAA Tent and Awning in Salt Lake City in order to learn the canvas business. He started out making horse blankets, wagon sheets and stockman's supplies and then began building cabin and umbrella tents. This led to the development of an original design, the "Springbar" tent. Mr. Kirkham now holds 16 patents for different components of this line of tents.

Springbar backpacking tents feature all domestic fabrics, aircraft-quality tubing, and polyester insect netting. All models have twin screened closable sky lights for extra ventilation or viewing the heavens on clear nights. Velcro closures are used on all doors. Outside zippers are protected by nylon flaps. Although somewhat unusual-looking in outward appearance, Springbar tents are stable and set up quickly. In a special contest held by the manufacturer in 1978, one contestant put up a model 9110 tent in 56.6 seconds.

Models 80 and 90 are of freestanding design. Model 60 is a four-person tent that weighs 10 pounds, 1½ ounces. The lightest tent is Model 850 at five pounds, 1½ ounces. It sleeps two people. It is also the least expensive tent, priced at about $100. Experienced outdoorsmen will recognize this as a very good value.

Springbar tents also come in a complete line of car-camping models made out of 100 percent cotton Army duck (the backpacking tents, of course, use synthetic fabrics such as 1.9 ounce Super K-Kote on floors and 1.9 ounce ripstop nylon on walls). Top of the car-camping line is a modular tenting system with a central living space and movable "bedrooms" that can be attached in various configurations. The modular system covers 200 square feet of floor space.

Springbar tents are sold direct from the factory to the customer. All tents are covered by a 10-year warranty.

PRODUCTS: Tents.

KLETTERWERKS
P.O. Box 1676
Bozeman, MT 59715

The Kletterwerks Terraplane may well be the ultimate soft pack. It certainly is one of the largest, with a 4,200-cubic-inch capacity in the X-Small size and a 4,600-cubic-inch capacity in the XX-Large size. Altogether there are six different sizes to insure a proper fit. A foam pad cushions the wearer's back from climbing hardware and other uncomfortable objects, and the load itself is used to create an internal frame. To this end, the main compartment is divided with a removable vertical partition to help organize the contents. Access to the interior of the pack can be had through a 10-mm covered coil zipper across the bottom, or via the fully removable top lid. The lid has two pockets and six lash points. There are two large pockets on the back of the pack where they will not interfere with arm movements. Compression straps allow you to reduce the pack's size when it is not carrying a full load. The two-inch-wide hip belt features a Velcro closure, and the shoulder straps have an adjustable sternum strap that goes across the front of the chest. A pair of optional sidepockets (450 cubic inches total) can be attached to the Terraplane.

The Bomb pack and the Matterhorn are smaller than the Terraplane, but have many of the same features. The Daypac and the Summit pack are useful around town as well as up in the high country.

The bag fabric of Kletterwerks packs is coated 11½-ounce Cordura nylon. The pack bottoms are tough 15-ounce ballistics nylon. Nylon thread is used exclusively with all seams stitched at least twice and stress points sewn four to seven times. Every piece of nylon fabric is individually hot cut, a technique that precludes mass production and insures quality. Every pack is carefully inspected before it is put on sale.

Kletterwerks also makes a deluxe fanny pack, a carry-on luggage bag, and Cordura cargo bags in three sizes.

PRODUCTS: Soft packs.

KNAPP OUTDOOR BOOKS
P.O. Box 2201
Jackson, WY 83001
307-733-5607 (credit card orders: 800-443-8610)
Accepts AMEX, MC, VISA. Four-color, 20 pp. Est. 1981. Kenneth J. Knapp, Pres.

The name is self-explanatory. The selection of titles is extensive. Knapp Outdoor Books stocks books by more than 40 publishers. The subjects include backpacking, skiing, sailing, mountaineering, canoeing, outdoor cooking, fishing, hunting, trail guides, wildlife identification guides, horsemanship, nature photography, environmental literature, children's books, bicycling, and more.

Reading about the outdoors is a fine vicarious substitute for actually being there, but it's much more than that. It is a way to draw on the diverse experiences of hundreds of other outdoorsmen, to learn about new outdoor techniques, to get ideas for future trips, to broaden and deepen your knowledge about all kinds of outdoor subjects. Tradition is an important part of the outdoor experience, and books are a primary repository of history and legend. The writings of John Muir, for example, can greatly enhance a backpacker's appreciation of the wilderness. Muir and Thoreau should be a part of every hiker's mental baggage. The written word, along with the color photograph, have also served as invaluable tools of the contemporary environmental movement and, again, you owe it to yourself to keep abreast of what is being published.

Outdoor books, of course, are available in bookstores and from equipment suppliers, but few retailers offer a selection that comes close to comparing with that offered by Knapp Outdoor Books. In addition, many outdoor publishing houses are not large enough to achieve national distribution. Knapp is the place to find their titles. Knapp also stocks foreign outdoor books, and will search for books not listed in the catalog. At Knapp, outdoor books are not a sideline. In fact, Knapp is the only distributor of strictly outdoor titles in the country.

PRODUCTS: Books.

KOMITO BOOTS
Box 2106
Estes Park, CO 80517
303-586-5391
Accepts MC, VISA. Illustrated brochure.

Komito Boots sells boots for rock climbing, ski touring and other mountain activities, and provides a shoe-repair service that specializes in mountain footwear. Steve Komito is an expert in all types of boot repair, including replacing soles and midsoles, replacing scree collars, rebuilding canvas rock climbing shoes, stretching boot uppers, replacing shanks, installing leather toe caps, and replacing eyelets, hooks, and D-rings. A number of replacement soles are available. The Galibier Varrape, Vibram Chouinard, Vibram Roccia, Insbrucker Super, and Galibier Contact are for rock-climbing shoes. The Vibram Montagna, Vibram Sestrograds, Vibram Ski Tour, and Galibier Makalu are for mountaineering, hiking and ski-touring boots. All repair work can be done by mail order. The average charge for replacing the soles and midsoles on hiking boots runs from about $22 to $40 per pair. An advance repair appointment—set up by a letter or phone call—will reduce the total time your boots are in the shop.

Komito Boots carries E.B. and Asolo Canyon rock-climbing shoes. The E.B., made in France, has been popular with climbers for years, although it is somewhat limited in durability and is not very comfortable for trail walking. This is definitely a shoe for the committed climber. The Asolo Canyon, made in Italy, is a bit stiffer than the E.B., and its all-leather uppers should increase durability.

Asolo ski-touring boots come in single-boot and double-boot models. These boots, which are much more substantial than low-cut sneaker-like cross-country racing shoes, are ideal for multi-day tours in the backcountry or the high mountains. The soles are designed to fit 75-mm Nordic Norm touring bindings.

Kastinger Hi Tour boots, also available in single-boot and double-boot models, are a little higher and a little stiffer than the Asolo boots. They should work a little better on steep downhill runs. One of the great things about a double boot, by the way, is that you can wear the inner boot inside the sleeping bag at night and spare yourself the agony of forcing stocking feet into iron-hard frozen boots the next morning.

Komito Boots is preparing a complete catalog that will offer a full range of mountain footwear.

PRODUCTS: Hiking boots, climbing shoes and boots, ski-touring boots.

KURT MANUFACTURING COMPANY
5280 Main St. N.E.
Minneapolis, MN 55421
612-566-5500
Information sheets on request.

There is no reckoning how many great photographs have never been taken because there wasn't enough time to take the pack off and get the camera out. Sometimes there *was* enough time, but it was just too much trouble. Of course you can always hike with a camera hanging around your neck, but then it constantly bangs against your chest or your stomach. And if you're scrambling over boulders or going through some other set of contortions, a swinging camera is more than a nuisance. Things can get very expensive very fast when the camera comes into violent contact with a solid object. One answer to this problem is a Kuban Hitch.

The Kuban Hitch, made by Kurt Manufacturing Company, is a clever harness system that holds a camera or a pair of binoculars firmly against you, ready for instant use, and does not restrict your freedom of movement. Basically, the Kuban Hitch consists of a set of straps that go over your shoulders and under your arms, and cross in back. Two elastic binders fit over the camera to keep it steady. A third binder can be used with oddly shaped cameras. The camera can be freed from the elastic restraining system at any time without undoing buckles or straps.

The Model D Kuban Hitch differs from the standard model in the use of non-reflective metal parts. The Kuban Hitch II has extra-wide straps that are striped yellow, white, and orange. The straps on the other models are black. All models function as a conventional neck strap when desired. One size fits all users and works with a wide variety of binoculars, 35-mm and medium format cameras. Aside from backpacking, the Kuban Hitch is extremely useful for activities such as bicycling, skiing, or any other active sport where you might want to carry a camera.

PRODUCTS: Sporting camera cases.

LAKOTA CORPORATION
7960 S.W. Cirrus Dr.
Beaverton, OR 97005
503-643-5424
Accepts MC, VISA. Est. 1976. George Baker, Gen. Mgr.

One of the problems with selecting a good knife is that there are so many to choose from. Dozens of manufacturers claim to use top-quality steel and painstaking production methods, and most of them actually do. Lakota knives stand out from the rest because they really don't look like anything else on the market. This in itself, of course, does not mean a great deal, but the unusual appearance of Lakota knives comes from total dedication to functional practicality, which is the essence of good design. In recognition of this, Lakota knives are included in the design collection of the Museum of Modern Art in New York City.

For a knife that is intended to be used in the field, strength and durability are important components of practicality. Lakota knives look strong and they are strong. They are simple and rugged. They aren't meant to be corkscrews or nail files. Lakota folding knives have one blade, a blade meant for cutting. With a folded length of 2³/₈ inches and a weight of 2¹/₂ ounces, the Lakota Falcon Model 275 is fine for backpackers. The Model 273 Fin Wing is a fixed-blade knife that should be good on the trail, too. It weighs four ounces. The Lil' Hawk Model 271, with a weight of seven ounces and a folded length of 4³/₄ inches, is one of the sturdiest folding knives ever made. The Model 280 Fish Hawk is a knife specially designed for fishermen. The Model 270 Hawk is a heavy-duty hunting knife designed for the ultimate in durability and handling ease.

The blades of all Lakota knives are 8A high-carbon stainless steel, heat-treated to Rockwell C56-59 hardness on the cutting edge. The knives are guaranteed for the life of the original owner. Leather sheaths are available for all Lakota knives.

PRODUCTS: Knives.

LANDAV DESIGNS
P. O. Box 4724
Portland, OR 97208
503-224-0996
Illustrated.

When it comes to equipment, a backpacker's first thoughts are quite naturally for basic items like packs, sleeping bags, and tents. Clothing is usually not given much attention. A few days in the wilderness, however, will reveal that some kinds of clothing are spectacularly ill-adapted for backcountry use. Wilderness apparel has to be tough. It should also be designed so you can move easily while clambering over rocks or balancing on a log. If you're in mosquito country, you don't want a shirt that bugs can bite through. Everybody has their own specific set of requirements for what wilderness clothes should or should not do.

The Landav Designs Easy Action Stretch shorts should please most hikers. The comfortable cotton/polyester stretch fabric lets you move freely. There is a flapped pocket in the rear and inset pockets in front.

The canvas Stand-Up pants and shorts are made for hard use, with a double seat and reinforced seams throughout. The colors are khaki and gray. The Classic Rugby short has taped side seams, full waistband and fly with elastic inserts and rubber buttons. The colors are green and blue.

The Tripsaver Gore-Tex is a nice little waterproof rainsuit that folds up into a pouch contained inside the jacket. Cuffs, waist, and leg bottoms are elasticized. The whole thing weighs 12 ounces.

The Snowfly Wading jacket is designed with fishermen in mind. It has a well-thought-out hood and inside pockets. The fabric is either Gore-Tex or Stormshed, a water-resistant breathable cloth. The Mallard Gore-Tex jacket is a short, flannel-lined garment with a removable hood. The Breathin' Easy Klimate Nor'wester is a West Coast version of the classic New England fisherman's foul-weather hat.

Landav Designs offers knickers in wool, poplin, and corduroy. Except with cross-country skiers, knickers have never really caught on that well in the United States, but they are immensely practical garments for wear in the mountains. Climbers and boulder-hoppers like them because they don't bind no matter what kind of bodily contortions you are going through. Also, there are no long cuffs to get wet from walking in snow. In the summer, knickers can double as a pair of shorts when you let down your knee socks. In addition to the knickers, Landav Designs makes wool pants, wool shirts, and wool jackets in various weights and styles. Synthetic garments are great, but there is many a hiker who would no more go into the wilderness without his trusty wool shirt than without his pocketknife or his matches. There is something about a wool shirt or jacket that is . . . well, wool is just *right*. You know what we mean.

PRODUCTS: Outdoor clothing, rainwear.

L.L. BEAN
Freeport, ME 04033
207-865-3111 for orders, any time
Cust. svc. 207-865-3161 8:00 am—4:30 pm EST Mon.—Fri.
Accepts AMEX, MC, VISA. Four times/year, free. Est. 1912. Leon A. Gorman, Pres.

In 1912, Leon Leonwood Bean started a small company in the coastal village of Freeport, Maine, to manufacture and sell his newly invented Maine Hunting Shoe, an outdoorsman's boot with rubber bottoms and lace-up leather tops. Today that little company in Freeport has 900 full-time employees and mails out eight million catalogs four times a year. It is one of the largest mail-order houses in the country. Because Mr. Bean originally catered to hunters and fishermen who tended to pass through town in the middle of the night, particularly on weekends, the retail salesroom stayed open 24 hours a day, 365 days a year. It still does. And, we might add, that salesroom is usually buzzing with activity. Stopping off at Bean's at four in the morning is a New England ritual.

But if the company grew beyond Mr. Bean's wildest dreams, some other things have stayed just the same. Bean's policy of providing honest Yankee value has never changed. Every item they offer is top quality, and usually priced somewhat lower than comparable goods in other stores. This, along with the Bean mystique, is what keeps the orders coming in year after year.

Like the original Levis or the Sierra Designs 60/40 parka, the Maine Hunting Shoe is a true classic. Woodsmen from Labrador to Alaska swear by Mr. Bean's rubber-bottomed boot. Indeed, the Maine Hunting Shoe is virtually indispensible in cold, wet terrain, and the Bean design has inspired a host of imitations. Bean's customer loyalty, however, remains high; 183,000 pairs of Maine Hunting Shoes were sold in 1980.

Bean's famous chamois cloth shirts, buffalo plaid Maine Guide shirts, chino pants, and canvas tote bags have spawned imitations too, but nothing quite beats the real item. The bulk of Bean's business today—some 85 percent—is mail-order. A 40-person customer-service staff is on hand to deal with special problems and questions. Bean's manufactures approximately 210 different products in its Freeport factory. These items are available only through the catalog or from the salesroom. In addition, Bean's stocks selected products from other manufacturers. The full line is strong on "country" clothing and footwear—we suspect that many an L.L. Bean customer has never cleaned a trout or shivered at the haunting wail of a loon—but the heart of the business is still very much devoted to supplying no-nonsense gear to serious outdoorsmen and outdoorswomen. This, after all, is what made L.L. Bean's reputation in the first place, and it is safe to say that the store in Freeport will be a North Woods institution for many years to come.

PRODUCTS: Outdoor clothing—pants, shirts, sweaters, jackets, footwear. Camping/backpacking/general outdoor equipment—packs, tents, sleeping bags, canoes, snowshoes, fishing tackle, waterfowl decoys, plus an extensive collection of gadgets and unusual items.

LOWE ALPINE SYSTEMS
802 S. Public Rd.
Lafayette, CO 80026
303-665-9220
Full-color.

A good external-frame pack is fine for carrying a heavy load on a well-graded trail. Some people never ask their packs to do more than that. Others like to travel cross country, scramble through boulder fields, climb mountains, or ski steep alpine terrain, and for these uses, an external-frame pack is not nearly so satisfactory. The load tends to be top-heavy, and it is held away from the wearer's body. The pack swings and sways and throws you off balance—very disconcerting while crossing a slippery foot-log over a roaring creek. The frame can also hang up on rocks and brush. It gets in the way in close quarters and interferes with arm movements. For all these reasons, climbers and skiers have long preferred rucksacks to pack frames, even though the entire weight of the load in a rucksack hangs from the shoulders and soon becomes uncomfortable, perhaps even painful, to carry.

The answer, of course, is the internal-frame pack. It combines the heavy-load-carrying comfort of a pack frame and the maneuverability of a soft pack. The Lowe brothers came up with one of the first practical models. Perhaps they did not actually invent the internal-frame pack, but most of the many internal-frame packs that have appeared on the market since then bear a suspiciously close resemblance to the original Lowe design. The Lowe Expedition pack, in fact, is *the* classic internal-frame pack.

The Lowe suspension system is designed for comfort and balance. A two-layer padded hip-belt carries most of the weight. Soft open-cell foam is placed next to the body, while closed-cell foam supports the load. The shoulder straps can be adjusted to bring the pack close to your back for stability, or loosened to put more weight on your hips. A chest strap that links the two shoulder straps across the front of your chest can be tightened or loosened to relieve pressure on the shoulder straps. The internal-frame components are 2024-T351 aluminum.

Lowe mountain packs come in three sizes: Triolet, Expedition, and Lhotse. At 5,300 cubic inches, the Lhotse is one of the biggest internal-frame packs on the market. Compression straps on all models allow adjustment of the pack's size. Accessory pockets are available. Pack fabric is eight-ounce coated pack cloth with an 11-ounce Cordura double bottom. Each Lowe pack is sewn start to finish by one person. Load-bearing seams are sewn at least twice, and stress points are reinforced with webbing and extra fabric.

The Trek I and Trek II packs are large-capacity internal-frame packs similar in many respects to the mountain packs, but with extra features for the convenience of serious hikers. The Loco pack is an internal-frame pack specifically designed for search and rescue and very difficult climbing. It has a built-in climbing/rappel/extraction harness. The Kinnikinnics packs are useful as soft luggage and also perform well as regular backpacks. Lowe Action packs are for the most demanding uses. They were chosen by the American Olympic Biathlon Team.

In addition to packs, Lowe Alpine Systems offers a unique selection of climbing tools, including the Hummingbird ice axe and hammer, the Chock Tocker, the Snarg ice piton, and the Lowe strapless crampons. The LowePRO camera case can be worn like a pack and is designed to meet the requirements of professional film makers.

PRODUCTS: Packs, mountaineering equipment.

LOWE INDUSTRIES
I-44
Lebanon, MO 65536
417-532-9101
Illustrated.

Not to be confused with the other Lowe, which makes packs and climbing equipment, Lowe Industries of Lebanon, Missouri, manufactures aluminum boats and canoes. Missouri, in case you are not familiar with the state, is bass-fishing country. During the summer, local television stations broadcast bass forecasts along with the news, weather, and sports.

You don't need a special boat to catch bass, but it helps. Lowe Industries makes five models. Basically, a bass boat is a scow-type craft with raised fishing chairs mounted on pedestals. The various Lowe models range from the Spartan to the deluxe. The fancier boats feature padded swivel fishing chairs with arm rests, control consoles with windshields, trolling motor panels, and carpeting. The big boats take motors of up to 70 horsepower.

A Jon boat looks something like a bass boat, but is more of a work boat. It has the same flat bottom and square bow, but has thwarts instead of raised seats. The Jon boat is the craft for shallow water, for marshes and swamps and bayous and lazy rivers, for duck hunters and fishermen. Lowe Industries makes 19 Jon boat models. The smaller sizes weigh less than 150 pounds and are suitable for car-top use.

The Lowe Industries line of Semi-V boats have pointed bows and resemble skiffs. Most are suitable for car-topping. Lowe also makes a line of large pontoon boats.

Lowe Aluminum canoes come in five models, including a square-stern 16-foot boat. These are all fine, sturdy canoes weighing between 69 and 92 pounds. Aluminum canoes have fallen somewhat out of favor these days, with the growing popularity of fiberglass and the new, exotic synthetics such as Kevlar 49, but the disadvantages of aluminum have been exaggerated. It is true that whitewater racers will not even consider an aluminum boat, but that may not have a great deal of relevance to the average canoeist. It is worth remembering that literally millions of aluminum canoes have been made over the years, and the boats have performed well in virtually every kind of canoeing situation. We recently took an aluminum canoe down 400 miles of wilderness river in the Brooks Range of Alaska, and couldn't have asked for a better boat. Aluminum canoes are tough, inexpensive and trouble-free when it comes to maintenance. The Lowe canoes will give their owners years of pleasure on the water, whether they paddle them on man-made lakes or on wild rivers.

PRODUCTS: Canoes, boats.

LYON HAMMOCKS
41 Galen St.
Watertown, MA 02172
617-923-2261
Accepts MC, VISA. Brochure. Est. 1976. Thomas R. Curden, Pres.

Popular in tropical countries all over the world, the hammock was actually invented thousands of years ago by the Mayan Indians of Central America. New World explorers responded enthusiastically to the idea, but because space on board ship is restricted, sailors slept in their hammocks lengthwise and thus did not realize the hammock's full potential for comfort. An authentic Mayan hammock is meant to be slept in crosswise. Spreader bars are not needed because the sleeper's own body acts as a spreader.

As luxurious as the softest feather bed, a hammock has an obvious appeal to backpackers because it is extremely portable and can be set up wherever there are two objects to suspend it from. A little ingenuity can provide protection from rain and insects, if needed. The same hammock can be used indoors, on the porch, or out in the backyard.

Lyon Hammocks are made in Mexico by hand out of cotton lace on long wooden racks called bastiadors. The regular size, which is 12 feet long and 11 feet wide, is woven from more than three miles of pure cotton and holds two adults. It weighs 3¼ pounds and folds up into a small bundle about the size of a rolled-up pair of pants.

The large hammock, which is 12 feet long and 12 feet wide, has waxed and polished end strings for mildew resistance. It holds three adults and weighs 3¾ pounds.

The extra-large hammock is 12 feet long and 16 feet wide and holds four adults. It weighs 4.6 pounds.

Considering the size of these hammocks, a large backpacking party would not have to provide a hammock for each individual. The hammocks could be shared or party members could take turns lounging in them around camp. Also, with a hammock in your pack, an afternoon rest stop takes on a whole new dimension. All you need to do is to select a likely looking pair of trees, string up the hammock, doze or read for an hour, and continue on your way, refreshed.

PRODUCTS: Hammocks.

MAD RIVER CANOE
Box 610
Waitsfield, VT 05673
802-496-3127
Four-color. James Henry, Pres.

The first canoes, of course, were made of birch bark. Wood and canvas canoes later became popular—if you're over 35 years old you probably paddled one at summer camp—but they had to be made by hand and they require a lot of owner maintenance. The few wood and canvas models still on the market appeal mainly to nostalgia buffs. A variant of this style, with fiberglass replacing the canvas, is fairly popular but expensive. Canoes made entirely of wood are things of incredible beauty and can be surprisingly lightweight and durable, but prices start around $1,500 and climb rapidly.

The first wave of mass-produced modern recreational canoes were aluminum. These have in turn been supplemented by canoes made of plastic-type materials. Aluminum canoes are faulted for heaviness, lack of design sophistication (aluminum cannot be controlled as precisely during the building process as plastic), noisiness, stickiness on rocks, and a tendency to transmit extremes of heat and cold. Nevertheless, they are relatively inexpensive and remain popular.

Serious canoeists today lean toward synthetic-material boats. They fall into three main categories: fiberglass, Kevlar and Royalex. Mad River Canoe makes all three.

"Fiberglass" is a fairly broad term that can mean just about anything from a cheap, sloppy boat to a carefully-thought-out piece of craftsmanship. A good fiberglass canoe is definitely not something that pops out of a mold. The fiberglass used by Mad River Canoe is specially woven and prepared to their own specifications. It employs numerous cloth layers laid in at specific angles for a good combination of rigidity and flexibility. Mat and filler materials are absent. Fiberglass canoes are relatively lightweight, moderately priced and durable.

Kevlar 49, a DuPont product developed as a substitute for steel in airplanes, produces the ultimate lightweight canoes. It also makes a strong and responsive boat.

Royalex (a cross-linked vinyl with a foam core made by Uniroyal) is heavier than fiberglass or Kevlar, but makes a canoe of extraordinary durability. Royalex tends to pop back into its original shape after being subjected to severe stress. An example of "severe stress" would be a canoe pinned against a rock in the middle of a roaring rapid. Mad River Royalex canoes have been bent nearly double in this situation and survived.

Mad River Canoe offers 10 different designs for wilderness tripping, whitewater, family paddling, fishing, and competition. The careful construction and high finish level is enhanced by cane seats and wood trim. Camouflage models are offered for duck hunters, and some Mad River canoes are adaptable to a Class C sailing rig. Mad River also offers paddles, motor mounts, portage yokes, car carriers, flotation bags, skid plates, and folding canoe chairs.

PRODUCTS: Canoes.

MAINE MARINE CORPORATION (Lincoln Canoes)
Route 32
Waldoboro, ME 04572
207-832-5323
Brochure. Est. 1961. Frederick Taska, Pres.

Lincoln makes a good-looking line of canoes in fiberglass and Kevlar. Most feature a shallow arch hull without keel, cane seats, black anodized aluminum gunwales, molded fiberglass or wood decks, ash carrying yokes and handles, and stainless steel fasteners.

The 16-foot, six-inch Concord I is an economy-priced fiberglass canoe. It weighs 70 pounds. The 16-foot, six-inch Concord II has cane seats and an ash carrying yoke. It weighs 70 pounds in fiberglass and 55 pounds in Kevlar. Maneuverable enough for a solo paddler, the Concord II can easily accommodate two people plus enough gear for a weekend trip.

The 16-foot Family Special is designed to be a very easy-paddling boat for its size. It is available with or without a keel and in fiberglass or Kevlar. Speaking in general terms, keels have fallen out of favor as a feature of modern canoe design.

The 18-foot Cruiser is a canoe designed for tripping on rivers and lakes. It weighs 76 pounds in fiberglass and 65 pounds in Kevlar. With a 950-pound capacity, this canoe will hold a lot of duffle. There is a substantial difference in price, by the way, between fiberglass and Kevlar canoes.

Designed by Bill Stearns, the Lincoln 5.3 Meter (17-foot, five-inch) canoe has an asymmetrical hull that offers the advantages of a long bow section without increasing the canoe's overall length. This is an ideal boat for river running or wilderness trips. The bow seat slides back and forth to allow adjustment to individual paddling positions and to trim the boat. The 5.3 Meter weighs 64 pounds in Kevlar and 74 pounds in fiberglass.

The Downeast 5.3 Meter has the same hull, but with mahogany decks and ash and mahogany gunwales. Both models have cane seats, ash carrying yokes and ash carrying handles, bow and stern. The Downeast 5.3 Meter weighs 68 pounds in Kevlar and 79 pounds in fiberglass.

Another Bill Stearns design, the 5.7 Meter, has a moderate rocker to give it fine maneuverability despite its 18½-foot length. This is the ultimate boat for big river trips in the wilderness. The 5.7 Meter has cane seats, a sliding bow seat, ash carrying yoke, and an asymmetrical hull shape. It excells in heavy whitewater even while carrying a big load. The 5.7 Meter weighs 72 pounds in Kevlar and 82 pounds in fiberglass.

The 14-foot Sportsman is a short, wide canoe designed to

provide a stable platform for duck hunters and fishermen. Its light weight (58 pounds) makes this boat easy to portage or to hoist on and off roof racks. The Sportsman is available with or without sponsons.

Lincoln also makes two Royalex canoes: the 16-foot Pemaquid and the 16-foot, two-inch Abenaki.

PRODUCTS: Canoes.

MARMOT MOUNTAIN WORKS
331 S. 13th
Grand Junction, CO 81501
303-245-3178
Accepts MC, VISA. Color.

Marmot Mountain Works manufactures down jackets, vests, sleeping bags, shell garments and tents. All uncoated nylon fabric is cut individually with a hot knife to eliminate fraying. Stress points are double or quadruple stitched with twelve stitches per inch. Many items are sewn entirely by one person to prevent assembly-line-type sloppiness. One ounce of Marmot goose down fills about 625 cubic inches. This is among the best-quality goose down available.

The Marmot down vest is made of 3.4-ounce nylon poplin. It features handwarmer pockets, a down-filled draft tube behind the front zipper, and a Velcro-sealed stash pocket. Marmot down parkas come in three basic models. The top-of-the-line Too Warm parka weighs just 26 ounces, but will meet the most demanding conditions. It is cut extra long to provide insulation around the lower back. Along with double hand-warmer pockets, this jacket features knit recessed cuffs, a Velcro-sealed flap over the zipper, a down-filled tube behind the zipper, and a storm skirt that fits around the hips to seal out drafts. The Too Warm is available in Gore-Tex or nylon poplin. An optional down hood is available.

The Marmot Gore-Tex Warm I parka weighs 17 ounces. It features the storm skirt and a down-filled draft tube behind the zipper. This jacket, with its high collar and trim fit, is excellent for skiing. The Marmot Warm II parka weighs in at 22 ounces, with 8½ ounces of down fill. It is available in Gore-Tex laminate or nylon poplin.

The Gore-Tex Powder jacket is a waterproof/windproof shell garment that offers Velcro-sealed cargo pockets, Velcro cuffs, a special inside "flash" pocket that is accessible without unzipping the main zipper, an elastic-banded storm skirt around the hips, and an optional hood. All seams are sealed at the factory, so the application of special liquid Gore-Tex sealant is not necessary.

The Marmot All-Weather Gore-Tex parka has all the features of the Powder jacket plus an attached hood. The matching All-Weather pants have full-length inseam zippers which allow the wearer to take them off or put them on while wearing crampons or skis.

Marmot down sleeping bags feature differential cut, slant-wall overlapping baffles or box baffles, seven baffled compartments in the foot section, 70-inch YKK #7 coil zippers with double sliders, and down-filled draft tubes. The various models are available in Gore-Tex or nylon taffeta.

Marmot makes two different styles of two-man Gore-Tex tents, one weighing four pounds, 14 ounces, the other, three pounds, 11 ounces. Both provide excellent roominess considering their extreme light weight, and feature novel ventilation systems, graphite-reinforced fiberglass poles, and good stability in wind.

In addition to the above items, Marmot's Berkeley store offers products from other manufacturers, including polyproplene underwear, angora underwear, Gregory packs, Kletterwerks packs, Moonstone sleeping bags, Robertson Synergy packs, Mojo Systems camera packs, Down Home mukluks, and Moss Tents. They are available by mail order from Berkeley only (address: Marmot Mountain Works 3049 Aseline St. Berkeley, CA 94703).

PRODUCTS: Down wear, sleeping bags, shell garments, tents.

MENGO INDUSTRIES
4611 Green Bay Rd.
Kenosha, WI 53142
414-652-3070
Annual, four-color, free. Est. 1970. Alfred Mengo, Sr., Pres.

Mengo's 12-page four-color catalog lists 48 boat ladders, seven rod holders, an outrigger pole, nine gaff hooks, a net holder, five aluminum and plastic paddles, seven boat hooks, 33 landing nets, and eight miscellaneous nets.

In the ladder category are models made for mounting on houseboats, docks or rafts, hand rails, transoms, bows, cockpits, decks, cruisers, and gunwales. The number of rungs varies from

two to six. All but the least expensive ladders are made of corrosion-resistant anodized aluminum.

Rod holders are made for attachment to rails, stanchions, gunwales, transoms, or decks. Three have swiveling bases that permit you to set the hook at the same time you retrieve the rod.

Five regular gaffs and four double-tine gaffs feature stainless steel hooks. Tested for 15 years by commercial fishermen, the double-tine models are said to prevent fish from twisting off.

All nets feature aluminum frames. Several have telescopic handles. Besides the ordinary nylon mesh, Mengo offers nets with collapsible molded-rubber netting, collapsible wire mesh and fine-mesh nylon. The strongest models have handles made of an aluminum tubing 1⅛ inches in diameter and netting made of heavy-duty green polypropylene. Replacement net bags are available for 15 models.

PRODUCTS: Boat ladders, boat hooks, fishing nets, rod holders, paddles.

MOSS BROWN & COMPANY
1522 Wisconsin Ave. N.W.
Washington, DC 20007
800-424-2774 (for orders)
Accepts AMEX, MC, VISA.

Depending as they do on covering distance with foot power, running and backpacking have always had a bit of overlap. In fact there is a sport in Great Britain called "fell running" where contestants race against the clock over mountainous terrain, often in atrocious weather conditions and without the refinements of a trail, much less a road. In this country, runners tend to be backpackers and vice versa. The two activities have even begun to share some of the same gear as more and more backpackers are hiking in running shoes. In part this is because heavy lug-soled boots have caused unacceptable levels of damage on popular trails, but running shoes have a lot going for them in their own right. Mainly, they're comfortable. There is no good reason to burden yourself with excessively heavy footwear if the conditions do not really call for it. Heavy boots are also much more likely to cause blisters or other foot problems, and we hardly need add that blisters are probably the primary source of backcountry misery.

By the same token, runners have borrowed a few tricks from the backpacking equipment industry. The Moss Brown 10-Miler Gore-Tex running suit is a good example. With a total weight of under 16 ounces, the suit offers complete wind and rain protection. The jacket has a hood, a high wind collar, front zipper, knit wristbands, and a venting system for air circulation. Leg zippers allow the pants to be put on over shoes.

The Moss Brown Gore-Tex warm-up suit also has careful design for freedom of movement plus a brush Antron flannel lining. Gore-Tex runner's mitts are available too.

The Moss Brown waterproof Runner's Backpack resembles a traditional day pack, but is designed for comfort while on the move. It has two storage compartments. The Early Warning runner's pack features 3M Scotchlite reflective-finish fabric. Day-glow orange reflective mitts are available.

The Boda belt is worn around the waist like a fanny pack, but instead of dry cargo, it holds 20 ounces of water. The Boda pouch fits over the Boda belt.

Moss Brown carries a complete line of New Balance running shoes plus the Reebok Gore-Tex running shoe. This durable and weather-resistant shoe would be a fine choice for trail use.

Consistent with its reputation as one of the top running-supply shops in the country, Moss Brown & Company also carries a full line of accessories from socks to computerized stopwatches.

PRODUCTS: Running apparel, shoes, accessories.

MOUNTAIN SAFETY RESEARCH
631 S. 96th St.
Seattle, WA 98108
206-762-0210
Accepts MC, VISA. Four-color, free. Larry Penberthy, Pres.

As the name implies, Mountain Safety Research originated as a testing service dedicated to alerting climbers to unsafe equipment. Since then, MSR has evolved into a manufacturing concern, utilizing data gleaned from the testing process. The MSR climbing helmet is probably the best-known example. Other helmets on the market were simply not up to MSR standards. The MSR helmet features a Lexan polycarbonate shell with a quarter-inch brim that increases side-to-side

rigidity, and 12 holes for ventilation. Three types of foam padding are used. A foam sweatband is easily removable for cleaning. A specially designed chin and nape strap keeps the helmet securely on the climber's head. MSR will replace, at no cost, any helmet involved in an accident, in order to protect the wearer and to add to the data on helmet performance. MSR also offers a bicycling helmet.

The MSR stove is another remarkable piece of technology. The Model G burns white gas, leaded automotive gas, unleaded gas, or aviation gasoline. The Model G/K burns kerosene, deodorized kerosene, Stoddard solvent, #1 diesel and #1 stove oil. It boils a quart of water in 3½ minutes. A built-in sparker eliminates the need for matches when burning gasoline. A quart of gas will boil 48 quarts of water or melt enough snow to yield 48 quarts of water. The stove itself weighs 15 ounces. A wraparound metal windscreen provides complete wind protection.

MSR also offers lithium-cell batteries and a headlamp to use them in. One D-size lithium cell gives as much light as four alkaline cells. In addition, the lithium cell lasts much longer and retains most of its power at extremely cold temperatures where other batteries fade or fail.

Aside from the above items, MSR offers ice axes, cooking gear, sunglasses, snow shovels, avalanche probes, rescue pulleys, and snow flukes. All of these products incorporate the technical brilliance, commonsense practicality and attention to detail that climbers have come to expect from MSR.

PRODUCTS: Climbing helmets, headlamps, stoves, climbing hardware.

MOUNTAIN SERVICES
P.O. Box 159
Elmer City, WA 99124
509-633-0130
Accepts MC, VISA with 5% surcharge. Price list on request. Est. 1979. Keith Dooley, Pres.

Mountain Services sells climbing and mountaineering gear on a mail-order basis. Their catalog is, without doubt, the least dandified of any we have seen. There are no illustrations, no write-ups—nothing except a list of the products and the prices. Serious climbers shouldn't need anything more. When it comes to hardware, ropes, and the like, if you don't know exactly what it is that you want, you shouldn't be buying it by mail. In fact, you probably shouldn't be buying it at all. The place to learn about technical climbing equipment and its safe use is from recognized instruction books, mountaineering journals, unbiased test results, and other climbers whose experience and judgment you trust, not from a catalog.

But climbers who *do* know what they need will appreciate Mountain Services for the breadth of its selection and for the prices which offer real savings over normal retail levels.

We can't duplicate the entire price list here, but it is possible to give a general outline. Mountain Services stocks carabiners by SMC, Bonati, Stubai, Salewa, and Liberty. Ropes are by Mammut, Interalp and Edelrid. Ice axes and hammers are by Forrest, MSR and Interalp. Pitons are by Leeper and SMC. Cleanware is by Forrest, SMC and Leeper. In addition, there are items such as snow saws, SMC crampons, Interalp crampons, MSR climbing helmets and stoves, SMC snow anchors, MSR snow flukes, SMC brake bars, MSR rescue pulleys, and more. Extra discounts may be available for large orders.

PRODUCTS: Mountaineering equipment.

MOUNTAINSMITH
12790 W. Sixth Pl.
Golden, CO 80401
303-238-5823
Accepts MC, VISA ($25 minimum on credit card orders). Descriptive brochure on request. Patrick Smith, Pres.

Mountainsmith offers an uncommon line of products that you may have difficulty finding elsewhere, particularly under one roof.

Cargo sleds have been popular with cross-country skiers in Europe for a long time, and now North Americans are starting to appreciate these versatile devices. On anything but steep alpine terrain, loads of over 40 pounds are easier to pull on a sled than to carry on your back in a pack. Smithsleds are made of fiberglass with rugged fitted covers. The bottom of the sled is flat with two aluminum runners. The Expedition series sleds are for the big loads. The freight model holds about 135 pounds. The passenger model has removable kid's seats with closed-cell foam padding and quick-release seat belts. Cover material is 11½-ounce Cordura.

The Safari series sleds are suitable for rescue work with room for a six-footer to lie down. The High Country series sleds were developed for sled skiing and are designed so that handicapped people with lower-body disabilities can use them. These sleds come with poles, quick-release restraint buckles, and a closed-cell foam pad on the bottom. They can be used as cargo sleds as well.

The Pro Pack is for skiers and climbers. It is long and narrow so you won't hit it with your arms. Waist-belt pockets zip on and off.

The Echo II transceiver, built by Paul Ramer, is an avalanche beacon. Other Ramer products sold by Mountainsmith include a practical snow shovel, adjustable-length ski poles, and climbing skins.

The Mountainsmith sled brake is heavy polypropelene cord that fastens across the back of the sled to keep it from slipping backward, or on the front to brake on steep slopes. Polypropelene ski climbers perform a similar function on cross-country skis. The Mountainsmith bottle thermos is an insulated cover that fits over the popular sizes of plastic bottles to keep liquid from freezing. The thermos comes with a belt loop.

Finally, Mountainsmith offers authentic tipis at a reasonable price. The fabric is cotton duck. Stakes and ties are included; poles are not.

PRODUCTS: Sleds, packs, tipis.

NATURAL FOOD BACKPACK DINNERS
P. O. Box 532
Corvallis, OR 97330
503-757-1334
Illustrated brochure.

Food is of tremendous importance on a wilderness trip. And the longer the stay in the backcountry, the more important food becomes. After a week or two—sometimes less—most people can think of little else. They start dreaming about food. At the same time, of course, a long trip intensifies the problem of carrying enough to eat. Canned goods, quite obviously, are too heavy and too bulky. So are many fresh foods. Dehydrated and freeze-dried backpacking meals are one answer, but you have to be careful. Some brands taste like cardboard. Others are loaded up with chemicals, artificial flavorings and preservatives.

Natural Food Backpack Dinners are an attractive alternative. There is nothing artificial in these meals. None contain meat. They cook up in 10 to 20 minutes and the portions are generous. The dinners are packaged in polyethylene bags for easy disposal.

The Middle Eastern dinner contains whole-wheat farina, soy grits, currants, pumpkin seeds, onions, salt, herbs and spices. The dry weight is eight ounces. It cooks in 15 minutes. The Loch Ness stew contains split pea grits, sunflower seeds, brown rice grits, onions, peas, salt, tomato powder, carrots, non-fat dry milk, herbs and spices. The lentil soup (you know there has to be a lentil soup) is a meal by itself. It contains lentil grits, non-fat dry milk, sesame seeds, onions, garlic salt, brewer's yeast, herbs and spices. The Mexican dinner is a concoction of pinto bean grits, cornmeal, soy grits, parmesan cheese, tomato powder, onions, garlic salt, chili powder, herbs and spices.

Other main courses include Meadow Mushroom soup, curried bean pilaf, vegetable minestrone, Country Corn chowder, and Mountain macaroni. All of these dinners weigh between seven and nine ounces in the package. Each package serves two people. Calories per serving range from 180 for the mushroom soup to 455 for the curried bean pilaf.

In addition to the main courses, Natural Food Backpack Dinners makes a naturally sweetened porridge that includes rolled oats, wheat, barley, rye, dates, date sugar, walnuts, soy grits, carob powder, spices and salt. And last but not least, there are the "Wha Guru Chews," high-protein honey nut crunch bars for trail snacks.

PRODUCTS: Natural backpacking food.

THE NATURE COMPANY
P.O. Box 7137
Berkeley, CA 94707
415-524-8340
Accepts MC, VISA. Full-color.

The Nature company does not sell parkas or packs or sleeping bags or boots. As a matter of fact, 95 percent of the items in their catalog are of no use whatsoever to backpackers out in the field. Nevertheless, we think you will be interested in what the Nature Company has to offer.

Take, for instance, their sundials. Or their weather vanes.

Or their rain gauges. Actually, one of the plastic rain gauges is small enough to carry in a backpack. So is the wind-chill meter, which comes with a nylon carrying case that can be worn on a belt. Outdoorsmen are always speculating about how cold it really is. This instrument will tell you.

Binoculars are useful in the wilderness. The Nature Company carries a good selection of Swift binoculars as well as spotting scopes and pocket telescopes. They also have the Astroscan 2001 telescope, made by Edmund Scientific for beginning astronomers.

The Nature Company carries a good selection of bird feeders, including several lucite models that mount directly on window glass with suction cups. Bird identification guides, books about birds, and ornamental items shaped like birds or with pictures of birds painted on them or woven into them are available in abundance.

The Nature Company's selection of records and tapes are particularly interesting. There are the obligatory whale songs, of course, and there is also a record that captures the early-morning sounds around a lake in the Canadian wilderness and another record that was recorded at a busy frog pond. Still other records feature a thunderstorm in a forest, the language of wolves, birdsongs, wood-masted sailboats, an English meadow, ocean waves, and the life of the Okefenokee Swamp. Listening to these records—or playing the tapes in your car while stalled in traffic—is just the thing to banish city blues.

The Nature Company has a special selection of games, books, and learning aids for children. For adults, the catalog is stuffed full of posters, jewelry, clothing, desk ornaments, note paper, sun bar prisms, and more curious odds and ends than you ever dreamed of, all with a nature theme.

PRODUCTS: Sundials, weather vanes, binoculars, telescopes, records, tapes.

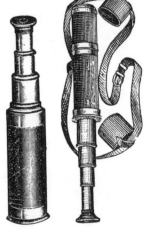

NORMARK CORPORATION
1710 E. 78th St.
Minneapolis, MN 55423
612-860-3292
Est. 1960. Ronald Weber, Pres. Barbara Ganzer, Cust. Svc.

Normark Corporation imports a line of top-quality Scandinavian-made knives, game shears, fishing lures, and compasses.

The Rapala Fish 'n Fillet knives come in four sizes, with blades four, six, 7½ and nine inches long. Hand-crafted in Finland, these knives have reinforced varnished birch handles and tooled leather Laplander sheaths. The blades are flexible Swedish stainless steel.

Normark's Presentation fillet knives feature a progressively double-tapered stainless blade made of a combination of carbon, molybdenum, and chromium for a long-lasting cutting edge. Hand-crafted like the Fish 'n Fillet series, the Presentation fillet knives come with tooled oxhide sheaths. There are three blade lengths in the Presentation series: four, six, and 7½ inches.

The Presentation hunting knife has a five-inch blade made of the same steel as the Presentation fillet knives and a molded handle in an ebony color.

The Swedish-made Presentation folding knives are surgical stainless steel blades in three lengths: 3⅛, 3⅝, and 3¾ inches. An optional leather belt sheath is available.

The Pocket Swede Dress knives are folding models with stainless steel blades, locking blades, resin-impregnated wood handles, and stainless steel combination bolster-liners. These knives come in three blade lengths: 2⅛, 2⅔, and 2¾ inches. Like all the other Normark knives, the Pocket Swede Dress knives feature an elegantly simple design that seems to be both classic and modern at the same time. These are exceptionally good-looking cutting tools.

Normark's Sportsman scissors are built with Swedish stainless steel blades, molded handles, and ball-bearing pivots. There are five models ranging in size from 4½ inches to eight inches long. The three smaller models all weigh less than one ounce. Backpackers may not immediately see the need to carry a pair of scissors in the field, but they can be convenient if you plan to do much angling. Other uses will inevitably come up.

A compass, on the other hand, is something no backpacker should be without. The Normark compass comes in a wrist model and a pocket model. Both feature four- to five-second setting times, a liquid-filled capsule and a fine jewel sapphire bearing. The pocket compass will float if accidentally dropped in water. Both models are waterproof.

PRODUCTS: Knives, game shears, fishing lures, compasses.

NORTHLAND OUTFITTERS
Route 2
Box 316
Marinette, WI 54143
Accepts MC, VISA. Illustrated.

A lot of backpackers think that binoculars are too much trouble. Others would not go into the woods without a pair. It used to be that binoculars that were worth anything weighed too much to take on an extended backpacking trip, especially if you were already carrying a camera, but this is no longer true. A variety of lightweight, high-quality binoculars are on the market today. Bushnell makes some of the best. Bushnell Custom Compact binoculars weigh 11 ounces, light enough for any pack. Northland Outfitters carries the Custom Compacts, along with a selection of other Bushnell binoculars and telescopes.

Aside from binoculars, Northland Outfitters stocks a complete line of outdoor equipment for backpackers: tents, sleeping bags, packs, cookware, compasses, knives, air mattresses, books, snowshoes, snowshoe furniture, bird feeders, and a folding lightweight (18-ounce) camp chair called the Sling-Light.

The packs are by Camp Trails, one of the most experienced pack frame manufacturers in the United States. Camp Trails packs have been on the market since the 1940s—when backpacking wasn't even a sport—and the company continues to stay abreast of the latest pack technology. The Centuri is a top-of-the-line Camp Trails frame pack that works either as a single- or a divided-compartment pack because of a zip-open internal partition. Other features include an extendable top with storm flap, a large pocket on the back, and tunnel pockets (which permit you to carry skis) on the sides of the pack.

Internal-frame packs have become popular in recent years for shorter trips and for activities, such as rock climbing or skiing, where agility and balance are important. Northland Outfitters carries three models of internal-frame packs by Camp Trails—the Wolf Pack series.

Northland Outfitters catalogs a wide variety of tents by Eureka!, including A-frame, dome and car-camping models. (Eureka! Tent and Camp Trails Pack are both owned by the Johnson Wax Company.) Other items in the Northland Outfitters catalog include sleeping bags for a variety of temperature conditions, Victorinox Swiss Army knives (the "genuine" Swiss knife), Primus propane camp stoves, and a Primus propane light with an output equal to that of a 100-watt electric light bulb.

PRODUCTS: Binoculars, tents, sleeping bags, backpacking equipment, books, snowshoes, cookware.

NORTHWEST RIVER SUPPLIES
430 W. Third
Moscow, ID 83843
208-882-2383
Accepts MC, VISA. Annual, four-color. Est. 1973. Bill Parks, Pres.

Northwest River Supplies specializes in whitewater rafts, kayaks, canoes, and accessories. It carries one of the most extensive lines of river-running equipment on the continent.

Along with rafts by Achilles, Avon, Camp Ways, and UDISCO, Northwest River Supplies has designed its own line of rafts which are manufactured by Kohkoku Chemical, Ltd., a major Japanese chemical company. The 14-foot, nine-inch NRS Sport II has the capacity for trips of a week or longer. The fabric is 5½-ounce 840 denier nylon coated with 80 percent DuPont Hypalon for durability. The raft weighs 120 pounds. Twenty-inch tubes provide a dry ride. The price of about $1,350 is very reasonable for a raft of this high quality. Further savings are offered by the Sport Universal Package which includes the raft, universal rowing frame, oars, oarlocks, and pump.

The Sprite II raft is a smaller boat for two or three people. It is priced at about $360. The Scout is an economical larger raft for extended trips. It features a 65 percent Hypalon coating over 420 denier tube fabric plus 840 denier floor fabric. This raft is 14 feet, six inches long, six feet, eight inches wide. It weighs 85 pounds.

The Achilles line of rafts is also made by Kohkoku Chemical. NRS carries two models in stock—both of them large, heavy-duty rafts—and can special-order others.

Avon, an English firm, makes the best-known inflatables in the world. Avon also has a reputation for top quality. As you might guess, Avon rafts are expensive. NRS carries several models in stock.

Camp Ways Blue Line is an economical and durable line of rafts. A large variety of sizes is available, and NRS stocks many of them, including a big 15-foot raft at a moderate price. UDISCO makes an inexpensive line of boats suitable for beginning rafters, although you have to be a little more careful with these rafts than the others. Sizes range from 11 feet, six inches up to 16 feet.

NRS manufactures its own rowing frame, the heavy-duty Universal. It also makes a more compact frame, the Expedition, that fits inside a car trunk easily. The Longhorn frame is lighter and less expensive. NRS offers a large selection of oars and paddles, along with pumps, repair materials, and an astonishing selection of raft hardware.

NRS carries several different kayaks, inflatable kayaks, and canoes. Canoes are not shipped; they must be picked up at the Moscow store. Other items in the catalog include canoe and kayak flotation systems, spray skirts, wetsuits, life jackets, helmets, roof racks, coolers, folding tables, camping equipment, etc. NRS makes its own waterproof storage bag out of bright blue 18-ounce PVC-coated Dacron. They also carry waterproof bags by Watersports International, Phoenix, and others. This may well be the best selection of waterproof bags, boxes, map cases, and camera cases you can find.

PRODUCTS: Rafts, kayaks, canoes.

OLD TOWN CANOE COMPANY
Old Town, ME 04468
207-827-5513

One of the two or three best-known canoe makers in the United States, Old Town's reputation has always been based on quality.

Old Town fiberglass canoes come in three models. The 17-foot, two-inch Canadienne is an all-around touring canoe designed by Ralph Frese, with a sharp nose and a keelless bottom that gathers into a V at both ends. This is a canoe that tracks well and is still maneuverable. A slight rocker enhances agility. Gunwales, decks, and coaming are mahogany. Inwales are Sitka spruce and seats are cane-filled ash. The Canadienne weighs 79 pounds.

The 16-foot fiberglass laker weighs 72 pounds and the 14-foot laker weighs 68 pounds.

Old Town Royalex canoes offer the ultimate in strength and durability. Royalex is an ABS plastic laminate with high resiliency and "memory." By memory they mean that when Royalex is dented it springs back into its original shape. Royalex canoes can take an incredible amount of abuse.

The Pathfinder is a solo expedition canoe that is 14 feet, 10 inches long and weighs 67 pounds. The Penobscott is an ideal general-purpose Royalex canoe for lakes or whitewater, with a length of 16 feet, two inches and a weight of 77 pounds. The Tripper is a 17-foot, two-inch, high-volume Royalex hull with high freeboard, high performance rocker and V-entry. This is a boat for running whitewater rivers in the remote wilderness. The Tripper weighs 79 pounds. The Ranger is a deluxe version of the Tripper with mahogany gunwales and brass fittings. The Voyageur has a Royalex hull 18 feet long and weighs 82 pounds.

Old Town also makes wood canoes. Actually, it has been making them for generations. There is no way to make a wood canoe quickly or cheaply—in a 20-foot canoe, for example, there are some 50 white cedar ribs that must be individually cut and steamed to shape—but the end result is a true thing of beauty. Moreover, these canoes are excellent performers. They don't weigh any more than their plastic counterparts, and their durability is excellent. The exquisite looking 17-foot Molitor canoe is so strong that it doesn't need thwarts. Other wood models include the Trapper, a 15-foot, 68-pound boat, and the Guide and OTCA series. A wood canoe kit is available too.

When it comes to kayaks, Old Town makes whitewater slalom models (three), touring models (three, including a two-man model), and Custom Order models, including the Prijon Dolphin, an ultimate sort of wildwater downriver boat, and the Berrigan, a three-hole decked whitewater canoe.

Old Town canoe and kayak accessories include a variety of paddles, sailing rigs, spray skirts, waterproof bags, rowing seats, portage yokes, canoe chairs, helmets, paddling jackets, roof racks, and T-shirts.

PRODUCTS: Canoes.

OLE TIME WOODSMAN
Box 731
Concord, MA 01742
617-369-5109
Annual, B&W, free. Est. 1978. Russell Beede, Pres.

DEET (Diethyl toluamide) has proved to repel insects effectively, even such tough little devils as Canadian blackflies, chiggers, and deerflies, not to speak of mosquitoes. While most insect repellents contain no more than 25 percent DEET, three Ole Time Woodsman repellents contain 40 to 75 percent. Jungle Formula is the strongest. It is said to contain 35 percent to 350 percent more DEET per dollar than any other brand. Just out of curiosity, I compared the cost of Jungle Formula and the cost of the powerful Canadian bug juice, Muskol. A two-ounce bottle of Jungle Formula retails for $3.30. Muskol, which contains 95 percent DEET, costs $5.95 for two ounces. Thus, the DEET in Jungle Formula costs $2.20 an ounce, while the DEET in Muskol costs about $3.14 an ounce. Of course, that says nothing of the comparative effectiveness or durability of the two.

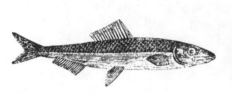

Ole Time Woodsman's aerosol Jungle Formula contains 60 percent DEET. Kampers Lotion, 40 percent DEET, is said to prevent sunburn and repel insects at the same time.

Another Ole Time Woodsman repellent is Liquid Fly Dope, said to be made of nothing but active ingredients. A company brochure does not elaborate on the content.

Another product is Skunk-Off, a chemical that is said to remove skunk odor from dogs, cars, homes, clothing, human skin, or hair. Skunk-Off is advertised as non-toxic and gentle on clothes.

PRODUCTS: Insect repellent, skunk-odor eliminator.

ORVIS
Manchester, VT 05254
802-362-1300 (order desk), 802-362-3434 (cust. svc.)
Accepts AMEX, MC, VISA. Color. Est. 1856. Leigh Perkins, Pres.

Backpacking and trout fishing are separate sports, but there is of course considerable overlap between the two. Indeed, fly fishermen were backpacking into remote lakes and streams long before the term "backpacking" was invented. The best piece of fiction ever written about backpacking, "Big Two Hearted River," by Ernest Hemingway, is also a fishing story.

In the old days, most people got interested in the wilderness because they wanted to hunt or fish. This is no longer true. People are going straight into sports like backpacking, climbing, cross-country skiing, and river-running without much knowledge of the old-time American outdoors traditions; in a way it's too bad, because the old way of doing things had a lot to offer. Fly-fishing in particular is compatible with backpacking. The gear is lightweight and compact, and the whole procedure of fly-fishing itself is an intensely contemplative activity that goes right to the heart of the wilderness experience. There is no better way to finish off a hard day on the trail than with an hour or two of quiet angling in some pristine mountain lake. And the best aroma, bar none, is a trout sizzling in a frying pan over your fire.

The Orvis catalog is a good place to become acquainted with the paraphernalia of trout fishing. Orvis has been making quality fishing gear for 125 years. It is the only company that makes bamboo and graphite rods, as well as boron/graphite and fiberglass rods. The bamboo rods have to be seen to be appreciated. They are things of rare beauty. Until you have actually used one, it is hard to believe that something so delicate-looking could be so sensitive and strong. All cane used in these rods comes from Kwangsi province in China. Less than five percent of the cane received is deemed good enough for an Orvis rod. The manufacturing process, all done by hand, calls for incredible precision. The bamboo is graded, impregnated with resins, and milled for final tapers to a tolerance of one thousandth of an inch.

Orvis also makes quality spinning rods, rod kits, rod cases, a wide variety of fly reels, spinning reels, fly lines, leaders, all kinds of flies, fly-tying materials and tools, knives, creels, nets, vests, hats, waders, shirts, and more. The Orvis Fly Fishing School offers three days of intensive instruction to neophyte anglers and to more experienced fishermen.

PRODUCTS: Fishing gear, clothing, instruction.

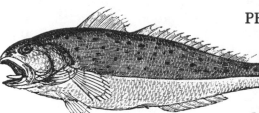

OUTDOOR SPORTS CENTER
141 Canal St.
Nashua, NH 03061
603-882-9500
Accepts AMEX, MC, VISA. Est. 1981. Thomas Little, Pres. Ruth Graney, Cust. Svc.

Outdoor Sports Center is oriented toward hunters and fishermen, but their 32-page catalog lists numerous items that will appeal to all kinds of outdoors people.

Wildlife photographers and bird-watchers will be interested in the complete line of camouflage clothing. The camouflage hunting jacket features Hollofil 808 insulation for all-weather use. This jacket has a detachable hood, inner map pocket, padded shoulder patches, fleece handwarmer pockets, and a two-way front zipper with a storm flap. A coated game pouch folds down to double as a dry seat on wet ground. The outer shell is a cotton/polyester blend. Bib camouflage overalls with Hollofil insulation are also available. They have large cargo pockets and two-way leg zips.

A camouflage jump suit made of 100 percent cotton duck is a good choice for warm-weather use. This suit has a bi-swing back for freedom of movement and slash side pockets for easy access to the pockets of whatever clothing is worn underneath. There are seven large cargo pockets on the jump suit itself.

The Johnson Guide pant, made by Johnson Woolen Mills of Johnson, Vermont, is a well-known cold-weather classic. The heavy 22-ounce 75 percent wool/25 percent nylon material is quiet, windproof and water repellent. These pants are cut roomy and they can take a lot of hard use. The color is dark green.

The Woolrich Stag jacket is another outdoors classic. Made of 20-ounce 85 percent wool/15 percent nylon material, the Stag jacket has a zip front, a double yoke, and slash handwarmer pockets. It comes in red and black check or green and black check.

The camouflage net parka will be of particular interest to wildlife photographers. This parka is almost a photography blind in its own right. A face cover folds down from the hood to give complete camouflage (as well as mosquito protection). Camouflage net gloves and head nets are also available.

In addition to these items, the Outdoor Sports Center also carries a complete line of boots, knives, compasses, fishing tackle, clothing, and unusual accessory items such as umbrella hats and floating wallets.

PRODUCTS: Camouflage clothing, outdoor clothing, fishing tackle, knives, boots.

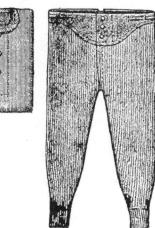

PACIFIC ASCENTÉ
1766 N. Helm
Fresno, CA 93727
209-252-2887
Accepts MC, VISA. Est. 1895. E.C. Bricker, Pres. Ed Solobei, Cust. Svc.

Pacific Ascenté manufactures its own line of goose-down jackets, vests, windshell clothing, rain gear, and sleeping bags.

Once standard outer wear for backpackers, goose-down jackets have been supplemented by synthetic-fill garments and pile garments, but goose down remains popular and probably always will. Nothing else is quite so lightweight, stuffs so easily or is as warm. Goose-down jackets are also adaptable to a number of other uses besides backcountry wear. Pacific Ascenté's Teton pullover down parka, for example, would be fine for watching a football game or for campus use. The Teton features a nylon taffeta outer shell with contrasting raglan sleeves, knit cuffs, down collar, and kangaroo zip pockets.

The Wasatch down parka has a zippered front, contrasting

raglan sleeves and side zip pockets. The Longhorn down parka features a nylon taffeta outer shell, an 80/20 cloth Western yoke across the shoulders and contrasting raglan sleeves. The Shorthorn vest is similar to the Longhorn jacket, but without the Western yoke.

The EIS is a no-nonsense down jacket for backpackers. It has inside body baffles and two-way cargo pockets. The Firn is a down-filled parka with a snap-closure front and a storm flap over the zipper. The Monterey vest is an 80/20 cloth down vest with a corduroy yoke and knit cuffs. The Minaret 80/20 cloth parka also has the corduroy yoke.

The Cascade Gore-Tex parka features raglan sleeves, attached hood, a drawstring at the waist, and two side pockets. The companion Cascade Gore-Tex pants make a complete waterproof outfit. The Ascenté Mountain Parka features Taslan Gore-Tex laminate material, a full lining, and four outside pockets plus an attached hood. The Taho Taslan Gore-Tex parka has a lined hood and two double-entry outside pockets. The Kings Canyon is a Gore-Tex pullover design with a pouch pocket in front. Pull-on and side-zip Gore-Tex pants are also available.

Pacific Ascenté's Wind River Paddling jacket features K-Kote nylon and Rubatex cuffs and collar.

The Ranier Mountain parka is made of 65 percent polyester/35 percent cotton Storm Shed Cloth and is lined with an 85 percent/15 percent wool/nylon fabric. This sturdy jacket features four outside pockets and a zip-off Thinsulate-lined hood.

The Rogue River is a Storm Shed Cloth pullover, and the Trekker is a snap-front Storm Shed Cloth jacket with four outside pockets and a wool lining. Bib pants and wind pants are available in Storm Shed Cloth, too. Pacific Ascenté also offers four styles of wool sweaters and four different types of hats.

Pacific Ascenté sleeping bags come in goose down and PolarGuard-insulated models. There is a bag here for most conditions, from the lightweight (33-ounce) Bivy model to the 73-ounce Mountaineer.

PRODUCTS: Sleeping bags, rain gear, windshell clothing, goose-down jackets.

PACIFIC MOUNTAIN SPORTS
910 Foothill Blvd.
La Canada, CA 91011
213-790-0087

Formerly known as "Lowa USA," Pacific Mountain Sports now imports a full line of European-made hiking and mountaineering boots designed to PMS specifications. The patented PMS contour sole allows easy break-in and lightweight comfort without the sacrifice of durability or support.

The Easy Walker is an excellent boot for trail hiking and for general outdoor use. It has suede leather uppers, nylon shanks, rubber midsoles, and padded leather scree collars. Size eight weighs about two pounds, 15 ounces. Light weight is extremely important in a hiking boot, because over the course of a full day of walking, heavy boots can become just as tiresome as a heavy pack. Lightweight, flexible boots are also much less likely to cause blisters, and blisters are 100 percent guaranteed to put you in a bad mood. In an extreme case, blisters can ruin a hike altogether. There is simply no reason to subject your feet to the torture of a pair of ill-fitting boots that are too heavy for your needs.

The PMS Easy Hiker is a bit more robust than the Easy Walker, and is probably as close as you can come to an all-around backpacking boot. It has one-piece uppers of full-grain leather, a sturdy Norwegian welt, a nylon shank, a removable innersole, foam padding, a padded and insulated tongue, and a padded scree collar. Size eight weighs approximately four pounds, four ounces.

The PMS Blazer is a lightweight hiking boot with a narrow profile. It has one-piece leather uppers, padded scree collar, and an integral tongue system. Size eight weighs about three pounds, 14 ounces.

The PMS Ranger is a high-top hunting style boot with full-grain leather uppers, padded scree collar, pull-on tab, and nylon shank. It weighs about three pounds, 14 ounces.

The Scout is a medium-weight boot for backpacking where more difficult terrain is the rule. This is a boot that will stand up to bushwhacking, scree fields, and boulder-hopping. It has cowhide uppers, contoured nylon shank, synthetic midsole, and a Norwegian welt. Size eight weighs about four pounds, seven ounces.

The Civetta is a top-quality mountaineering boot for summer and winter use on alpine terrain. It has full grain Swiss Gallo-Montagna leather uppers, nylon shank, leather and synthetic midsoles, Norwegian welt, and Vibram Montagna Block soles.

PRODUCTS: Mountaineering boots, hiking boots.

PACIFIC WATER SPORTS
16205 Pacific Hwy. S.
Seattle, WA 98188
206-246-9385 or 242-9278
Illustrated brochure. Est. 1974. Lee Moyer, Pres. Judy Moyer, Cust. Svc.

Kayaks are usually associated with foaming whitewater and remote wilderness rivers, but there is another side to the sport: ocean touring. The Pacific Northwest, from Puget Sound all the way up the coast of British Columbia to Alaska, is the promised land of saltwater paddlers. Thousands upon thousands of islands, bays, coves, fjords, and untouched beaches cry out for exploration. Whales, dolphins, eagles, salmon, and waterbirds provide a magnificent wildlife spectacle.

Cruising kayaks are different from whitewater boats or flatwater racing designs. The cruising kayak hull is long, the keel straight and the decks are high and peaked to shed water, although the bow and stern ends should be low to reduce wind sensitivity. The comfort of the paddler is a primary consideration. The cockpit should be roomy and the coaming should be cut low enough so the paddler does not need to hold his arms in an awkward position while paddling. A comfortable seat with good back support is essential.

Pacific Water Sports' Sea Otter single cruising kayak incorporates these design features. The hull material is fiberglass. Exotic materials are not necessary in cruising kayaks, since rigidity is the primary objective. Fiberglass accomplishes this quite well. Because the hull does not have to flex, a bulkhead is placed behind the cockpit to make the aft half of the Sea Otter watertight. Access to this compartment is through a hatch on the deck.

The Sea Otter's seat is removable, and the footbraces are adjustable. There are grab lines bow and stern. Deck cleats allow the stowage of cargo on deck. A forward access port is standard equipment. A removable, deck-mounted fishing-rod holder is optional. Because of the Sea Otter's design, a rudder is unnecessary, but one can be added if the customer insists. The Sea Otter is 16 feet, two inches long, 25½ inches wide. It weighs 40-45 pounds.

The Sisiutl is a double cruising kayak. It is 20 feet, two inches long and 30 inches wide. It weighs about 75 pounds. The two cockpits are spaced far enough apart so the paddlers do not have to paddle in unison to avoid striking each other's paddle blades. The semi-round bottom, long waterline, slender shape, and thoughtful design yield stability and paddling ease. Selective hull reinforcement increases strength.

Pacific Water Sports also stocks some 35 models of canoes, one of the largest selections in the Northwest. The kayaks are available in kit form. There are daily and weekly rental programs. In addition, Pacific Water Sports runs a kayak and canoe training program.

PRODUCTS: Kayaks, canoes.

PEAK 1, THE COLEMAN COMPANY
260 N. Francis St.
Wichita, KS 67201

Long famous as a maker of stoves and lanterns for general outdoor use, the Coleman Company introduced its line of Peak 1 backpacking equipment in 1977. It now offers a full range of packs, sleeping bags, and tents, plus a lightweight gasoline-burning stove and lantern for use in the backcountry.

The need for some sort of stove by backpackers and climbers who travel above the treeline is self-evident, but with the incredible popularity of wilderness sports today, it is becoming harder and harder to find adequate firewood even in heavily timbered areas, and in some places open fires are flatly prohibited. Backpacking stoves have traditionally fallen into two basic categories: those that burn butane or some similar fuel in a sealed canister, and those that burn liquid fuel, such as gasoline or kerosene. The butane stoves have the advantage of extremely easy operation. You just turn the stove on and light it. Gasoline stoves tend to be more complicated. Some require pumping. priming or elaborate cleaning procedures. Poorly designed gasoline stoves are very difficult to light in cold or windy conditions, and there is always the possibility of making a mess with spilled fuel. On the plus side, gasoline stoves are efficient. They burn hotter than butane stoves and thus boil water and cook meals quicker. Butane stoves perform poorly at high altitudes or in extreme cold, while gasoline stoves are more dependable in these conditions.

The Coleman Peak 1 gasoline stove has eliminated many of the drawbacks of the gasoline stove. It offers full control over the intensity of the flame, from simmer to full-blast, requires priming only in the most severe conditions, has a built-in windscreen, burns quietly (some other stoves sound like blow torches), and has no separate pieces such as cleaning needles or control keys. This stove will boil a quart of water in a closed container in less than two minutes, 50 seconds. It will burn wide open for 1¼ hours on a 10-fluid-ounce tank of fuel. It weighs 38.5 ounces with a full tank. The 125-candle-power lantern will burn three hours on an eight-ounce tank of fuel.

The novel Peak 1 pack frame features a one-piece molded frame of flexible high-impact material. The flexibility allows this frame to imitate a soft pack, bending and twisting as you walk, and at the same time providing the stability and support of a traditional frame pack. The one-piece construction eliminates all seams, welds, and joints. With an abundance of slots to attach harness parts, more than 2,000 different combinations of adjustment are possible. Five different pack bags to fit this frame are available. Peak 1 also offers a large-capacity internal-frame pack, and a variety of rucksacks and day packs.

Peak 1 sleeping bags are either rectangular or mummy in shape, and feature DuPont Hollofil II insulation, double quilt stagger seam construction to eliminate cold spots, zipper baffles, and #5 two-way polyester coil zippers. A full selection of bags is available for summer, three-season, and winter use

Peak 1 Alpha tents have A-frame poles front and rear joined across the top of the tent by a domed self-tensioning ridge bar that increases interior room and gives the tent added stability. Tent walls are 1.6-ounce nylon taffeta, and the floor is urethane-coated 1.9-ounce nylon ripstop.

The Alpha tents, as well as the more conventional A-frame tents, are freestanding, and built with lap-felled seams, overlock stitching, and reinforcement at stress point.

PRODUCTS: Backpacking equipment, stoves, lanterns, sleeping bags, tents.

PERCEPTION
P.O. Box 686
Liberty, SC 29657
803-859-7518
Accepts MC, VISA. Est. 1975. Bill Masters, Pres. Ken Horowitz, Cust. Svc.

Perception kayaks are made out of a rotationally molded cross-linked polyethylene material called Marlex. This material, combined with the advanced construction technique, produces a boat with no seams and extraordinary durability. Perception kayaks are tailor-made for rugged whitewater use and can generally be expected to have a longer service life than comparable fiberglass boats.

The Mirage is Perception's ultimate kayak. Unlike most other "big water" boats, the Mirage does not have a high-volume hull. Nevertheless, it will accommodate a large paddler comfortably on a multi-day trip, along with a reasonable amount of gear. Maneuverability in demanding conditions is excellent. This is a boat for "unrunable" rivers in the wilderness, or for playing in a favorite rapid closer to home. The Mirage is 13 feet, one inch long, 24 inches wide and weighs 39 pounds.

The Quest is a bow weighted, medium-volume (79 gallons, compared to the 65-gallon Mirage) kayak designed for whitewater use. The Quest is 13 feet, two inches long, 24 inches wide and weighs 39 pounds.

The Cruiser is a large-volume kayak for less demanding whitewater use and for cruising on large bodies of open water. A large paddler can spend all day sitting in this boat without feeling cramped. The cruiser is 13 feet, two inches long, 28 inches wide and weighs 41 pounds.

The Sage is a C-1 (fully decked, one-man) canoe built with the same rotational molding process used in Perception kayaks. The high-volume (110-gallon) hull is perfect for extended river trips. The Sage is 13 feet, two inches long, 28 inches wide and weighs 42 pounds.

The HD1 is a solo open canoe with the maneuverability and quick handling of a kayak or C-1. The hull material is Royalex for ruggedness. The HD1 Sola offers white ash hardwood trim, while the HD1 Solus features polycarbonate gunwales for extreme durability. The HD1 is 13 feet, six inches long, 30 inches wide and weighs 48 pounds.

The Chattooga is a two-man open canoe designed for whitewater rivers. It has overside anti-glare splash decks, tempered aluminum gunwales, and an eight-member internal bracing system. Polycarbonate gunwales are available as an option. The hull material is Royalex. The Chattooga is 16 feet long, 34 inches wide and weighs 75 pounds.

The Nantahala is a two-person open canoe with white ash gunwales, a varnished portage thwart, and lace rawhide seats. This is a general-purpose canoe. The hull material is Royalex. The Nantahala is 16 feet long, 33 inches wide and weighs 68 pounds.

The Harmony K-1 paddle has epoxy-impregnated fiberglass cloth blades, aluminum blade tips and an oval fiberglass shaft that allows the paddler to feel the orientation of the blades during a roll. The Harmony canoe paddle features similar attention to detail. Other accessory items available from Perception include helmets, life jackets, paddling jackets, spray skirts, canoe solo seats, floatation bags, knee braces, portage bags, dry bags, knee pads, car-top carrier brackets, flashlights, socks, and sunglasses. It should also be mentioned that the Perception catalog shows a high degree of sensitivity to the spiritual aspects of kayaking and is a pleasure to read. Newcomers to the sport will particularly appreciate the no-nonsense advice about learning basic techniques.

PRODUCTS: Kayaks, canoes, paddles, accessories.

PHOENIX PRODUCTS
U. S. 421
Tyner, KY 40486
606-364-5141
Accepts MC, VISA. Annual. Est. 1973. Thomas Wilson, Pres. Mark Watson, Cust. Svc.

Anyone who runs rivers probably already uses a Phoenix waterproof bag. At the very least, he will have met someone who owns this functional piece of equipment. Dry storage, of course, is essential in a canoe, kayak, or raft. On a day trip, you need to protect wallets and cameras. On wilderness expeditions, it is important to keep clothing and food dry, not just from the rain, but from unexpected dunkings.

Phoenix bags are made of clear vinyl so you can see what's inside. To close the bag, you roll up the top and then secure it with nickel-coated brass fasteners. Then the bag is inflated. The Phoenix camera bag has two air-tight chambers that are inflated separately so a cushion of air protects fragile objects.

Phoenix also manufactures high-quality kayaks. As with

canoes, no one kayak is suitable for all uses. It is important to select a boat that will do what you want. Design characteristics determine what a specific kayak does well. A kayak with a steep V hull section tracks (travels in a straight line) well, but is not particularly maneuverable. A kayak's rocker (the curvature of the hull from bow to stern) affects tracking and maneuverability too, as does length. A long boat tracks well, a short boat turns easily. Obviously, there are a lot of different combinations possible, and this is why Phoenix carries eight different kayak models.

In building a kayak, it is necessary to achieve the proper balance of strength and lightness, rigidity and flexibility. A kayak has to be rigid to respond quickly (an important safety factor), but it also needs a certain amount of flex in the right places so it will not shatter when it strikes a hard object, such as a rock. Phoenix kayaks achieve a good combination of flex, functional rigidity, strength, and light weight (26-33 pounds) by using careful fiberglass construction that employs a special flat-woven fiberglass cloth. Selective reinforcement is used in critical areas. Different Phoenix kayaks are intended for slalom racing, whitewater river tripping, difficult whitewater, long-distance tripping, and downriver racing. The Phoenix Match II won the downriver gold medals in the 1973 and 1975 world championships. Phoenix also makes a recreational two-person kayak.

In addition to boats and bags, Phoenix offers paddle jackets, whitewater helmets, life jackets, spray skirts, kayak paddles, and kayak flotation systems.

PRODUCTS: Kayaks.

PORTA-BOTE

P.O. Box 2287 C
Menlo Park, CA 94025
415-961-5334
Accepts AMEX, MC, VISA. Quarterly, four-color, free. Est 1973. Sandy Kaye, Pres.

If your car is too small to haul a large boat, or if you don't have room in which to store a boat, consider a folding craft. Porta-Bote comes in three lengths—eight, 10 and 12 feet—and folds into a surfboard-shaped package about four inches thick. It's light; a 10-footer weighs 49 pounds. Because of its shape, the company says it is stable. A 10-footer can carry a load of 420 pounds. A small outboard motor to a maximum of three horsepower can be attached to a 10-footer.

Because of the Porta-Bote's small size and light weight, it can be carried on top of a car as small as a VW Rabbit. It makes a fine dinghy for sailors of even small cruisers or sailboats and can be stored under a bed. The polypropylene hull is guaranteed for 10 years.

An optional kit turns a Porta-Bote into a small sailboat with leeboards for added stability. Porta-Bote also sells an 18-pound outboard motor that is said to run all day on a gallon of gasoline.

PRODUCTS: Folding boats, miniature outboard engines.

P&S SALES
Box 45095
Tulsa, OK 74145
918-622-7970
Accepts MC, VISA.

The P&S catalog is oriented toward hunters, fishermen, and general outdoorsmen, but backpackers are bound to find some interesting items here, especially in the clothing department. Everyone, for example, can put a bush shirt to good use. The P&S bush shirt is made of 65 percent polyester/35 percent cotton and comes with long or short sleeves. The design features pleated bellows pockets and epaulets at the shoulder. The color, of course, is tan.

Cargo shorts and jeans made from 65 percent polyester/35 percent cotton are extremely practical and durable items for wear in the backcountry. These pants feature a grand total of six roomy pockets. Painter's pants of 100 percent cotton are also a good choice for durability and freedom of movement while on the trail. The model stocked by P&S features double stitching and bar tacking at stress points.

Ghurka shorts of 100 percent cotton are warm-weather classics. Corduroy shorts with extra pockets and an elastic waistband should be good for wear around camp, for day hikes, or just about anything else.

For colder days, P&S has a very nice two-tone chamois shirt in a western design with snaps down the front and on the pocket flaps. Color combinations are camel body with a brown yoke and steel-blue body with a navy yoke. Standard-design chamois shirts are also available, as is a handsome 70 percent wool/30 percent nylon buffalo plaid shirt, a true outdoors classic.

Sweaters from P&S come in ragg, Navy and British Commando styles. The commando sweater has a crew neck, extra-long length and abrasion-resistant patches at the shoulders and elbows. It is made of 100 percent new worsted wool.

P&S also carries field pants, jeans, chinos, western hats, Hollofil II insulated jackets and vests, leather vests, belts, camouflage clothing and accessories, camp furniture, rain gear, mountain parkas, long underwear, bomber jackets, moccasins, boots, insulated shoe-pacs, knives, sunglasses, mounted steer horns, pickup-truck saddle-blanket seat covers, binoculars, kerosene lamps, and much, much more.

PRODUCTS: Hunting and fishing equipment; outdoor clothing.

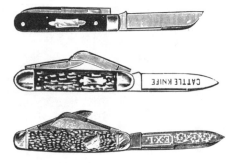

RANDALL MADE KNIVES
P.O. Box 1988
Orlando, FL 32802
305-855-8075
Illustrated.

Is a knife an essential piece of backpacking gear? No, it is not, at least in the strictest sense of the word "essential." You can set up a tent, prepare a meal of freeze-dried food, and do dozens of other camp chores without ever having to cut anything. As long as nothing unusual comes up, you don't need a knife. But it's awfully nice to have one. With a knife you can clean a fish, slice cheese, or effect emergency repairs on a broken pack. A knife may not be absolutely necessary, even in a survival situation, but it is extraordinarily useful. Most outdoorsmen would not go into the woods without one.

What kind of knife is best for a backpacker? Some people have strong feelings about that, but to tell the truth, you don't need anything fancy. The average pocketknife—not too big, not too small—is perfectly adequate. If you're going to skin an elk, you need a large knife with a special blade, but for general camping use there are no rules written in stone. Some hikers like a knife with a lot of attachments—screwdrivers, can openers, files, etc.—while other people insist on something simple. It's a matter of personal preference.

Nevertheless, many outdoorsmen like knives for their own sake; this is easy to understand, because a high-quality knife can be a beautiful object. There are practical reasons for buying a good knife—an inferior blade deteriorates quickly—but beyond that, what it boils down to is that knives have a certain mystique, and handmade knives carry the heaviest magic of all. Perhaps it has something to do with the American frontier tradition. Perhaps there are other reasons. A knife, after all, can be used as a weapon—some knives are good for little else—and this is definitely part of the fascination. A big knife on the belt gives some people a macho feeling. Other people simply enjoy owning a finely crafted tool.

Randall Made Knives are among the best available. The blades are Swedish tool steel or high-carbon domestic stainless steel. The entire knife, from start to finish, is made by hand. There are no concessions to mass production. No jigs or patterns are used, and no two Randall knives are exactly alike. A customer may have to wait as long as a year for his knife after placing an order, but he will be rewarded with a collector's item. This term is not used loosely. Randall Made Knives are in museum collections around the world.

Naturally, Randall Made Knives are not inexpensive, but people have been lining up to buy them since 1937. The Randall catalog describes a wide variety of designs and contains a mass of information about how the knives are made. Randall also carries Schrade and Solingen pocketknives.

PRODUCTS: Knives.

RECREATIONAL EQUIPMENT
P. O. Box C-88126
Seattle, WA 98188
206-575-4480
Accepts MC, VISA. Full-color. Jerry Horn, Pres. Sharon Deibert, Cust. Svc.

Although you do not have to be a member to make purchases, REI is a co-op. It costs five dollars to join. Members receive an annual cash dividend based on how much they bought during the year. REI was founded back in the 1930s, when quality mountaineering equipment was hard to come by, and has since grown into one of the largest suppliers of outdoor gear in the United States, offering its own line of clothing and equipment plus those of other manufacturers.

The range and variety of merchandise is immense, almost to the point of defying summation, but basically it includes outdoor clothing (shirts, pants, hats, sweaters), goose-down sweaters, jackets, parkas (including an expedition model with 18½ ounces of down fill), mountain shell parkas, running gear, underwear, down vests, Gore-Tex rainwear, gaiters, gloves, socks, cross-country ski wear, alpine ski wear, sunglasses, compasses, flashlights, knives, stoves, cookware, trail food, downhill skis, cross-country skis, bicycles, canoes, kayaks, snowshoes, binoculars, technical climbing equipment, hiking boots, leisure shoes, soft luggage, frame packs, soft packs, tents, and sleeping bags.

Some of these items are old standards; others, such as the Gore-Tex hiking boots, are brand-new designs. The emphasis is on quality and competitive prices. Although REI is by no means a discount-house-type operation, its own-brand products in particular provide excellent value for the money, especially when you consider the member dividend.

Despite REI's large size (one million members to date) it has managed to avoid an atmosphere of bureaucratic impersonality. Customers are spared slick merchandising techniques and get the feeling that they are dealing with people who share their own interests and enthusiasms. REI's Social/Advisory Committee sponsors outreach activities that include environmental resource centers, member volunteer service projects, climbing expeditions, and support of environmental-preservation campaigns; $86,000 has been allocated to various projects.

REI employs strict quality-control standards at the research, manufacturing, distribution, and retail levels. Special attention is given to items, such as climbing gear, which might endanger life if they failed in a critical situation. The REI tensile test machine meets internationally approved standards and is the only such installation in the country. In addition to laboratory tests, many products are subjected to field testing in the alpine environment by REI staff members.

All of this has made REI something of an institution in the backpacking/mountaineering community. More than a store, REI is a concept, a near-lengendary symbol of quality and involvement that has a been winning converts for longer than most of us have been alive.

PRODUCTS: Outdoor clothing, running gear, camping equipment, ski equipment, sporting accessories, climbing equipment.

RED BALL
95 McGregor St.
Manchester, NH 03105
603-669-0708
Annual, four-color, free. Mitchell Ridnick, Pres.

A familiar brand name to American hunters and anglers, the Red Ball trademark is now owned by Prevue, a maker of women's and children's molded fashion boots. Until 1981, Red Ball was owned by Uniroyal, which imported many rubber boots from Korea. One of Uniroyal's best-known Red Ball products, the Flyweight chest wader, however, was manufactured by Hampshire Manufacturing of Nashua, New Hampshire. Prevue also has bought Hampshire, and an improved version of the Flyweight has been introduced.

Made of a tough but thin nylon fabric, the Flyweight is a stockingfoot wader. An inflatable air chamber provides stability in deep water and helps prevent water from pouring into the waders if you get in water over your chest. The improved version is said to be made of a tougher fabric than the original Flyweights. Designed for use with stockingfoot waders are felt-sole wading shoes.

A cheaper stockingfoot wader is the Sportster. There are also six boot-foot chest waders. They're made in three quality levels, and there are insulated and uninsulated models. Most expensive is the Master, offered in regular sizes 7 to 11 and in tall sizes 10 to 13. Less expensive Brookfield and Sportster waders are made in sizes 7 to 13.

Hip boots are also made in three quality levels. Masters hip boots are made in insulated and uninsulated versions. Another has a felt-sole boot foot for maximum traction on slippery river bottoms. Sportsters also are made insulated and uninsulated. The only Brookfield hip wader is insulated, something you'll appreciate unless you venture outdoors only in bluebird weather.

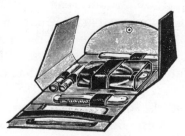

Wading accessories include suspenders made of elastic webbing, insulated insoles, patch kits and boot hangers. An interesting concept is the Bama Sokket, a pair of removable boot liners that wick moisture from your feet. I've used them and can give them my highest recommendation.

Red Ball makes air mattresses for camping and floating. A dozen models range from 44 to 78 inches long. One mattress, 51 inches wide, is designed for use in vans and wagons and with double sleeping bags. Two backpacking models each feature six separate air chambers that are said to promote comfort, and they're made of light urethane-coated fabric.

Royal's boot line features three over-the-boot vinyl boots from 12 to 16 inches high and six over-the-boot vinyl overshoes.

PRODUCTS: Waders, air mattresses, vinyl boots.

RIVERS & GILMAN MOULDED PRODUCTS
Maine St.
Hamden, ME 04444
207-862-3600
Est. 1962. Paul River, Pres.

Fiberglass and Royalex are two of the most popular canoe-building materials in use today. Fiberglass is popular because it is lightweight, quiet in the water, durable, and economical. Royalex is more expensive, but it offers incredible strength.

Rivers & Gilman Indian Brand canoes come in a wide range of fiberglass models. The 16-foot Renegade is specifically designed for economy, but not at the cost of durability or handling. With a beam of 36 inches and a depth of 13 inches it weighs 68 pounds.

The 13-foot Brave weighs 61 pounds and excells as a one-man whitewater slalom racer or as a hunting and fishing canoe that has to be portaged frequently. A wide beam, comparatively flat bottom, and low, full ends give the Brave admirable stability.

The 15-foot Squaw is an all-purpose canoe. It can carry two people and all their gear on a four-day camping trip. The Squaw weighs 73 pounds.

The 16-foot Penobscot has a square stern for use with a motor of up to five horsepower. This canoe weighs 108 pounds and has a roomy 38½-inch beam.

The 17-foot Princess has a graceful, classic design with high, narrow ends. This is a speedy, easy-paddling canoe with excellent maneuverability. Cargo capacity, however, is somewhat limited. The weight of the boat is 84 pounds.

The 18-foot Chief is a stable, roomy canoe with good handling characteristics and a large load-carrying capacity. This is the boat for rough whitewater and extended wilderness trips. The Chief weighs 90 pounds. The 17-foot Sagamore is Rivers & Gilman's Royalex canoe. An all-around design, the Sagamore is fine for whitewater or camping trips or portaging. It weighs 82 pounds. Extreme durability is the outstanding feature of the Sagamore. Rivers & Gilman was one of the first manufacturers in the United States to build Royalex canoes, and the Sagamore

is the result of many years of experience in quality canoe construction.

All Rivers & Gilman canoes are designed without keels. A keel is a hindrance in any canoeing situation that calls for maneuverability. Rivers & Gilman canoes also feature vinyl bang plates and vinyl outside gunwales. Canoe accessories available from Rivers & Gilman include hardwood paddles, portage yoke shoulder pads, motor mounts, and car-top carriers.

PRODUCTS: Canoes.

ROBBINS MOUNTAINGEAR/MOUNTAINWEAR
Box 4536
Modesto, CA 95352
209-529-6913
Accepts MC, VISA. Catalog on request.

The 1960s were the Golden Age of North American climbing, and Yosemite Valley was the center of the action. Big-wall climbs were the most dazzling side of the sport. You would stand there in the Valley and look up at El Capitan or Half Dome and just not be able to believe that a human being could possibly make his way up those towering granite walls.

The men who climbed those faces became, quite literally, legends in their own time. More difficult climbs have been done since, both in the Valley and in high ranges around the world, but the Yosemite climbers of the 1960s were the first Americans to attempt climbs at this level of difficulty and succeed. It was a tremendous leap from traditional mountaineering to a multi-day all-out climb on a 2,500-foot face, especially when no one else had ever done it before. These people were the pioneers and the luster of their achievements remains undimmed.

There is not much point in trying to say who was the best of those climbers, but certainly Royal Robbins had to be counted among the elite. Every time you picked up a climbing magazine or journal, his face seemed to be staring out of a summit photograph. Certainly no one else was doing harder climbs or doing them with more style.

Like some other Yosemite climbers, Mr. Robbins gradually got into the equipment business. Robbins Mountaingear is the major importer of Edelrid climbing ropes. Edelrid was the first kernmantle rope to be widely used in this country and it is still

very popular, for good reason. No Edelrid rope has ever been broken by the impact of a fall. It also has an excellent combination of low impact force and impact force elongation. Just as important, Edelrid feels right when you handle it; it is easy to use and tends not to kink or curl. Robbins Mountaingear carries seven different types of Edelrid climbing rope for various applications, including the Royal Robbins Lifeline which is specially designed for the most difficult climbs.

Robbins Mountaingear imports Galibier boots made in France. Long-time climbers know these boots by reputation, but their quality is evident even in a casual inspection. The Galibier double boot is extremely warm, but no bulkier than many single boots. The PA Varappe smooth-soled climbing shoe is a legend in its own right. A number of other models are offered, including the Super Guide, which may well be the most popular mountaineering boot in the world.

Robbins stocks Laprade ice axes, Salewa crampons, Robbins/Robersson harnesses, Edelrid harnesses, various carabiners, Ultimate helmets, and CMI ascenders and descenders. The catalog also includes lines of cookware, stoves, glacier glasses, headlamps, flashlights, and a most extensive line of books. In the clothing department, there are Swiss shirts, pants and shorts, canvas shirts, cotton sweaters, and Clarke's Craghoppers, a line of English-made knickers and climbing trousers.

PRODUCTS: Climbing ropes, boots, climbing equipment, camping equipment, clothing.

ROBERTSON HARNESS/SYNERGY SYSTEMS
P. O. Box 217
Westminster, CO 80030
Accepts MC, VISA. Est. 1970. Ken Koerwitz, Pres.

Robertson Harness manufactures hang-glider harnesses and sail bags, industrial safety harnesses, technical rock-climbing harnesses, camera cases, day packs, rucksacks and Synergy Systems internal-frame packs.

Robertson offers six different climbing harnesses, all of them designed and tested by the famous Scottish climber Brian Robertson. The Mountain Belt is a basic swami belt design with a hauling-line loop and equipment cord ties. The stitching is covered with Cordura. Adjustable leg loops are available for the Mountain Belt. The Guide is a one-size-fits-all economical

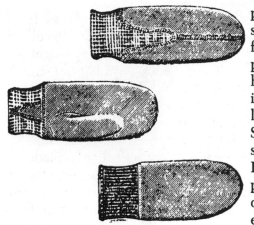

protection harness ideally suited for use by clubs and climbing schools as well as individual climbers. The Chest Harness is a fully adjustable, lightweight harness that can be used with a pelvic harness for full body support. The Pro is an all-purpose harness that works well on big-wall or aid climbs. It has a three-inch waist belt, rear pelvic straps, adjustable leg straps, hauling-line loop, and equipment cord ties. A step up from the Pro, the Super Pro features a fully padded waist belt, sewn-in holster, side equipment rings, accessory cord, and a belay anchor. The Big Wall is the ultimate Robertson Harness design. It has a padded waist belt, a pelvic support area with "floating padded quick-adjustable mid-butt strap," two sewn-in holsters, two side equipment rings, an accessory cord, and a floating belay anchor. Robertson also makes an extremely versatile mountain-rescue harness system, and one-inch tubular webbing etiers, a belay seat, chalk bags, gear slings, and a variety of runners.

Robertson camera cases come in two models: the Fanny Pack and the Pro System Bag. The Fanny Pack, which is made of vinyl-lined waterproof Cordura, can be swung around to the front for quick access to its contents. The walls of the pack are padded with foam, and the main interior compartment is filled with foam that can be cut to the exact shape of individual pieces of camera equipment. The Pro System Bag is a large, over-the-shoulder camera bag with D-rings for optional backpack straps. The interior of the main compartment is fitted with a padded, Velcro-fastened divider to keep individual pieces of equipment from banging into each other.

The Synergy Systems internal-frame packs come in four basic models. The 5.9 FL front-loading pack has a 4,500-cubic-inch capacity with pockets attached. The 4.6 FL is a smaller version of the 5.9. The 7.4 TL is a top-loading model with a 5,900-cubic-inch capacity. The 9.2 TL is an extra-high-volume (6,600) top-loader. Like the 7.4 TL, it will expand to carry still more gear or contract to carry smaller loads.

There are more internal-frame packs on the market today than you can shake an ice axe at, but along with the Lowe Expedition pack and the Gregory Mountain pack, the Synergy System packs have an almost legendary reputation for quality construction, load-carrying comfort and ingenious design. Synergy System packs feature fully adjustable yoke suspension straps that lift the weight of the pack off shoulder nerves and muscles, a patented internal X-frame, a mesh-panel back, a conically cut waistbelt, anatomically shaped shoulder straps, adjustable anti-sway straps, a sternum strap, and a quick-release pocket system. The suspension system is detachable for air travel, and the pack has a side handle so you can carry it like a suitcase.

Robertson also makes a full line of soft luggage, garment bags, rucksacks, stuff sacks, polyurethane foam coolers, locking bicycle covers and bicycle-touring gear.

PRODUCTS: Packs, harnesses, bicycle-touring gear.

SAFARI CAMERA CASE
Box 19972
Houston, TX 77024
800-232-1753 for orders
Accepts MC, VISA. Descriptive brochure on request.

The Safari camera case should not be confused with a camera bag or a piece of luggage. We are talking here about an actual case, a greatly improved version of the cases that come with most 35-mm single-lens reflex cameras. With thick foam padding inside and a high-impact polypropelene shell outside, the Safari case provides excellent protection against shock, weather and dirt. Its modular design offers extraordinary versatility. The basic unit fits over a 35-mm camera body. A hinged back affords quick access. To this unit you can add a screw-on lens case to protect a "normal" (50-mm) lens. The addition of a second lens case will accommodate a 135-mm lens. Further extension tubes can be added to fit telephoto or zoom lenses up to 10$\frac{1}{8}$ inches long.

Lenses can also be carried separately, since the extension tubes function as cases in their own right. In other words, you custom-design your own carrying system. The camera case can be worn around the neck, over the shoulder, or hung holster-style from the belt. This rig is ideal for backpacking, skiing, or any other outdoor activity where expensive cameras are subjected to rugged conditions.

PRODUCTS: Modular camera cases for 35-mm SLR cameras.

SALMON RIVER BOATWORKS
P. O. Box 1804
Salmon, ID 83467
208-756-4321
Illustrated brochure on request. Est. 1978. Jeffrey Bevan, Pres.

The Salmon River in Idaho offers the premier whitewater wilderness river running in the United States. You would expect to find a boat builder in the vicinity, and in fact there is one—the Salmon River Boatworks.

Salmon River Boatworks kayaks come in three basic models. The SRB I is a large-volume kayak for large paddlers and for carrying gear on extended river trips. It maneuvers well in close quarters and surfs very well in big water. The weight is about 27 pounds in Kevlar, 29 pounds in fiberglass.

The SRB II has the same design features as the SRB I, but has less hull volume, making it suitable for medium-sized people.

The SRB III is what kayakers call a "play boat"—a boat for playing in big whitewater. Compared to the SRB I and II, the deck and hull of the SRB III are radically reduced in profile. Sharper chines insure quick responsiveness, and a flatter hull in the tail end enhances surfing characteristics. The SRB III weighs 25 pounds in Kevlar, 27 pounds in fiberglass.

SRB's Kevlar models feature a hull laminate of three layers of Kevlar on the inside, three layers of S-glass on the outside, and S-glass reinforcement to improve rigidity. Kevlar 49 Aramid is manufactured by DuPont, and is used in sailboats, ropes, and bulletproof vests as well as kayaks. S-glass is a special fiberglass noted for strength and abrasion resistance.

SRB's fiberglass boats are a little heavier and less expensive than the Kevlar models. The hull consists of five layers (three of them half-layers, overlapping lengthwise), and is built using the vacuum-bag technique and vinylester resin. In vacuum-bag lamination, the reinforcement fabric is laid in a mold, saturated with resin under a vacuum, and heat treated. This method provides better control of the resin-cloth ratio than contact-lamination techniques, and results in a lighter and stronger boat.

SRB kayaks also feature a removable seat to facilitate gear stowage, adjustable Yakima footbraces, and built-in knee hooks. A repair kit is available.

PRODUCTS: Kayaks, boats.

SAWYER CANOE COMPANY
234 S. State
Oscoda, MI 48750
517-739-9181
Color, on request.

Like a number of other manufacturers of quality canoes, Sawyer offers boats made of fiberglass, Kevlar or Royalex. Fiberglass is the most economical of the three materials, and with the construction techniques used by Sawyer, it makes a sturdy, lightweight canoe. The ultimate lightweight canoes, however, are made of Kevlar 49. Made by DuPont, Kevlar is half the weight of fiberglass for the same tensile and stiffness strength. Sawyer builds Kevlar canoes with an all-Kevlar layup or with Kevlar and a foam core. The all-Kevlar is stronger; the foam core is lighter. Both cost the same. Royalex ABS, made by Uniroyal, is a patented thermoplastic laminate used in canoes where strength and durability are the most important considerations. Royalex, while not indestructible, has a fantastic ability to spring back into its original shape when dented. It is heavier than fiberglass or Kevlar.

Hull material is critical to a good canoe, but design is just as important. Most canoes are fairly versatile, but some are designed for versatility while others are designed for specific purposes. There will always be some degree of compromise. A boat, for example, that is designed for maneuverability in whitewater will not be as satisfactory on a big, windy lake as a canoe with a low profile and good tracking qualities. Sawyer makes a wide range of canoes for general purpose and special uses.

The Saber falls in the latter category. Designed for unlimited racing, it is built like a rowing shell with a thin hull and extremely sharp bow and stern entry lines. Despite a length of 24 feet, it weighs just 35 pounds in foam-core Kevlar. Obviously, the Saber is not a family boat or a work boat.

The Yankee Rebel 13, on the other hand, is a short, stable 13-foot canoe for duck hunters and fishermen. The Safari is a square-stern, flat-bottomed 18-foot canoe that will take a five-horsepower motor. And the Kaynoe is a decked, 17-foot one-man (C-1) canoe suitable for saltwater cruising.

The Cruiser is a 17-foot, nine-inch canoe that is excellent for all-around use by serious canoeists, whether they are interested in cruising, camping, or amateur racing. It weighs 68 pounds in fiberglass, 54 pounds in Kevlar, and 44 pounds in Kevlar with foam core.

The Charger is an 18½-foot canoe for whitewater and

open canoe class competition. It is roomy enough for big loads. It weighs 82 pounds in fiberglass, 68/58 in Kevlar.

In addition to these canoes, and a number of other models not mentioned (such as the Champion, which has won the USCA National Championship five times), Sawyer offers a variety of accessories, including car-top carriers, motor mounts, portage yokes, adjustable foot braces, whitewater end caps, paddles, cushions, life vests, and repair materials.

PRODUCTS: Canoes, boats.

SCHNEE'S BOOT WORKS
411 W. Mendenhall St.
Bozeman, MT. 59715
406-587-0981
Illustrated brochure. Steve Schnee, Pres.

With the price of good-quality hiking and climbing boots hovering around the $100 level, you want to get as much use out of your mountain footwear as possible. Climbing boots can be resoled several times if you take them into the shop before the leather midsole is severely damaged, but finding a good shoemaker isn't easy. A lot of shoe-repair shops won't touch heavy mountaineering boots. In fact, most shoe-repair shops simply don't have the experience to work on mountain boots at all. If they attempt it, they may well do more harm than good.

Schnee's Boot Works specializes in the repair of hiking boots, climbing boots, and rock shoes. They can put on new soles, repair midsoles, replace steel shanks, add additional midsoles, replace scree collars, reline heel counters, and replace broken hooks, D-rings, and eyelets. They also specialize in mail-order repairs. The exact cost of repairs will be given after you send in the boots. All repair work is unconditionally guaranteed.

The various replacement soles available include the Vibram Montagna Block (the original Vibram sole), the Vibram Roccia Block (with shallower tread than the Montagna), the Vibram Security (with tiny suction cups), the Vibram Sestogrado (for technical mountaineering), the Vibram Oil Resistant (for work boots), the Vibram-Vasque (for rock climbing), the Galibier Makalu (a mountaineering sole for Galibier boots), the Galibier Raid (with a shallower tread than the Makalu), the Innsbrucker Super (for light hiking and rock climbing), and the Galibier PA/RR for smooth-sole friction shoes used by technical rock climbers.

Schnee's Boot Works also carries nylon boot laces, wood shoe trees, Sno Seal, Barge Cement, Leath-R-Seal, and Shoe Saver liquid silicone.

PRODUCTS: Repair hiking boots, climbing boots, rock shoes.

SEATTLE MANUFACTURING CORPORATION
12880 Northrup Way
Bellevue, WA 98005
206-883-0334
Listing and description of products on request

Twenty-five years ago, almost all the technical climbing hardware used in the United States was imported from Europe. The prices were steep, the technology primitive, and it was difficult to find exactly what you wanted. More importantly, the quality was uneven. American climbers were not familiar with the reputations of all the different European manufacturers. You didn't know if you were getting a first-class item or one that was likely to wear out quickly or perhaps even fail in a life-or-death situation.

Fortunately, this has changed. With the immense growth in the popularity of climbing, customers and dealers alike have become considerably more sophisticated. For the most part, unsatisfactory and unsafe items have disappeared from the marketplace. Although European merchandise is still popular with some climbers, it is now possible to put together a hardware rack that consists entirely of American-made products.

Like as not, at least some of the items on that hardware rack will be stamped with the familiar initials SMC, Seattle Manufacturing Corporation. SMC products are well known for solid dependability, practicality and reasonable price. SMC aluminum carabiners are available in oval and "D" configurations, and come in either bright or anodized finishes, as do the brake bars that are designed to fit them. SMC chrome-molly steel angle pitons are available in 15 sizes. There are four different styles of climbing nuts, including the patented Camlock. SMC also manufactures "Straight 8" rappelling devices, weldless descending rings and chrome-molly bolt hangers.

SMC chrome-molly crampons come in two models: hinged, for general mountaineering, and rigid, for extreme ice climbing. The SMC ice axe has a drop-forged chrome-molly head and a PVC-coated tubular aluminum shaft. Aluminum snow pickets and snow anchors are available. A special aluminum handle converts the two sizes of snow anchor into a sturdy snow shovel that can be indispensible for leveling tent sites and doing other jobs. The SMC snow saw makes building igloos considerably easier.

SMC also imports Clan Robertson equipment slings, Mannut-Civetta climbing harnesses, Mummut Dynaflex climbing rope, and attractive Icelandic wool sweaters, hats and scarves.

SMC's line is rounded out with a complete selection of tent stakes, plus tent line adjusters, drawstring clamps, replacement aluminum tent poles, and a Sierra Club style drinking cup. All of these products can be purchased or ordered at outdoor shops throughout the country. A complete listing and description of SMC merchandise is available by writing the manufacturer at their Bellevue, Washington, address.

PRODUCTS: Technical climbing equipment—carabiners, pitons, nuts, ice axes, crampons, etc. Camping equipment—tent stakes, drawstring clamps, replacement tent poles, snow saws. Clothing—Icelandic sweaters.

SEDA PRODUCTS
P. O. Box 997
Chula Vista, CA 92010
714-425-3222
Accepts MC, VISA.

Seda was founded by a whitewater champion kayaker, and Seda canoes and kayaks have been accumulating gold medals ever since. Racers are already aware of Seda's outstanding competitive record, but recreational boaters stand to benefit from it too. As with sports cars and skis, racing improves the breed.

Seda uses four basic hull layups. The standard fiberglass layup uses fine-quality fiberglass cloth and high-impact isophthalic resin. The Competition lightweight construction incorporates fiberglass cloth and Kevlar laminated with vinylester resin. Heavy Duty construction includes Kevlar, S-glass and fiberglass cloth laminated with vinylester resin. There

are internal seams, two layers of outside seams, and full-length foam walls. This is the construction to choose if your main interest is running Class 5 whitewater. Sedaflex construction is nearly 100 percent Kevlar laminated with epoxy resin and stiffened with graphite fiber ribs. Sedaflex construction produces the lightest racing boats. All Seda boats are non-gel-coated. This doesn't look as pretty, but it weighs less, as much as five pounds less.

The Vagabond kayak is a great touring boat with good whitewater agility and straight-line tracking qualities (of course there is always some compromise here), a dry ride, a roomy cockpit, and a large-volume hull. The Climax is a slightly less roomy touring kayak that can double as a racing boat. It is stable enough for beginners. The Dart was introduced some years ago as a slalom racing boat, but is now in use by a wide range of river runners.

The Strike is Seda's most successful slalom racing boat. It also makes a good general-purpose boat for paddlers weighing 130 pounds or less. The Equipe, manufactured by Seda under license from Pyranha, Ltd., of England, is a flat-out slalom racing boat.

The Spirit is a downriver racing kayak that can be used in some cruising applications, although it is too tricky for beginners to handle. The Vertex is a lot like the Spirit, but will accommodate heavier paddlers. It is a little slower in flatwater, a little faster in big whitewater.

The Seasurf is a kayak specifically designed for surfing ocean waves. It is not adaptable to any other use.

Seda makes three models of recreational canoes, all of which are excellent for long trips on wilderness rivers. One model features Royalex ABS construction for extreme durability.

The Explorer canoe is a 15-foot boat that combines the qualities of a regular canoe, a kayak, and a C-2 whitewater canoe. The Explorer is partially decked with a spray skirt covering the space between the two paddlers. Thus it can take on big whitewater and still function as an open boat on less demanding stretches of the river. It is also much easier to load with gear than a fully decked C-2 canoe. It can be paddled solo from the center when an appropriate spray cover (three-hole or one-hole) is used.

The Cobra is a C-2 decked canoe that has chalked up an impressive list of competition victories. Orion and Supermax are C-1 (one-man) canoes. While Orion is more of a general-purpose boat, the Supermax is strictly for racing.

Seda also carries an exceptionally complete line of kayaking and canoeing accessories, including their own make of wetsuits, knee pads, booties, wind gloves, paddling jackets, life vests, paddles, helmets, spray covers, waterproof gear bags, roof racks, and flotation bags. The Seda quick-opening camera bag is one of the nicest on the market.

PRODUCTS: Canoes, kayaks.

SHERPA
2222 Diversey
Chicago, IL 60647
312-772-6200
Descriptive brochure on request.

Anyone who has traveled the backcountry in winter knows that traditional snowshoes have limitations. Steep, hard-packed slopes present a particular problem. The shoes slip and slide and become virtually useless if the snow surface turns icy. Strapping on metal creepers or crampons is a stopgap solution, about as ineffectual as it is inconvenient. With Sherpa snow-claw snowshoes, however, the traction device is an integral part of the binding, offering a sure grip and unparalleled agility on the steepest hills. In fact, snow-claws can go where other snowshoes simply cannot, and it is for this reason that snow-claws are so popular on winter mountaineering expeditions.

The Sherpa binding holds the foot firmly aligned in the direction the shoe is pointed, without any of the slip or give of traditional leather bindings, and the patented Sherpa hinge rod allows unrestricted heel lift for a natural walking motion. You can put on a pair of snow-claws in as little as twenty seconds, without taking your mittens off. Because snow-claws are narrower than most other snowshoes, you do not have to walk bowlegged. In addition, the smaller size of snow-claws makes them more maneuverable in heavy brush as well as easier to carry on your pack when not in use.

Snow does not stick to the Sherpa gold-anodized aircraft aluminum frames or to the solid (as opposed to webbed) neoprene decks. The aluminum-neoprene construction makes snow-claws about half as heavy as other shoes. It also makes snow-claws stronger and eliminates the need for maintenance. Traditional snowshoes, of course, need to be revarnished every few years.

With all this going for them, you have to wonder why snow-claws have not completely replaced old-style shoes.

Appearance, no doubt, is part of the reason. Snow-claws have a high-tech, space-age look about them. It is difficult to imagine a pair of snow-claws hanging over the fireplace. Then, too, traditional wooden shoes are perfectly adequate for the majority of casual outings in the woods. But when the going gets tough, Sherpa snow-claws really come into their own.

Snow-claws are available in five sizes: The Featherweight, the Lightfoot, The Tracker, The Bigfoot and the Musher. There are three types of bindings. The price of shoes and bindings is about $100 per pair. Snow-claws are sold through outdoor shops around the country. Technical information and the name of the nearest dealer are available by writing the manufacturer, Sherpa, Inc., at their Chicago address.

PRODUCTS: Snowshoes, bindings.

SIERRA DESIGNS
247 Fourth St.
Oakland, CA 94607
800-227-1120 for orders
Accepts AMEX, MC, VISA. Color.

The word "classic" is often abused, but the Sierra Designs 60/40 mountain parka is the genuine article, a true classic in the best sense of the term. In fact, the 60/40 parka is probably the most imitated piece of outdoor specialty clothing in the country. 60/40 refers to the composition of the parka fabric: 60 percent cotton and 40 percent nylon. It is breathable, windproof and water repellent. The design of the 60/40 parka, with its four patch pockets, hood, Velcro cuffs, waist drawstring, and front zipper with snaps is instantly recognizable anywhere.

Sierra Designs also makes down-filled vests, canvas shirts, Billy Goat pants, and a variety of men's and women's shorts.

Sierra Designs down sleeping bags come in two lines: the Cloud series and the Cocoon series. The Cocoon series uses goose down with a fill power of 550 cubic inches per ounce, and the Cloud series uses down with a fill power of 700 cubic inches per ounce. All Sierra Designs bags use stretch baffle material which reduces stress on baffle seams and increases the life of the bag. Other features include differential cut, down-filled draft tubes, a baffled foot section, spring-lock adjustable neck drawcord and two-way nylon zippers. All seams are sewn with eight to 10 stitches to the inch, and a unique tuck stitch is used to sew baffles into place. There are three models in the premium Cloud series and five models in the Cocoon series including a super-lightweight mummy bag that weighs two pounds, six ounces.

Sierra Designs makes seven different tents. The Glacier tent is almost as much of a classic as the 60/40 parka. This is a mountain tent of traditional double A-frame design, which is built to stand up to the most severe kinds of high altitude storms. It sleeps two climbers and weighs seven pounds, 11 ounces. The Starflight, on the other hand, is a lightweight (four-pound, 11-ounce) backpacking tent for two people. With a single A-frame in front, it tapers down, almost to the ground, in the rear.

The Three-Man Tripod tent is a roomy nylon shelter that is light enough (eight pounds) for two-person trips. The peak of this tent is 72 inches high. The Terra III is a luxurious two-man, three-season tent with an exceptionally roomy interior space and a clever external arc support system. The floor plan is hexagonal to eliminate unused corners. Aside from being a delight to live in, this tent has a strange kind of beauty, which is a great deal more than can be said for most backpacking tents. The Terra III weighs eight pounds, 10 ounces.

The Terra IV is a four-season tent for three persons. It is much like the Terra III in shape and design, but has additional foul-weather features. It weighs nine pounds, five ounces.

The Aireflex is an A-frame mountain tent with an arch bow support system—no guy lines necessary. It sleeps two and weighs six pounds. The Octadome II sleeps three or four people under its self-supporting arch bow pole system. Four big arch windows afford superb ventilation. An integral fly sheet simplifies set-up procedure. The Octadome II weighs nine pounds, four ounces complete.

PRODUCTS: Parkas, vests, clothing, sleeping bags, tents.

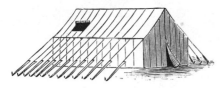

SIMS STOVES
Box 21405
Billings, MT 59104
406-259-5644
Accepts MC, VISA. Descriptive brochure. Graham D. Sims, Pres.

Some time ago we were invited to supper at a Basque sheepherder camp way back up in the mountains of central

Idaho. Thick lamb stew was on the menu, but the camp itself was what really impressed us. It was a scene that could have been lifted out of the century before. It was like stepping into an old photograph of the American West. Those sheepherders had a wood stove inside their tent and it heated the place up to where you were comfortable in shirt sleeves. You could cook up a storm on it, too, and ever since then a woodburning stove has seemed like the pinnacle of backcountry luxury.

Wood stoves, of course, are far too heavy for backpacking use, but Sims Stoves of Billings, Montana, makes a folding model—the "Sportsman"—that is well adapted to horse packing or car camping. The basic stove, including damper, side shelf, nesting seven-foot stovepipe and carrying case, weighs 28 pounds. The erected dimensions are 15 inches by 13 inches by 22 inches. It folds down flat and sets up in 30 seconds. If you want to get fancy, a reflector oven and a 6½-gallon hot-water tank are available. With the oven attached, the stove is capable of roasting a 12-pound turkey.

According to company literature, these stoves are in use by the Forest Service, the National Park Service, the U. S. Geological Survey, the Bureau of Land Management, and the Wyoming Fish and Game Commission. As we say, you couldn't slip one in your pack and skip off down the trail, but a Sims stove would be ideal for a semipermanent base camp or for a large group that had a few horses to carry some of their duffle. It would certainly go a long way toward warming up chilly autumn nights in the high country—something that big-game hunters have appreciated for years.

The basic stove is priced at $74. The reflector oven and hot-water tank are $40 and $45, respectively. Accessories such as stovepipe extensions, rain caps and tent-flue shields are available. Sims Stoves also sells canvas wall tents, tipis, pack saddles, and panniers.

PRODUCTS: Folding woodburning stoves.

STEPHENSON'S
RFD #4
Box 145
Gilford, NH 63246
603-293-8526
Four-color, $3. Jack Stephenson, Pres.

With well over 150 manufacturers of backpacking equipment in the United States, it has become inevitable that most product lines are more notable for their similarities than their differences. When one company comes up with something good, other companies, quite naturally, tend to imitate it. Nevertheless, a few firms have managed to preserve a high degree of individuality, but none have been more successful in this regard than Stephenson's.

You can tell that Stephenson's is unique the minute you first lay eyes on their catalog. People who have already seen it know what we are talking about, but for those who have not, perhaps the best thing to say is simply that they will be amazed. What other catalog pontificates about nuclear power? Then, too, the illustrations, particularly the centerspread, are beguiling in a way that you could never anticipate.

None of this, however, would mean very much if the products themselves were not highly original. Fortunately, they are. Jack Stephenson has come up with a line of sleeping bags, tents, packs, and clothing that turns conventional design wisdom on its head.

Everyone knows, for example, that rubber boots promote damp feet. The same thing (sweaty clothing) happens when you wear a waterproof rain jacket while exercising. This has led to the quest for "breathable" fabrics that allow perspiration to evaporate. So far so good, but evaporation leads to further sweating, which eventually soaks clothing and makes you cold. Why not place a waterproof layer between the skin and the clothing and stop the evaporation at its source? Why not indeed? It is the evaporation of perspiration, not the perspiration itself, that produces cold, clammy skin. Your skin, after all, is naturally moist. If you wear a plastic bag inside your socks, your feet stay warm and your socks stay dry. Try it sometime. It really works, and Stephenson's has applied the same principle to sleeping bags and to their "No Sweat" vapor-barrier shirt.

But the innovation does not stop there. The Stephenson Warmlite sleeping bag is actually three bags in one, giving the sleeper a choice of adding or subtracting three different insulation thicknesses for versatility over a wide range of temperature. A foam pad or a down-filled air mattress is sewn into the bottom of the bag. With the air-mattress option, the bag will actually float on water—with a sleeper inside!

Stephenson tents (among the lightest available anywhere) and packs demonstrate an equally radical approach to problems most backpackers have experienced. We can't possibly go into all the details here, or even scratch the surface, but the Stephenson catalog offers a massive amount of information on the subject. The catalog and the products it describes are truly extraordinary. They are obtainable only from the manufacturer.

PRODUCTS: Sleeping bags, tents, packs, clothing.

STOW-A-WAY SPORTS INDUSTRIES
166 Cushing Hwy.
Cohasset, MA 02025
617-383-9116
Accepts MC, VISA. Semi-annual. Est. 1963. William B. White, Pres.

Stow-A-Way Industries offers one of the largest selections of freeze-dried and dehydrated food available anywhere. Before looking at the Stow-A-Way catalog, you may not have realized just how much variety there is. When it comes to beans, for example, Stow-A-Way has dehydrated baby lima beans, cut green beans, garbanzo beans, mung beans, navy beans, pinto beans, red kidney beans, and soy beans.

Aside from offering a wide variety of food items in trail packs, cans and bulk containers, Stow-A-Way has considerable expertise in unusual food requirements. They have supplied provisions to space capsules, to submersible research vessels, and to expeditions sponsored by the National Geographic Society, the Smithsonian Institute, the Arctic Institute of North America, and the National Science Foundation. Whatever the condition—high altitude, extreme heat, extreme cold—Stow-A-Way can design a menu. As a special service to long-distance backpackers, Stow-A-Way will mail out pre-selected food packs to post offices along the route.

In addition to food, Stow-A-Way carries stoves, grills, and cookware. They have a good selection of water-purification apparatus and water distillers. For people interested in preparing food at home, Stow-A-Way has grain mills, Kenwood mixers, dehydrators, pressure canners, and ice-cream freezers. They also offer a nice selection of books that cover topics such as homesteading, self-sufficiency, small-scale farming, underground houses, food (*100 Ways To Use Wheat, The Sprouters Cookbook, Commercial Foods Exposed*, etc.), cheese making, solar energy, and survival.

Survival, in fact, is a major focus of the Stow-A-Way catalog. By this we don't mean survival in the woods, but survival in the home in case of natural disaster, economic calamity, war or whatever. This type of planning ahead is not to everyone's taste, but it is by no means fair to characterize all survivalists as doomsday fanatics or gun-toting zealots. The media has emphasized this aspect, but survivalism, when you come right down to it, consists mainly of commonsense precautions. In an earlier day and age, when most people lived in rural areas and grew all or part of their own food, just about everybody was a "survivalist" to some degree. They just couldn't run out to the store every time they needed something. That kind of self-sufficiency cannot be duplicated today—things have become far too complicated—but a number of remedial measures are quite feasible. It's worth thinking about.

PRODUCTS: Freeze-dried, dehydrated food, outdoor cooking equipment, home food-preparation apparatus, do-it-yourself books.

SUNSHINE LEISURE
20310 Plummer St.
Chatsworth, CA 91311
213-886-2940
Est. 1966. Taiji Sakai, Pres. Lorrain Pritkin, Cust. Svc.

Tents and tarps are what Sunshine Leisure is all about. Models include backpacking designs, family camping designs, and backyard screen houses.

The Four-Season Geodesic tent has a clever design that gives you 43 square feet of living space for a total weight of nine pounds. This tent comes complete with fiberglass poles, rain fly, stuff bag, and insect netting. The geodesic design offers superb wind stability with virtually no flapping. It will sleep three or four people. The Octadome tent is a four-person dome model with excellent stability, easy set-up, and a big roof window for superb warm-weather ventilation. The Octadome weighs in at nine pounds, eight ounces.

The Moonlite is an unusual looking three-season tent that features exceptional roominess for its weight of seven pounds. It

also has a roof window and a full-size door on either side. The Moonlite will sleep two or three people.

The Trail's Edge Dome has a hexagonal floor plan, ample head room, large door and window, and a urethane-coated fly. It sleeps two or three people and weighs seven pounds, eight ounces.

The Sequoia is an all-season, tunnel-style tent with arch poles and a door at each end. The rain fly has web and buckle attachments for quick set-up. The Sequoia weighs six pounds, eight ounces and sleeps two or three people.

The Catalina is a roomy four-man modified dome tent with a square floor plan and a large door plus three big windows for ventilation. It weighs nine pounds.

As the name suggests, the Ten-Second Automatic tent offers an unusual feature: It virtually sets up by itself. The frame is built right into the tent. Stakes and guy lines are not needed. The Ten-Second Automatic weighs ten pounds and sleeps two.

The Super Dome features a hexagonal floor plan, outstanding head room, fiberglass poles, large door, good ventilation, and an economical price. The weight is five pounds, twelve ounces. It sleeps two.

The Shelter Dome is a two-person tent that weighs in at just four pounds, four ounces. The Summit Wedge is a freestanding semi-dome that weighs five pounds, twelve ounces with rain fly.

Sunshine also makes a number of A-frame backpacking tents including the three pound, six ounce Mountain Pac tent that sleeps two people. The Bivy Shelter features hoop poles front and rear, and full insect and foul-weather protection. In a pinch, two people can get inside. It weighs three pounds, eight ounces.

PRODUCTS: Tents, tarps.

TERRAMAR INDUSTRIES
P.O. Box 114
Pelham, NY 10803
914-668-0022
Est. 1974. M. Shapiro, Pres.

Terramar Industries offers a line of imported and domestic sweaters, shirts, hats, jackets, and underwear of interest to backpackers, sailors, and other outdoorsmen.

Terramar's American-made black wool sweaters are made of pure, naturally dark sheep's wool. The body and sleeves of the sweater feature a tubular knit design for strength rather than stretch. This is a lightweight, durable garment. It comes in four styles: crew, chevron, shawl, fatigue, and hooded. Sweaters are an old answer to the problem of keeping warm in the backcountry, but they continue to be popular for a number of reasons, not the least of which is that people simply like them. A good warm sweater is a real comfort on a brisk day. Terramar offers some of the nicest looking and most practical sweaters on the market.

Ragg wool garments have long been popular with back-packers, and Terramar offers American-made ragg wool sweaters in three styles: crew, shawl, and fatigue. The fatigue sweater features a collar with three buttons down the front. The material in these sweaters is 85 percent wool and 15 percent nylon for added durability. The color is black and bone ragg.

Terramar's American-made Dri-Wool sweaters are 100 percent wool treated with a lanolin-like substance for water-repellency. The design features a high crew neck, raglan sleeves and a close knit. The available colors are navy, bone, brick mari, tan mari and grey mari.

Terramar's British-made mountain and boating sweater comes in crew neck and five-button placket-front models. It is 100 percent wool with a dense, tightly woven double-knit construction to prevent snags and keep out wind.

The British-made mariner sweater is a heavy-duty navy blue sweater with a zip front. The American-made U.S. Navy Submarine Sweater is a lightweight 100 percent wool garment with a tight weave and a mock turtle neck. The Aran Style Fisherman's Knit sweater is handmade in Portugal. The English-made oiled wool sweater is a classic, ribbed sweater with natural water repellency.

Terramar also offers a line of cotton sweaters, French-made cotton pullovers, English-made canvas and chamois shirts, and a line of hats, including "crusher" hats and wool watch caps. One of the most interesting items in the Terramar selection is pure silk thermal underwear made in the People's Republic of China.

PRODUCTS: Outdoorwear.

TODD BIBLER TENTS

14240 S.E. 41st St.
Bellevue, WA 98006
206-641-5283
Illustrated.

Bibler is a tent specialist. The Bibler I-Tent is a two-man dome tent built to take the punishing weather conditions of the high mountains. It was chosen for use in the Karakorum by the 1980 American Gasherbrum IV Expedition. It sets up in less than two minutes, and the freestanding dome design allows it to be used where it is impossible to place stakes. A tunnel vent near the top of the tent provides all-weather ventilation. This is an exceptionally rugged shelter for the most demanding environments. Incredibly, it weighs just three pounds, three ounces, including poles and stuff sack. The packed size (without the poles) is five inches by 12 inches. Obviously, the I-Tent is ideal for bicyclists, kayakers, and backpackers, as well as high-altitude climbers.

The Ahwahnee is a larger tent than the I-Tent, but has the same basic dome design. It sleeps two people luxuriously and three snugly. A full-width front door provides lots of nice-weather ventilation. The Ahwahnee weighs four pounds, eight ounces.

The Solo Dome is a one-person tent that really is a tent rather than a glorified sleeping-bag cover. The height at the center of the tent is 40 inches and the steeply angled walls give plenty of usable room inside. A lone hiker or bicyclist can cook, read, meditate or weather out a storm inside this tent without feeling like he is sealed up in a cocoon. The Solo Dome weighs two pounds, six ounces.

All Bibler tents are single-wall designs with the poles inside the tent rather than outside. The fabric is stretched skin-tight over this framework to eliminate flapping. The poles are anodized gold aluminum and shock corded to break down into easy-to-pack 24-inch lengths. Tent walls are Acapulco gold Gore-Tex laminate. The floors are rust-colored Super K-Kote nylon taffeta. Zippers are YKK nylon coil. Polyester thread is used throughout. All seams are at least double sewn. Every piece of fabric is individually cut, and the tents are put together one at a time, from start to finish, instead of on a production line.

The conventional wisdom has it that single-wall tents (as contrasted to tents with rain flies) are not practical because condensation forms inside the tent during the night, but through our own experience we have found that this is not necessarily so. We used a prototype single-wall tent (not a

Bibler) for an entire year in the mountains of Idaho, winter and summer, fair weather and foul, and had no problems whatsoever. Proper ventilation design is part of the answer. And the tent that we used was made of heavy-duty coated fabric—not breathable in the slightest. The Gore-Tex tents made by Bibler should be even more efficient.

PRODUCTS: Tents.

TRAIL FOODS COMPANY
P.O. Box 9309
North Hollywood, CA 91609
213-785-3202
Accepts MC, VISA. Illustrated brochure.

Trail Foods Company carries products by Mountain House, Dri-Lite Backpacker's Pantry, Rich Moor, and Alpine Aire. Mountain House freeze-dried items include main courses like beef stew, spaghetti with meat sauce, beef chop suey, beef Stroganoff, etc. Breakfast packs include omelettes, scrambled eggs, granola with raisins and milk, and the like. Freeze-dried meats, vegetables, fruits and snacks are available too, as are pudding-type desserts.

Dri-Lite's Backpacker's Pantry foods come in packages that serve two or four people. They can be classified into supper entree, breakfast food, fruit, no-cook spread and dessert categories. There are also complete packaged meals—breakfast, lunch and dinner—that serve four people. A sample breakfast might include pancakes, syrup, orange drink, bananas, and margarine. Another includes scrambled eggs, orange drink, cocoa, margarine, and coffee cake. A representative dinner includes chicken and dumplings, peas and carrots, and butterscotch pudding.

Rich Moor Foods offers no-cook main course entrees, cook-in-the-bag entrees, specialty main-course entrees, freeze-dried quick meals, breakfast items, vegetables, spreads, fruits, desserts, meats, and trail snacks.

Alpine Aire offers natural foods for backpackers. They contain no flavor enhancers or additives. The shrimp Newburg with sherry sounds interesting. In fact, all of the Alpine Aire items have a slightly exotic ring.

Aside from food, Trail Foods Company carries Eureka! tents and Camp Trails packs and sleeping bags. The bags are

insulated with PolarGuard or goose down. The packs come in external- and internal-frame models. A discount plan is available for large food orders. The larger the order, the bigger the discount. A bonus discount is available to nonprofit institutions. The discount plan does not apply to equipment, but the tents, packs, and sleeping bags are priced very reasonably.

PRODUCTS: Food, tents, packs, sleeping bags.

TWIN PEAKS
253 E. Harris St.
South San Francisco, CA 94080

Twin Peaks manufactures a no-nonsense line of sleeping bags and clothing that feature top-quality fabrics and PolarGuard or Thinsulate insulation. All PolarGuard products use Twin Peaks' "Uniquilt Construction" technique where quilting is done seam by seam, individually, rather than on a large multi-needle quilting machine. Twin Peaks' more painstaking process results in better lofting. Thinsulate is an insulating material developed by the 3M Company with patented microfiber construction that traps air within the insulating material much more effectively than other synthetics or even prime goose down. Thus, the Thinsulate-insulated garment does not have to be as thick to produce the same warmth.

The Twin Peaks Sleeper is a rectangular bag for moderate weather. The Yosemite is a rectangular PolarGuard bag for chillier nights. The Summer Sack is a mummy with two offset layers of 5.3-ounce PolarGuard for lightweight (three pounds, six ounces) warmth. The Tri-Season is a semi-mummy for spring, summer and fall. The Sierra Sack is a three-season bag that is a little more compact and a bit lighter. The All Season is warm enough for winter and light enough to use during the rest of the year. The Expedition, a bag for severe climates, features three 10-ounce PolarGuard layers on top, and 10-ounce, 5.3-ounce and 10-ounce layers on the bottom. The average sleeper should be warm in this six-pound, 12-ounce bag at minus 20 degrees.

The Dana parka has PolarGuard insulation, a Western-style yoke in a contrasting color across the shoulders, hidden knit cuffs, and an optional PolarGuard hood. It is a garment that will appeal to urbanites as well as wilderness travelers. The Summit vest has a water-repellent poplin yoke like the Dana, a corduroy collar, deep pockets, snap closure in front, and an optional hood. The warm-when-wet qualities of PolarGuard make the vest practical on a sailboat as well as up in the mountains.

The Meadow vest has 10-ounce PolarGuard insulation, a satiny taffeta shell, and handwarmer/cargo pockets. The Yosemite vest has a 65/35 shell, making it more practical for rough outdoor work. The Shasta shell is a well-thought-out mountain parka that is water repellent and windproof. The Klamath parka features Thinsulate insulation, an inner drawstring at the waist, knit cuffs, and a built-in hood. The Minaret parka has 10-ounce PolarGuard in the body of the jacket, with eight-ounce PolarGuard in the sleeves. The Expedition parka is a cold-weather jacket built like a sleeping bag, with double offset layers of eight-ounce PolarGuard. Mittens and booties round out the Twin Peaks line.

PRODUCTS: Sleeping bags, outdoor clothing.

TYROL SHOE COMPANY
100 Front St.
Keenesville, NY 12944
518-834-7411
Illustrated brochure.

Although some backpackers wear running shoes on the trail, and others make do with inexpensive work boots or high-topped hunting boots, there is no real substitute for traditional European-style hiking boots. A running shoe is fine for carrying a moderate load on a nice smooth trail in dry weather, but as soon as things get wet or rocky, your feet begin to suffer. Nor do running shoes or work boots provide the ankle support that you need for carrying a heavy load or for scrambling over a scree slope.

Tyrol USA offers a full range of hiking boots for everything from weekend backpack trips to general mountaineering. Top-quality leather, either chrome-tanned or vegetable-tanned, or both, is used throughout. Construction is either Norwegian welt or Littleway, the preferred methods for durable boots. Tyrol boots are available in men's and women's sizes.

The Arlberg is a lightweight trail boot with Littleway construction, leather insole, calfskin lining, padded scree collar and tongue, steel half-shank, and Vibram Roccia Bloc outsole. This is a fine boot for general backpacking on average trails.

Similar in appearance to the Arlberg, the Packer is a bit more boot. It has Littleway construction, steel half-shank, padded inside collar and tongue, laminated leather board and rubber midsole, Vibram Montagna Block outsole, and heavy, one-piece, full-grain, smooth leather uppers.

The Sierra is heavier and has a higher top than the Packer. It features Norwegian welt construction, steel half-shank, split-leather lining, leather insole, padded insole, scree collar and tongue, and Vibram Montagna Security outsole. The Sierra is a good choice for longer trips, off-trail hiking, and occasional mountaineering.

With heavy-gauge one-piece rough-out uppers, the Banff is a boot built for hard use in the wilderness and for cross-country travel above or below the treeline. It has Norwegian welt construction, gussetted, padded double tongue, steel half-shanks, full-grain calfskin lining, padded inside collar, and Vibram Montagna outsole.

The Yukon is a full-fledged mountaineering boot with Gallusser one-piece, full-grain uppers. It is too stiff and heavy for normal backpacking, but this is true of any boot that is built to take the punishment to which alpine climbers continually subject their footwear.

In addition to hiking boots, Tyrol USA offers a full line of cross-country racing shoes and touring boots and touring binding.

PRODUCTS: Hiking boots, cross-country racing shoes.

UNIQUE 1
Box 744
Camden, ME 04843
207-236-8717
Accepts AMEX, MC, VISA. Four-color brochure and mail-order form on request.

Although goose-down-filled jackets and vests have become a standard item in virtually every backpacker's kit, old-fashioned wool sweaters are still extremely popular and probably always will be, for a number of excellent reasons. In the first place, wool retains warmth when wet, while goose down does not. A sturdy wool sweater is also much more durable and resistant to abrasion than the nylon fabric of most down jackets. A good sweater can last a lifetime, while even the best down garments must eventually wear out. But aside from this, sweaters are simply nice things to own and wear, particularly the sweaters made by Unique 1.

Every Unique 1 sweater is handmade from 100 percent natural wool from Maine farms. Natural sheep oils are left in the yarn when it is spun, producing an exceptionally water-repellent and warm garment. The sweaters come in classic V-neck, turtleneck, boat-neck, and round-neck styles, as well as in a unique hooded and pocketed design, the most popular item in the line. All sweaters are sized for men and women, with child's sizes for the hooded and boat-neck styles. Sweaters are made to order for people with unusual measurements.

In addition to sweaters, Unique 1 makes premium-quality hats, scarves, knee socks, over-the-knee socks, skirts, vests, and long- and short-sleeved dresses. A variety of solid colors and patterns are available. We suspect that there is something here that will appeal to everyone, as all of these garments are extraordinarily attractive. The prices, which range from $10 for knee socks to $85 for the long-sleeved dress, are most reasonable when you take the handcrafted quality into account.

PRODUCTS: Sweaters, hats, socks, scarves, dresses.

UNIVERSAL SPORTS
Box 1514
428 St. Augustine
Valdosta, GA 31601
912-244-9941
Flyer, B&W, free. Est. 1977. Connly Carter, Pres.

Universal Sports was founded in 1977, and its product line is still limited. But several items are of special interest to fishermen and hunters. Perhaps most significant is the One Man Econo Boat. Essentially, it is nothing more than a molded swivel seat mounted on two attached pontoons. The whole thing is made of high-impact ABS plastic. Cost is about $260. The boat is only six feet, five inches long and three feet, three inches wide, and its capacity is only 325 pounds. But the 60-pound boat would be ideal for certain uses, such as bass fishing in small farm ponds, or maybe duck hunting in tiny marshes. The boat is powered by an electric trolling motor or a miniature outboard. A motor is not included.

Identical except in size is the Two Man Econo Boat. Its two

seats are mounted on connected pontoons eight feet long and capable of carrying 500 pounds. The width is two inches short of four feet. Weight is 85 pounds. The price is $370.

Universal carries a matching 1½-horsepower outboard engine. Called the Cruise 'N Carry, it features solid-state ignition and has a clutch. Weight is just 12 pounds, and the price is about $250. An optional nylon carrying case with hand and shoulder strap is priced at about $30.

Another item is an odd fish stringer called the Fish Ringer. It consists of polypropylene cord and a plastic ring, to which steel fish-holding snaps are mounted. A crossbar in the ring acts as a support and carrying handle, a feature not found on conventional fish stringers.

The Gripper is a gadget with six advertised uses. Made of heavy-gauge steel, it is a wicked-looking clip that can be used to anchor a boat on brush or tree limbs, hold tent guy lines to trees or brush, hold fish, boat fish, hang hammocks and hang lanterns. An advertisement makes the claim, "The harder you pull, the tighter it gets."

Something new is the Fisherman's Mate, a live bait tank made from a Gott ice chest. An electric pump aerates water in the chest and keeps fish supplied with plenty of oxygen. The bait well comes ready to plug into a car or boat cigarette-lighter jack. An optional Mini Power Mate provides enough electricity for eight hours of aerating action. A 50-quart Fisherman's Mate costs about $80, an 80-quart model $110.

Other products include a tow strap made of reinforced nylon, three models of car-top racks, portable soft-foam coolers, rod holders, and Zynco, a chemical said to eliminate fish and game odors and stain.

PRODUCTS: Small boats, live bait chests, fishing and hunting accessories.

UPTOWN SEWING
135 N. Glenwood
Jackson, WY 83001
307-733-4684
Illustrated, $1. Est. 1972. C'Anee Baker, Pres. Cindy Shanholtser, Cust. Svc.

Located in the shadow of the Tetons, Uptown Sewing began as a custom-design service that produced one-of-a-kind items to meet the special needs of individual customers and later expanded its operations to include a line of equipment for serious mountaineers and backcountry travelers. The firm may be best known for its "Supergaitor," a design that originated with climber Peter Carman more than 15 years ago and has since become the standard against which all other gaiters are measured.

The Supergaitor is not just an anklet that keeps snow and scree out of the boot; it provides waterproof protection and insulated warmth from the welt of the boot up to the knee. The model 374 Supergaitor is lined with an 80/20 wool/polyester blend. The uppers are eight-ounce Parapac, and the lowers are 11½-ounce Cordura. The fit is adjustable to virtually any mountaineering boot. The Model 380 Supergaitor features a tightening system that is not quite so adjustable, but is lighter and simpler.

The Lev boot, with Parapac uppers and urethane-coated, insulated lowers, is a heavy-duty overboot that will fit over Supergaitors. The Watergaitor is more of a conventional knee-high gaiter that fits over a wide range of boots from shoepacs to cross-country racing shoes. Minesota Spats are durable, easy-to-put-on gaiters with side zippers, snap tops, a neoprene under-arch strap, and a front boot-lace hook.

Uptown Sewing also offers a line of internal-frame packs. The larger models carry heavy loads with the comfort of a standard frame pack, but they are more durable and versatile. Because of the way these packs ride, they facilitate difficult climbing, skiing and bushwhacking. The lack of fragile external frames also makes them less susceptible to damage when subjected to airport-style baggage abuse.

The Pumori I and Pumori II are the monsters of the line. Pumori II has a capacity of 5,050 cubic inches with the extension in use. Side and lid pockets provide additional capacity. The suspension system features a chest harness, padded shoulder straps, beveled waist pad, and shoulder cinch straps.

The Northridge is a scaled-down (2,826-cubic-inch) version of the Pumori. The Excalibur is a pack for difficult climbs where the climber's pack has to do double duty as a haul sack. The Pichstone is a multi-purpose pack with a main-body capacity of 3,060 cubic inches. Day packs, dog packs, and pocket packs complete the line-up.

The Uptown Sewing mummy bag is PolarGuard-insulated and designed to minimize stuffed bulk. It weighs three pounds, six ounces with the breathable, waterproof Klimate weather shell, three pounds without. Windproof and waterproof shirts and pants are also available from Uptown Sewing.

PRODUCTS: Mountaineering equipment, backpacking equipment.

UTICA DUXBAK

815 Noyes St.
Utica, NY 13502
315-797-1320
Accepts AMEX, MC, VISA. Biennial, four-color, free. Est. 1904.
Gilbert Jones, Pres.

Many hunting clothes are cheaply made and cannot withstand hard use. What's more, many are offered in only a limited number of sizes, so a person with extra-long legs or an extra-long torso often can't find hunting clothes that fit properly.

Utica Duxbak says a hunter won't have those problems with its clothing. The company, which has been making hunting clothing since 1904, says its philosophy is to provide customers with the best possible value in excellent fabrics, proper sizing, superior workmanship, and well-designed clothing. Gilbert Jones, president of the firm, says he has received many letters from hunters who are still using Duxbak coats 50 and 60 years old.

The company's coats are full cut, and many are sized in chest sizes for better fit. Duxbak pants have always been made on dress-pant patterns with waistband and outlet construction, and are said to have the proper fit and proportionate rise not found in the usual work-pant construction of most hunting pants.

The company prefers to sell through its dealers, but if there is no dealer close to you, you can order from Duxbak's outlet store; Outdoor Outfitters, 1322 Sunset Ave., Utica, NY 13502, phone 315-797-1320.

Besides a wide variety of coats and pants, Duxbak offers parkas, jackets, shirts, hunting vests, game bags, insulated vests, coveralls, rainwear, beach and summer wear, fishing vests, fishing clothing, underwear, 20 styles of socks, 17 styles of mittens and gloves, 13 hats, mesh head nets, net parkas, and such accessories as belts and suspenders.

Most pieces of clothing are offered in a variety of colors. There are several styles and shades of camouflage.

Though quality is high, prices don't seem outlandish to me. The most expensive insulated jacket, for example, lists at $100. The least expensive costs $20. A green camouflage rain parka lists for $27.50, while the top-of-the-line rain parka costs $110.

PRODUCTS: Hunting and fishing clothing.

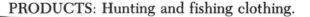

VERMONT TUBBS
Forrestdale, VT 05745
C. Baird Morgan, Jr., Pres.

A well-known and respected maker of classic wooden snowshoes since the 1800s. Vermont Tubbs also offers a modern aluminum snowshoe that was used on the 1979 International Mt. Everest Expedition. Known as the Alum-A-Shoe, this snowshoe features a one-piece non-tubular aircraft-quality aluminum frame and the Super A binding that is factory-mounted on maintenance-free nylon bearings. Front and rear flotation pads are made of rugged Hypalon, the material used in whitewater rafts. The lacing is steel-reinforced Hytrel for abrasion and moisture resistance. Stainless steel crampons give the Alum-A-Shoe traction going uphill or downhill or on wind-packed traverses. The crampons are attached to the shoe at the factory. The Super A binding, which features a nylon strap laced through D-rings and a two-ply polyester nitrile-coated toe piece is available separately and can be used on conventional snowshoes. Tubbs neoprene and leather bindings are also available.

Tubbs wooden snowshoes feature full-grain rawhide lacing and carefully selected straight-grain New England ash frames. Most models are available with neoprene lacing.

The Green Mountain Bear Paw is a Vermont Tubbs original designed for New England snow conditions and for use in the woods and in thick brush. The Cross Country snowshoe is similar to the Green Mountain Bear Paw, but has a tail that acts as a stabilizer. The Alaska Trapper is a long, narrow shoe with up-turned tips. It is a fine shoe for deep, light powder snow. The Standard Bear Paw is a short, wide shoe suited to backpacking and maneuvering in close quarters. The Michigan snowshoe is a tailed, all-purpose model that supports a lot of weight and is good for most snowshoeing conditions except thick brush. The Junior Alaska Trapper is a children's model of the full-size Alaska Trapper. The Green Mountain Bear Paw and the Cross Country and Alaska Trapper snowshoes are available in kit form. The kits include bent frames, neoprene lacing, varnish, rivets, bindings, etc.

Vermont Tubbs also makes a full line of snowshoe furniture that includes rocking chairs, love seats, coffee tables, end tables, armchairs, footstools, magazine racks, and other pieces.

PRODUCTS: Snowshoes, snowshoe furniture.

WE-NO-NAH CANOES
P.O. Box 247
Winona, MN 55987
507-454-5430
Annual. Est. 1968. Mike Cichanowski, Pres.

Eugene Jensen designed his first canoe in 1949 and used it to win the 500-mile Bemidji-Minneapolis Marathon. He won the same event in 1950. Two decades later, after piling up victories around the country, he returned to the scene of former glories and won the Bemidji-Minneapolis race in 1971 and again in 1973. Jensen-designed canoes have won nearly every marathon in the United States and Canada. Mr. Jensen's whitewater designs have done very well too.

But a good hull design is only part of what makes a great canoe. Materials, construction technique, attention to detail, and the dedication of the canoe-builder are critically important. Mike Cichanowski, the owner of We-No-Nah Canoes, has been building canoes since he was in the Boy Scouts. Today all We-No-Nah canoes, many of which utilize Jensen designs, are built by hand from the best of modern materials.

Because one canoe cannot do all things equally well, We-No-Nah offers 12 models for flatwater, whitewater and recreation. Most are available in Fiberglass or Kevlar. A chief advantage of fiberglass over aluminum is that fiberglass allows much better control of the hull shape by the builder. Fiberglass is as durable as aluminum and weighs less. A good fiberglass canoe is stronger than a wood canoe and much less expensive. Kevlar makes the lightest canoes of all (about 10 pounds less per canoe compared to glass), but costs a little more. Royalex is an ABS "memory" plastic—it springs back to shape when dented—of excellent durability. It's good for bouncing off rocks. On the other hand, Royalex is heavy, lacks stiffness and is fairly expensive. We-No-Nah offers three hulls in Royalex.

For performance reasons, no We-No-Nah canoes have keels. To regain the stiffness provided by a keel, We-No-Nah uses several different methods. Extra layers of fiberglass add stiffness to some hulls. Extremely lightweight hulls use core-stiffening method. Hulls with flexible bottoms (for shallow rocky water) use stiffening ribs. Special whitewater layups use a center rib with shock absorbers.

The We-No-Nah 18½-foot Cruiser was created for USCA marathon racing. The 18½-foot Pro-Boat is like the Cruiser, but sleeker. In Kevlar (with Sitka spruce gunwales) it weighs an incredible 31 pounds. The 17-foot C-1 Flatwater (26 pounds in Kevlar) and the 16-foot C-1 Flatwater are designed for one-man flatwater racing. The C-1 Whitewater is for solo whitewater racing. It is also excellent for solo wilderness trips. The Whitewater II is a two-man canoe for racing and for experienced wilderness paddlers. The Sundowner is an economical whitewater and tripping hull. The 18-foot Jensen is an all-around hull for touring and occasional racing. The 17-foot Jensen is a little more stable in the water and costs less. The 17-foot Wenonah is a sturdy recreational canoe. The Packer is an ultra-light (30 pound) 14-foot canoe for fishermen. The Echo is a 16½-foot canoe for beginning canoeists.

PRODUCTS: Canoes.

WESTERN CUTLERY COMPANY
1800 Pike Rd.
Longmont, CO 80501
303-772-5900
Est. 1911. Harvey Platts, Pres. Chuck Hoffman, Cust. Svc.

Western Cutlery Company has been making top-quality knives for outdoorsmen since 1911. Stainless steel blades are made of 44A high carbon stainless steel. Carbon steel blades use a special high-carbon, chrome vanadium steel. Every step in the knife-making process—and some knives require 150 separate operations—is done at Western Cutlery's own plant. This includes stamping, heat treating, grinding, honing, polishing, assembly, inspection, etc. No work is contracted out. Western even has an in-plant aluminum foundry to produce the aluminum end knobs that go on handles. Total control of all knife-making operations insures a better product.

Western Cutlery offers a wide variety of two- and three-blade pocketknives that should be of interest to backpackers. The No. S-901-S Campers' knife is especially attractive. It has a large stainless steel main blade, a leather punch, a can opener, a screwdriver, a bottle-cap lifter, and a stag pattern Delrin handle. This knife measures 3⅝ inches with the blades closed.

The No. 822 Barlow knife with two carbon steel blades, nickel-silver bolsters, brass scales, and a saw-pattern Delrin handle is a good choice for a simple and rugged camping knife. It measures 3⅜ inches.

The No. S-751 Fishing knife, with stainless blades, yellow Delrin handle, clip blade, scaler blade, hook disgorger, cap lifter, and a small one for hook sharpening, is an excellent knife for backpackers who plan to do some serious angling.

Western Fillet knives, which come in three models, have a nationwide reputation for excellence. The No. SW764 Fish-Camp knife—which can be used as a general-purpose knife as well as a precision filleting tool—would be a good choice for a canoe trip in Alaska when salmon, arctic char, and grayling are on the menu. This knife is nine inches long overall and features a resin-impregnated hardwood handle with brass rivets. It comes with a molded leather sheath.

The No. SW769 Super Fillet is designed for the big fish. It has a long, flat-ground nine-inch flexible stainless steel blade with a satin finish and has an overall length of 14 inches.

Western also carries a full line of sheath knives—many of which would be good choices for backpacking—and a full selection of folding lock-blade knives that feature the patented Westlock mechanism.

PRODUCTS: Knives.

WILDERNESS EXPERIENCE
20120 Plummer St.
Chatsworth, CA 91311
800-423-5331 (213-998-3000 in Calif.)
Accepts MC, VISA. Four-color. Greg Thomsen and James Thomsen, Founders.

Wilderness Experience is a specialist in the design and manufacture of packs—day packs, fanny packs, kid's packs, internal-frame packs, external-frame packs, climbing packs, expedition packs, and soft luggage. They also offer sleeping bags and clothing.

Internal-frame packs have become very popular in recent years, particularly among people who also use their pack as a piece of luggage. There is no protruding frame with sharp corners and metal parts to hang up or break on airport baggage conveyors. Internal-frame packs also tend to ride more like a part of the wearer's body, a characteristic much appreciated by rock climbers, cross-country skiers, and boulder-hoppers who might be thrown off balance by a top-heavy, swaying load.

With sophisticated suspension systems, well-designed waist belts and carefully placed internal-frame components, an internal-frame pack can carry a moderate load as comfortably as a conventional external-frame pack. Internal-frame packs are ideal for a two- or three-day backpacking trip, and

Wilderness Experience offers several designs for this purpose. Internal-frame packs in the Alpinist series are larger. They are designed for serious mountaineers for use on the most difficult climbs.

External-frame packs come into their own on extended trips when heavy loads must be carried. Unlike many manufacturers, Wilderness Experience fabricates its own frames instead of relying on an outside supplier. The frame material is 6061 T6 thick-wall aircraft aluminum tubing. All frame joints are heliarc welded. Frames come in conventional and wraparound designs. Pack bags are offered in front- and top-loading models in various capacities up to 4,782 cubic inches. The adjustable "Little Big Man" frame is appropriate for growing kids.

Soft luggage comes in suitcase, shoulder bag, duffle bag, carry-on bag, and travel pack (with shoulder straps like a pack) styles. The vast selection of Wilderness Experience day packs makes up one of the most comprehensive lines on the market.

Wilderness Experience sleeping bags feature PolarGuard insulation and 50 denier nyl-silk as a top-shell fabric and 70 denier nylon taffeta as a bottom-shell fabric. The interior shell is a soft material, pleasant against the skin, that is a blend of 25 percent cotton, 25 percent polyester, and 50 percent nylon. Wilderness Experience jackets and vests are insulated with PolarGuard or Hollofil II. The top-of-the-line Blue Max parka is designed for extreme conditions in the big ranges with two layers of eight-ounce PolarGuard and an outer shell of Gore-Tex.

PRODUCTS: Sleeping bags, outdoor clothing, packs.

WILDWATER DESIGNS

230 Penllyn Pike
Penllyn, PA 19422
215-646-5034
Accepts MC, VISA. Est. 1972. C. Walbridge, Pres.

Wildwater designs offers a line of accessory items for canoeing, kayaking, and rafting. Many of the Wildwater Designs products are available in kit form, an option that saves a significant amount of money and also allows custom sizing and modifications.

Throw-Line rescue bags were standard equipment on Navy

lifeboats in World War II, and Wildwater Designs now makes an updated version of this proven piece of equipment for recreational boaters and professional rescue organizations. The rescue bag is superior to a heaving line or a ring buoy because it is lighter and much easier to use. The rope does not have to be coiled; it is simply stuffed into the bag. It never tangles when thrown. The bag itself contains an Ethafoam disk for flotation. The three-eighths-inch polypropylene line is 70 feet long.

Bonnie Hot Pogies are gloves specially designed to fit over a kayak paddle. You put your hands inside the gloves after they are in place on the paddle. In an emergency, you simply let go of the paddle in the normal fashion and your hands slide out of the gloves. The glove material is heavy-duty coated nylon. An optional liner of polyester pile is available for extremely cold conditions.

The Hi-Float life-vest kit has bouyancy far in excess of U. S. Coast Guard specifications. A full 1½-inch thickness of PVC foam gives added protection to the wearer's back and padding in the shoulder area makes a fine portage pad. The vest shell is six-ounce nylon pack cloth sewn with polyester thread. The vest is also available in a custom-made version.

Wildwater Designs sprayskirt kits offer the advantage of a skirt that is specifically tailored to the dimensions of your own boat. The deluxe neoprene kit features glued seams and a built-in grab loop for quick release. Oversize kits are available. The nylon sprayskirt kit is a less expensive model and can be sewn by beginners.

Wildwater Designs wetsuit kits are available for vests, short pants, long pants, long tops, gloves and booties, pogies and booties, gloves only and pogies only. Material is one-eighth-inch neoprene, nylon backed.

Other items available from Wildwater Designs include paddle-suit kits, paddle jackets, helmets, pile jackets, duffle bags, shock-proof, waterproof camera boxes, and flotation bags.

PRODUCTS: Canoeing, kayaking, and rafting accessories.

WINONA KNITTING MILLS
910 E. Second St.
Winona, MN 55987
507-454-4381
Accepts MC, VISA. Annual, four-color, free. Est. 1883. Pat Woodworth, Pres.

There are hundreds of sweater manufacturers, but Winona is included in this book for two reasons. It is one of the few mills that sell directly to individual customers through the mails, and it has a special line of sweaters and vests made for sportsmen. Recently a friend gave me a unique Winona sweater that is fluorescent orange with black blotches. It would be ideal for a blackpowder hunter or for a bowhunter active during firearms seasons, but I think it also has a strong future as a garment for other big-game hunters. There is recent scientific evidence that deer have the ability to discern colors, contrary to what hunters have been told for decades, and some authorities believe a deer would have more difficulty seeing a blotched pattern of colors than a solid color. Even if deer are color-blind, as some experts still hold, a blotched pattern would break up a hunter's outline effectively, thus making him harder to see.

I've used the sweater while hunting whitetail deer and bear, and I found it warm, resistant to snagging in brush, quiet, stretchy enough to fit over several layers of bulky clothing, and well-designed. The zipper was easy to use, even in cold weather, and it was quiet, an important consideration to a hunter.

Winona also sells sweaters, vests, and masks in a winter camouflage of brown, black, and white. I bowhunted last winter with a fellow wearing one of those sweaters. The photographs I took of him during the trip turned out poorly because he was so hard to see against snow and brush!

Other sweater and vest patterns include more conventional brown-black-green and brown-tan-black patterns. All sweaters, vests, and hats also are available in solid fluorescent orange.

I think prices are reasonable for high-quality wool clothing. A pullover costs $19.50 while a zippered cardigan with or without pockets costs $27.75.

Winona's socks are another indication of good price. I wish I'd seen the company's catalog before I recently bought several pairs of wool socks at almost $10 a pair. Winona prices its 85 percent wool socks from $3.50 to $5 depending on style.

PRODUCTS: Sweaters and other knitwear.

W. R. CASE & SONS CUTLERY COMPANY
20 Russel Blvd.
Bradford, PA 16701
Illustrated brochure.

One of the best known quality knife makers in the United States, W. R. Case & Sons has been manufacturing knives for sportsmen since before the turn of the century. All Case pocket knives are hand assembled and have specially formulated high-carbon steel blades for sharpness and long life. More than 100 different styles of pocketknives are offered.

A knife of interest to backpackers is the #640045R with chrome vanadium blade, can opener, screwdriver/cap lifter, and punch. It is 3¾ inches long when closed. The #6143 Grandaddy Barlow is an excellent single-blade heavy duty pocketknife that is five inches long closed. The #32095 FSS is a fisherman's knife with a stainless steel California clip style blade and a scaler/hook disgorger and a yellow plastic handle with a hook hone attached.

The #6318 is a trim pocketknife 3½ inches long (closed) with three blades: California clip, sheep and spey. It comes with either stainless steel or chrome vanadium blades and either a bone or a yellow plastic handle. The #A62033 is a compact (2⅝ inches closed) penknife with two chrome vanadium blades and a bone handle.

The #SR62027 is a small 2¾-inch-long pocketknife with rounded ends and two chrome vanadium blades. The #2138 Sodbuster is a rugged single-blade stockman's knife with a skinner-type blade in either chrome vanadium or stainless steel. Stainless blades take a little more work to sharpen but are extremely corrosion resistant. The Sodbuster has a smooth black plastic handle and is 4⅝ inches long in the closed position. The #6265 SAB DR folding hunter is a knife for the big jobs, with a skinner and a saber, ground chrome vanadium blades and a brushed metal handle 3¾ inches long. The #6165 SAB DR LSSP folding hunter has a stainless steel lock-open blade and a lamistag handle 5¼ inches long. The rear bolster is drilled to take a lanyard.

Case hunting knives come in a wide array of styles and feature quality American steels and cowhide sheaths. Case also makes sharpening tools, household knives, fishing knives, and scissors.

PRODUCTS: Pocket knives.

YAK WORKS
2030 Westlake Ave.
Seattle, WA 98121
206-623-8053
Accepts MC, VISA. Color.

The Yak Works carries a full line of backpacking equipment, from tents and clothing to compasses and flashlights, but with an emphasis on unusual and advanced designs. A good example is the Fastent. This is a tent which sets up by itself. You take it out of the stuff sack and it springs into the full erect position. The Fastent has a coated floor and sidewalls and a full rain fly. The Superlight model weighs four pounds and the standard model weighs 5.9 pounds.

Yakpaks are advanced-design soft packs that use the load as the frame of the pack. The patented X-suspension system includes crossed straps that reach across the hiker's chest and stomach from the waist belt to the shoulder straps and automatically lengthen or shorten to compensate for body movements. This arrangement shifts pack weight from shoulder muscles to chest muscles and allows exceptionally free arm movement, an important consideration when rock climbing or skiing. The pack itself has a smooth outside shape, vaguely like a teardrop, and is wider and thicker at the bottom than the top. This pack wraps around the wearer's hips with a full-circle free-floating conical hip belt. All load-bearing seams are triple stitched and pockets are double stitched.

The Trail/Super Trail models have a capacity of 4,300 cubic inches (larger than most frame packs). The Super Alpinist has a 4,000-cubic-inch capacity and a streamlined outer shape for rock climbing. The Trekker has a giant 5,400-cubic-inch capacity, slotted pockets, and other features.

Yakwear pile clothing is as warm as wool but weighs only half as much. Yakwear Borglite Pile retains warmth when wet, and dries quickly from body heat alone. Yakwear pile garments come in pants, bib overalls, mitts, vests, and jackets with underarm zippers for ventilation.

The Yakwear Gore-Tex Actionsuit offers complete protection from foul weather with a coverall-type hooded garment made of 1.9-ounce Gore-Tex nylon taffeta with double-sewn seams and oxford reinforced seat and knees. Other Yakwear Gore-Tex garments include parkas, bib overalls, pants, and rain jackets.

In 1980, the Yak Works purchased Rivendell Mountain Works, formerly run by Larry Horton in Victor, Idaho. Over the years, such Rivendell products as the Jensen pack and the

Bombshelter tent had become classic designs. The Jensen pack is a soft pack which, like the Yakpak, uses the load as a frame. The Bombshelter tent is one of the strongest tents ever made and is built and designed to stand up to intense winds. The Bombshelter doesn't flap, it hums.

In addition to the above items, the Yak Works also carries sleeping pads, bivy sacks, flashlights, altimeters, socks, wool underwear, polypropylene underwear, Dachstein sweaters, Gore-Tex gaiters, day packs, camera packs, soft luggage, shorts, shirts, running suits, food, stoves, roller skis, and technical climbing equipment by Chouinard, MSR, SMC, CMI and Lowe.

PRODUCTS: Backpacking equipment.

Index